THE FAMILY ROMANCE OF THE
FRENCH REVOLUTION

THE FAMILY
ROMANCE OF THE
FRENCH REVOLUTION

LYNN HUNT

University of California Press
Berkeley · Los Angeles

University of California Press
Berkeley and Los Angeles, California

© 1992 by
The Regents of the University of California

First Paperback Printing 1993

Library of Congress Cataloging-in-Publication Data

Hunt, Lynn Avery.
   The family romance of the French Revolution / Lynn
Hunt.
     p. cm.
   Includes bibliographical references and index.
   ISBN 0-520-07741-5 (cloth)
   ISBN 0-520-08270-2 (pbk)
   1. France—History—Revolution, 1789–1799—
Psychological aspects. 2. Louis XVI, King of France,
1754–1793—Death and burial. 3. Symbolism in politics—
France—History—18th century. 4. Regicides.
5. Family—France—History—18th century. I. Title.
DC148.H86 1992
944.04—dc20   91-26852
                                  CIP

Printed in the United States of America

9 8 7 6 5 4 3 2 1

The paper used in this publication meets the minimum
requirements of American National Standard for
Information Sciences—Permanence of Paper for Printed
Library Materials, ANSI Z39.48-1984. ⊗

To Peg

Contents

Illustrations

Preface

Since the title of this book may be obscure to some readers, I will begin with a few words of explanation about what I mean by family romance. The term is Freud's, though it is now used, especially by literary critics, in ways that are only loosely related to Freud's original formulation.[1] By "family romance" Freud meant the neurotic's fantasy of "getting free from the parents of whom he now has a low opinion and of replacing them by others, who, as a rule, are of higher social standing."[2] When the child feels slighted by his parents, he (he, in particular, since Freud thought this tendency was much weaker in girls) retaliates by imagining that these are not in fact his parents and that his real parents are important landowners, aristocrats, or even kings and queens. In Freud's formulation, the family romance was located in the individual psyche and was a way for individuals, especially boys, to fantasize about their place in the social order. Thus the individual psyche was linked to the social order through familial imagery and through intrafamilial conflict.

Rather than using this term in the strict Freudian sense as applying to the individual psyche, I use it to refer to the political—that is, the collective—unconscious, and I give the term a positive connotation. By *family romance* I mean the collective, unconscious images of the familial order that underlie revolutionary politics. I will be arguing that the French had a kind of collective political unconscious that was structured by narratives of family relations.[3] I do not claim that

1. See, for example, the useful discussion in Christine van Boheemen, *The Novel as Family Romance: Language, Gender, and Authority from Fielding to Joyce* (Ithaca, N.Y., 1987). The idea of family romance also informs, among others, Janet L. Beizer, *Family Plots: Balzac's Narrative Generations* (New Haven, 1986).

2. From "Family Romances," in vol. 9 of *The Standard Edition of the Complete Psychological Works of Sigmund Freud*, trans. James Strachey (London, 1959), pp. 238–239. I am indebted to Ruth Leys for this reference and for several other helpful suggestions.

3. The term *political unconscious* became current in literary studies after Fredric Jameson elaborated it in *The Political Unconscious: Narrative as a Socially Symbolic Act*

this is a universal phenomenon; other peoples at other times might well experience politics in other terms. But most Europeans in the eighteenth century thought of their rulers as fathers and of their nations as families writ large. This familial grid operated on both the conscious and the unconscious level of experience.

The French in a sense did wish to get free from the political parents of whom they had developed a low opinion, but they did not imagine replacing them with others who were of a higher social standing. They imagined replacing them—the king and the queen—with a different kind of family, one in which the parents were effaced and the children, especially the brothers, acted autonomously. Needless to say, however, the French revolutionaries did not stand at the tribune and lay out their psychosexual fantasies about the political order. As a consequence, many readers may question the very terms *political unconscious* and *family romance;* what evidence could possibly prove their existence? My case for using these terms is simply that they help us make sense of evidence that would otherwise remain confounding and mysterious. I hope to present enough of this evidence to convince my readers that such an approach is fruitful, because it brings previously overlooked evidence into clearer focus and because it raises important questions about the meanings of modern politics. The ideology of absolutism explicitly tied royal government to the patriarchal family, and the use of the term *fraternity* during the French Revolution implied a break with this prior model. It makes sense, then, to ask what this break in the family model of politics meant.

By introducing the term *family romance,* I do not mean to suggest that the French revolutionaries were acting out of some kind of pathological fantasy rooted in warped individual psychologies. The revolutionary family romances (and they were plural) were not neurotic reactions to disappointment—as in Freud's formulation— but creative efforts to reimagine the political world, to imagine a polity unhinged from patriarchal authority. I use the term *family romance(s)* in order to suggest that much of this imaginative effort went on below the surface, as it were, of conscious political dis-

---

(Ithaca, N.Y., 1981). My analysis is not much informed by Jameson, though I do endorse his claim that "the structure of the psyche is historical, and has a history" (p. 62). It might be said that I am trying to uncover some of that history.

course. I try to get at its constitution and changes through a variety of documents, ranging from speeches about the killing of the king to paintings and engravings of ordinary families.

I do not offer this analysis of family romances as a replacement for traditional political history, as if feelings about paternal authority, for instance, somehow predetermined the nature of overt political conflicts. I do not mean to reduce politics to fantasies, either individual or collective. Yet politics do depend on imagination and hence to some extent on fantasy, and family experience is the source of much of that fantasy. Family issues divided political groups on a conscious and on an unconscious level. It is significant, for example, that differences over family policy divided a broadly defined political left, which proposed sweeping changes in family laws, from a broadly defined right, which resisted those changes. In many and sometimes surprising ways, family romances, both conscious and unconscious, helped organize the political experience of the Revolution; revolutionaries and counterrevolutionaries alike had to confront the issues of paternal authority, female participation, and fraternal solidarity. They had to tell stories about how the republic came to be and what it meant, and those stories always had an element of family conflict and resolution. Some of the elements of the stories were perennial—the relations of fathers to sons, husbands to wives, parents to children, men to women—but their particular configurations were contingent on the social and political patterns produced by the revolutionary process.

Over the years of preparation of this book, I have benefited from the help and encouragement of countless individuals and institutions. My work on this project first got off the ground during the academic year 1988–89 thanks to a National Endowment for the Humanities fellowship at the School of Social Science of the Institute for Advanced Study in Princeton. The School of Arts and Sciences at the University of Pennsylvania made it possible for me to take a year's leave in 1988–89 by supplementing the fellowship at the Institute for Advanced Study and has also generously supported my research since 1987 through the Joe and Emily Lowe Foundation Term Professorship in the Humanities. This research fund provided me with the invaluable help of two research assistants, Jeffrey Horn and Victoria Thompson. The Society for the Humanities at Cornell University provided me with a semester's leave and an intellectual home during the spring of 1990. To all these institutions and my colleagues at them, I am very grateful.

I had the good fortune (at least it usually seemed like good fortune) of working on this book during the bicentennial celebrations of the French Revolution. As a consequence I had the opportunity to give various parts at conferences and lectures around the world. Many of the central themes of my argument were first elaborated in the Gauss seminars that I gave at Princeton University in the fall of 1988 and in the Hagey lectures at Waterloo University in the fall of 1989. It is impossible to recognize adequately all of the helpful suggestions made to me by colleagues at those lectures and at meetings in Rouen, Paris, Tokyo, Edinburgh, Milan, and many other places. Special recognition is due to the participants in my seminar on sexuality and republicanism at the Folger Institute in the spring of 1991. They graciously sat through weeks of discussion on matters most dear to me, read large portions of the manuscript of the book, and freely gave of their own ideas on the subject. The two readers for the University of California Press, Sarah Maza and Dena Goodman, offered many valuable suggestions; and Sheila Levine, as usual, shepherded me and the book through all the necessary stages toward publication. Margaret Jacob has shared all my worries and hopes for this book and has read its various versions with immense good cheer and good sense.

Since I have been studying the forms of French revolutionary politics for two decades now, I suppose that it is about time that I recognized the importance of the family in constituting the political order. Sometimes the things closest to home are the hardest to see. My own interest in politics emerged from the experience of growing up in a very political household. My mother was involved in many political and public-interest organizations, sat for ten years on the city council of St. Paul, Minnesota, and now is a county commissioner. My father first tolerated and then actively enjoyed the excitement. I learned an immense amount about the way local politics worked by watching my mother and have always been encouraged in my intellectual endeavors to understand them by my father. I only hope that they will see in these pages a tribute to their influence (though I do not mean to imply that the family and gender relations of the French Revolution remind me of home!).

1

The Family Model of Politics

It was a cold and foggy morning in winter when the king of France met his death. At 10:22 A.M. on 21 January 1793, the executioner dropped the guillotine's blade on the neck of Louis Capet, the former Louis XVI (see figure 1). The recently installed guillotine had been designed as the great equalizer; with it, every death would be the same, virtually automatic, presumably painless. The deputies hoped that by killing Louis in this way, they would prove "that great truth which the prejudices of so many centuries had stifled; today we have just convinced ourselves that a king is only a man and that no man is above the laws."

In these few words, the newspaper writer captured the meaning of the event in the most accessible terms: the French killed the king in order to *convince themselves* that the king was only a man like other men, that the magic of kingship which had been so powerful during so many centuries could be effaced. "Capet is no longer! Peoples of Europe! Peoples of the world! Look carefully at the thrones and you will see that they are nothing but dust!"[1] As if to ensure the return of this particular throne to dust, the severed head and body of the king were immediately deposited in a deep grave in the Madeleine Cemetery and covered with quicklime. All remaining traces of the king's physical presence were effaced.

The newspaper article's tones of hope and tenses of conditionality belie a great anxiety. France has given a great example to the people of the world and a great lesson to kings, the writer proclaims, but will the one and the other profit from it? The day is forever memorable, but will it survive for posterity? "Never let insult come near you. Historians! Be worthy of the time; write the truth, nothing but the truth."[2] The writer writes to reject all semblance of guilt. The

1. "Paris. Journée du 21," *Journal des hommes libres de tous les pays*, no. 82, 22 January 1793. Unless otherwise noted, all translations from the French are my own.
2. Ibid.

Louis Capet étant monté sur l'échafaud les mains liées derrière le dos, considéra pendant quelques minutes les objets qui l'environnoient, son confesseur lui dit allez fils ainé de St. Louis, le ciel vous attend .Cette exécution eut lieu place de la Revolution .ci - devant place Louis XV.

1. Engraving of Louis XVI at the guillotine. From *Révolutions de Paris*,
no. 185, 19–26 January 1793. Photo: author.

20,000 spectators jammed into the Place de la Révolution had been
there to share the experience, and 80,000 armed men had stood
guard to make sure that there would be no breaches of security.[3] If
guilt was felt, it was presumably widely shared.

The killing of the king was the most important political act of the
Revolution and the central drama in the revolutionary family romance. Everyone recognized its symbolic significance, yet the revolutionaries had various and often contradictory views about the
meaning of the act. Even though the deputies in the Convention
frequently cited the historical precedent of the execution of England's Charles I, for example, they drew no single consistent meaning from it. In any case, everyone knew that kingship had been
restored in England and the regicides punished; it was not a particularly encouraging precedent.

Revolutionaries and royalists alike considered the king the head

3. For the best account of the trial and execution, see David P. Jordan, *The King's
Trial: The French Revolution vs. Louis XVI* (Berkeley, 1979).

of the entire social order, even though the political position of Louis XVI had been undermined in some respects before 1793, perhaps even before 1789. The status of Louis Capet was very much in question at the time of his execution. Had the executioner killed a king or a man long since deprived of his sacred status? Whatever the answer, whether the king was symbolically dead in 1793, 1789, or before, his actual death in 1793 drew attention to a sacred void, marked by the empty pedestal facing Louis during his execution. The pedestal had supported a statue of his grandfather, Louis XV.

The government which ordered the execution of the former king was a republic whose legitimacy rested on popular sovereignty. Establishing a republic on paper took a stroke of the pen; winning the allegiance of the population and establishing an enduring sense of legitimacy required much more. What would make people obey the law in the new social order? The king had been the head of a social body held together by bonds of deference; peasants deferred to their landlords, journeymen to their masters, great magnates to their king, wives to their husbands, and children to their parents. Authority in the state was explicitly modeled on authority in the family. A royal declaration of 1639 had explained, "The natural reverence of children for their parents is linked to the legitimate obedience of subjects to their sovereign."[4] Once the king had been eliminated, what was to be the model that ensured the citizens' obedience?

No one understood better than the English critic of the Revolution, Edmund Burke, the connection between filial devotion and the willingness of a subject to obey. He feared that the whole community would be destroyed by the subversion of "those principles of domestic trust and fidelity which form the discipline of social life."[5] In reviewing the early events of the French Revolution and in particular the demeaning of the royal family during the October Days of 1789, Burke bemoaned the passing of what he called the age of chivalry and its replacement by the age of "sophisters, oeconomists, and calculators":

4. Marcel Garaud and Romuald Szramkiewicz, *La Révolution française et la famille* (Paris, 1978), p. 135.
5. *Letter to a Member of the National Assembly*, quoted in Steven Blakemore, *Burke and the Fall of Language: The French Revolution as Linguistic Event* (Hanover, N.H., 1988), p. 42. Blakemore offers an excellent discussion of Burke's understanding of patriarchy.

In the new age, all the pleasing illusions, which made power gentle, and obedience liberal, which harmonized the different shades of life, and which, by a bland assimilation, incorporated into politics the sentiments which beautify and soften private society, are to be dissolved by this new conquering empire of light and reason. All the decent drapery of life is to be rudely torn off.

Without that "decent drapery," without "the sentiments which beautify and soften private society," Burke predicted, the revolutionaries would have to rule by the force of terror. "In the groves of *their* academy, at the end of every vista, you see nothing but the gallows."[6]

My analysis in the following pages is much influenced by Burke's fundamental insight into the interweaving of private sentiments and public politics, even though I have a very different view of the Revolution from his. Burke saw that political obedience rested on something more than rational calculation: "To make us love our country, our country ought to be lovely."[7] Political obedience always rests on a set of assumptions about the proper working of the social order, and obedience—in modern terms, consent—is never automatic, even when it most appears to be so, as in so-called traditional societies. It was certainly not automatic in the new republic, as tax collectors and military recruiters discovered every day.

The revolutionaries were ripping the veil of deference off society. Unlike Burke, however, they did not see this as the end of all decency; they wanted to make their government "lovely" too. From 1789 onward, supporters of the Revolution were engaged in the great adventure of the modern Western social contract; they were trying to replace deference and paternal authority with a new basis for political consent. Many of them had read the great theorists of this adventure: Machiavelli, Hobbes, Locke, Montesquieu, and Rousseau. But the theorists, with the exception of Rousseau, offered little in the way of advice about the affective relations that might cement a new contract.

In the absence of any clear model for the private sentiments that might make a new order lovable, the revolutionaries fumbled their way through a thicket of interrelated problems. If absolutism had rested on the model of patriarchal authority, then would the de-

---

6. Edmund Burke, *Reflections on the Revolution in France* (New York, 1973), pp. 89–91.
    7. Ibid., p. 91.

struction of absolutism depend on the destruction of patriarchy, what the French called "la puissance paternelle"? How far should the moderation of paternal authority go? Would the restriction of paternal authority make everyone in the political family equal, brother with brother, brother with sister, and children with parents? In other words, what kind of family romance would replace the one dominated by the patriarchal father? If paternalism was to be replaced by a model of fraternity, what were the implications of that new model? How, for instance, was the idea of the political exclusion of women to be maintained in the absence of the old justifications of "natural" family order? Would the model of the family be thrown out altogether in favor of a model based on isolated, independent, self-possessing, contracting individuals? The attack on absolutism brought in its turbulent wake a necessary reevaluation of the shape of the individual self.

Although these questions might seem to be obvious, they did not present themselves very clearly or even all at once to the leaders of the French Revolution. To a great extent these questions have also dropped out of much modern, contract-based political theory. Contract theory pretends that questions about the family and the relations between men and women belong in a private sphere separate from the public arena. All of the great political theorists from the seventeenth century onward struggled with the question, in particular, of women's place in the new order, and all of them tried to devise solutions that would ensure the continued subordination of women to their husbands after the breakdown of patriarchy. Yet most of these theorists showed little interest in elaborating what Carole Pateman calls the "sexual contract" between men and women that logically accompanied the social contract.[8] The one great exception is Freud. Although hardly known as a political theorist—indeed his forays in this direction are among his most maligned works—Freud tried to imagine a story about the original social contract that would explain the genesis of "the law of male sex-right," the right of men as men to dominate women.[9]

---

8. Carole Pateman, *The Sexual Contract* (Stanford, 1988). Although Pateman's analysis is very important, I do not follow her on all points. I have written this book to show how difficult it was to enforce a patriarchal version of fraternity.

9. Pateman takes the term "law of male sex-right" from Adrienne Rich. See ibid., p. 2.

In *Totem and Taboo* (1913), in particular, Freud offered his own version of the origins of the social contract, or what might be called the original family romance. He located those origins in a kind of prehistoric fall from life in the primal horde, the first amorphous gathering of humans. In "the first great act of sacrifice," as he called it, the sons banded together to kill the father and eat him.[10] They killed the father because he had kept all the females for himself and driven away the growing sons. By eating him, they accomplished their identification with the father. The deed once accomplished, the brothers felt a sense of guilt, so they undid their deed by creating two taboos: a taboo against killing the totem animal that was substituted for the father; and the incest taboo, which denied the liberated women to the brothers. These taboos gave rise to religion and social organization (kinship) respectively, and they effectively repressed for the future the two main wishes of the Oedipus complex: the desire to kill the father and to sleep with the mother.

By instituting the taboos, moreover, the brothers solved the major problem facing them after the killing of the father: their feelings of competition with each other for the women. "Sexual desires do not unite men," claimed Freud, "but divide them."[11] If the brothers were to live together in peace, they had to deny themselves the women previously controlled by the father. Freud suggests that the brothers' social organization had a homosexual tinge that was worth preserving. By creating the incest taboo, the brothers "rescued the organization which had made them strong—and which may have been based upon the homosexual feelings and acts, originating perhaps during the period of their expulsion from the horde."[12] Through their new social organization, the brothers were able to reconcile themselves with the dead father, whom they also loved and admired, maintain their feelings for each other, and at the same time enforce a heterosexual system of marriage to ensure the survival of the group.

An inevitable "longing" for the father led to a recreation of him in the form of gods and social organization itself. Because of the pres-

---

10. *Totem and Taboo: Some Points of Agreement between the Mental Lives of Savages and Neurotics,* in vol. 13 of *The Standard Edition of the Complete Psychological Works of Sigmund Freud,* trans. James Strachey (London, 1958), p. 151.

11. Ibid., p. 144.

12. Ibid.

sure of competition within the band of brothers, no one could be allowed to gain "the father's supreme power," but the desire to mimic the father could be accommodated in new systems of rank and status. "The original democratic equality" of each member of the tribe was relinquished, and individuals who distinguished themselves above the rest were venerated.[13] Thus the social contract as envisaged by Freud was not only based on a concomitant sexual contract, in which women were subject to men's power; it also implied complementary bonds between men. Social organization sublimated an underlying, highly charged, male bonding. Women had no place in the new political and social order except as markers of social relations between men.

Freud's own inability to work himself out of a patriarchal model of psychopolitical organization was revealed in one of the throwaway lines of *Totem and Taboo*. Speaking of the move toward deification of the murdered father, Freud inserts: "I cannot suggest at what point in this process of development a place is to be found for the great mother-goddesses, who may perhaps in general have preceded the father-gods."[14] Freud's vision was so patriarchal that the only contests he could imagine were between fathers and sons; women were merely the objects of these conflicts. In a telling passage, he asserted: "The psychoanalysis of individual human beings, however, teaches us with quite special insistence that the god of each of them is formed in the likeness of his father, that his personal relation to God depends on his relation to his father in the flesh and oscillates and changes along with that relation, and that at bottom God is nothing other than an exalted father."[15] The same might be said of the law and of social organization generally.

In the essays in this book, I do not intend to apply Freud or Freudianism to the French Revolution, as if Freud's theories of human development could be simply superimposed as a grid on the raw data of the revolutionary experience. Indeed, many of the central Freudian concepts such as penis envy, castration fears, or even the Oedipal complex will appear infrequently or not at all in these pages. I find Freud's analysis in *Totem and Taboo* suggestive

13. Ibid., pp. 148–49.
14. Ibid., p. 149.
15. Ibid., p. 147.

because it sees a set of relationships as being critical to the founding of social and political authority: relationships between fathers and sons, between men, and between men and women. In addition, Freud's own need to write a myth of human origins demonstrates the centrality of narratives about the family to the constitution of all forms of authority, even though Freud's account cannot fruitfully be read as an analysis of an actual event in prehistory or as a rigid model for social and political relationships. I will be arguing that the experience of the French Revolution can be interpreted to put pressure on the Freudian account, even though that account provides an important point of departure.

The very mention of the name Freud by a historian is for some a red flag of danger. Among historians, psychoanalytic interpretation has been largely confined to the analysis of individual biographies or, more rarely, to the analysis of group psychology in times of crisis. The connection between individual psyches and social and historical development is an interesting subject of research, but it does not directly concern me here. I do not, for example, offer an analysis of a figure such as Robespierre in Freudian terms. I am interested rather in the ways that people collectively imagine—that is, think unconsciously about—the operation of power, and the ways in which this imagination shapes and is in turn shaped by political and social processes. Central to this collective imagination are the relations between parents and children and between men and women.

To put it in specific historical terms, once the French had killed the king, who had been represented as the father of his people, what did they imagine themselves to be doing? What figure did they imagine to take his place? What was the structure of the new political unconscious that replaced the old one? Answers to these questions require an analysis of the political imagination that is at once historically specific and capable of illuminating generally the basic metaphors of modern political and social life.

Freud's apparent insistence that the ritual sacrifice of the father was an actual deed—"in the beginning was the Deed";[16] his fondness for analogies between the thought processes of "savages" and neurotics; and his incredibly intricate, if not fanciful analyses of particular individuals are all grounds for worry about the verifiabil-

---

16. The concluding sentence of *Totem and Taboo*, ibid., p. 161.

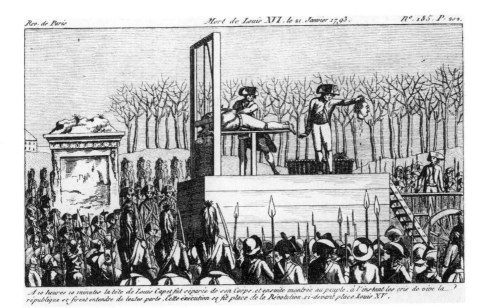

2.   Engraving of the execution of Louis XVI. From *Révolutions de Paris*,
no. 185, 19–26 January 1793. Photo: author.

ity or scientific grounding of psychoanalysis. Yet they do not vitiate
the importance of the questions raised by Freud or of the general
metaphorical structure that he outlined. Freud, like Burke, saw that
obedience was not automatic, and he tried to provide an explanation
for how it works. In so doing, he suggested several themes that will
appear again and again in this book: the killing of the father, the
nature of fraternity, the assignation of guilt, the fate of the "liberated women," the choice of new totems to replace the dead father,
and the enforcement of the incest taboo.[17]

The French killed the father in an act that comes as close as
anything does in modern history to a ritual sacrifice (see figure 2).

17. A very brief suggestion of the importance of this "primal scene" can be found
in Ronald Paulson, *Representations of Revolution (1789–1820)* (New Haven, 1983). See
especially p. 26: "It is here that we find the central and most important aspect of the
self-representation inside Paris: a tension of the stereotypic and the unique, of the
symbolic and the representational, which is to say the regressive, which urges a return
to the primal scene which Père Duchesne and others (in England Burke) knew as the
real heart of the matter, a scene more primal than republican Rome or Lycurgan
Sparta."

The radical newspaper that published the engravings reproduced in figures 1 and 2 put it just that way:

> We owe to the earth, since we have in a manner of speaking conse-crated slavery by our example, we owe a great lesson in the person of the 66th king, more criminal than all his predecessors taken together. The blood of Louis Capet, shed by the blade of the law on 21 January 1793, cleanses us of a stigma of 1300 years. . . . Liberty resembles that divinity of the Ancients which one cannot make auspicious and favor-able except by offering to it in sacrifice the life of a great culprit.

It is worth noting that in this passage the editor did not describe the "great culprit" as a father figure. By 1793 the revolutionaries wanted to reject any such role for Louis Capet, the former Louis XVI. Nevertheless, the father is implied because the paper went on to refer to the brothers who had killed him, and it described a scene in which the victim was metaphorically devoured. A crowd of people ran up to the scaffold after the execution to dip their pikes and handkerchiefs in the blood of the former king. One zealot sprinkled blood on the crowd and shouted, "Brothers, they tell us that the blood of Louis Capet will fall again on our heads; well, so be it, let it fall. . . . Republicans, the blood of a king brings happiness."[18]

This is one of those rare occasions when revolutionary discourse provides its own revealing glimpse into the psychosexual founda-tions of the political order. Yet even in this case, the evidence is subject to more than one interpretation. In a major rereading of Freud's analysis, the literary critic René Girard has offered a dif-ferent psychoanalytical perspective on just such a scene. He argues that ritual sacrifice is not fundamentally about parricide and incest but rather is a way of concealing and disguising the community's terror of its own violence. The ritualization of violence—the sin-gling out of a scapegoat—serves to reinstitute differences, limits, and boundaries and thereby displaces violence from the interior of the community. He insists, "The purpose of the sacrifice is to restore harmony to the community, to reinforce the social fabric." Bound-aries are especially important because any "sacrificial crisis," accord-ing to Girard, threatens sexual differentiation. The singling out of

18. "Mort de Louis XVI, dernier roi de France," *Révolutions de Paris*, no. 185, 19–26 January 1793. I have compared Durkheimian and Freudian analyses of the killing of the king in "The Sacred and the French Revolution," in Jeffrey Alexander, ed., *Durkheimian Sociology* (Cambridge, 1988), pp. 25–43.

the scapegoat, who might be anyone and not just the father, is for Girard the true origin of all myths, rituals, kinship systems, indeed, symbolic thought itself.[19]

The Girardian reading provides a different angle on the passage from the revolutionary newspaper about the execution of the king. In a Girardian account, the emphasis would not be on the king's position as father of his people. The brothers do not kill him because they want to share his power but rather because the French fear their own capacity for violence and need a ritual act in order to reinstitute community boundaries. In other words, the king has to die to erase the guilt that the French themselves feel *before the act has been committed*. As the editor of the *Révolutions de Paris* wrote: "We owe to the earth, since we have in a manner of speaking consecrated slavery by our example, we owe a great lesson in the person of the 66th king."

In order to displace its own violence, which follows from the disintegration of Old Regime cultural and political codes, the revolutionary community has to focus its guilt on a surrogate victim, the scapegoat, who is, as Girard puts it, a kind of "monstrous double": "The surrogate victim constitutes both a link and a barrier between the community and the sacred."[20] The king has to be transformed into a kind of sacred monster, whose expulsion will return the community to itself. His monstrousness is defined by his outrageous culpability; he is, the newspaper claims, "more criminal than all his predecessors taken together." He has to be in order to be a suitable victim. As a consequence, his blood (another sacred allusion) "cleanses us of a stigma of 1300 years." Only the sacrifice of a great culprit would be sufficient to the task of community redefinition and redemption.

Several themes from Girard's reinterpretation of Freud will appear in the essays that follow: the moment of sacrificial crisis, the need for the community to define itself through the choice of victims, and the threat of the loss of boundaries, especially sexual boundaries. It is not enough, however, to replace Freud with Girard. In the French Revolution, the king was victimized for several reasons; he may have been a great culprit and hence a monstrous

19. René Girard, *Violence and the Sacred*, trans. Patrick Gregory (Baltimore, 1977), pp. 8, 188, 235.
20. Ibid., p. 271.

double of the community, but he was also the father. So, in a sense, I want to have it both (Freudian and Girardian) ways. The French Revolution is a drama about conflict between father and sons *and* about the threat of violence to the community.

Girard denies the validity of the Oedipal triangle between father, mother, and son and replaces it with a more generalized mimetic model of desire which emphasizes the identification between men; nevertheless, he too accords some importance to the role of women.[21] Women are often blamed for violence in order to exonerate men; women are associated with delirium in order to reassure male dignity and authority and in particular to eliminate the blurring of sexual boundaries that accompanies the sacrificial crisis.[22] In the end, however, Girard, like Freud, refuses all independence of action to women; in both psychoanalytic scenarios they are simply the *objects* of desire, whether directly (in the case of Freud) or indirectly through male mimesis (in the case of Girard). It is one of my aims here to redress that balance, to insist that women were viewed as threats because they could act and not just because they were convenient figments of the male imagination.

The French revolutionaries did talk self-consciously about "fraternity," the least understood of the values in the revolutionary triad of "liberty, equality, and fraternity." In conscious discourse fraternity was an idea associated with political solidarities and the drawing of political and social boundaries within the community. The notion of fraternity gradually evolved during the revolutionary decade, as a recent study by Marcel David has shown. In the early years of the Revolution, fraternity had a large and confident meaning because almost everyone could be imagined as participating in the community. For example, at the Festival of Federation of 14 July 1790, Lafayette swore on behalf of all the federated national guards present "to remain united to all the French by the indissoluble bonds of fraternity."

21. Girard rejects the family model, whether it privileges fathers or brothers, and insists instead on the centrality of rivalry to desire. As he puts it, "rivalry does not arise because of the fortuitous convergence of two desires on a single object [such as the mother]; rather, *the subject desires the object because the rival desires it.*" It follows, then, that "the incest wish, the patricide wish, do not belong to the child but spring from the mind of the adult, the model. . . . The son is always the last to learn that what he desires is incest and patricide, and it is the hypocritical adults who undertake to enlighten him in this matter." Ibid., pp. 145, 175.

22. Ibid., pp. 139–41.

During the radical years, 1792–94, *fraternity* was used more often in a narrow and fearful sense; fraternity defined a kind of "us" and "them" of revolutionary politics, especially on the popular level. One Parisian sectional assembly proclaimed in February 1793, "For a free people, there should be no neutral being. There are only brothers or enemies." The slogan "fraternity or death" seemed to capture this sentiment in dramatic fashion. A reaction against such a belligerent notion of fraternity accompanied Robespierre's fall from power. In the first months after his execution, most representations of fraternity associated it with symbols of sweetness, purity, innocence, and union.

Domestication of fraternity did not prove to be enough, however. Progressively after the fall of Robespierre, "fraternity" dropped out of revolutionary slogans to be replaced by liberty and equality standing alone. Official engravers no longer included fraternity in their repertoire of themes, and royalist engravers represented it in derisory contexts. An engraving of 1797, for example, shows a sansculotte trampling on the constitution. The word *fraternity* is written on his dagger. Fraternity and fraternization were now cynically limited to the relations with the "sister republics," the satellites and dependents of the conquering French nation. Under the Consulate, prefects were expressly forbidden to use the word.[23] This brief history suggests that the word had a political charge that was indissolubly linked with radical revolution.

Getting at the affective charge implicit in the notion of fraternity is more difficult. Revolutionaries rarely explained their emotional motives for, or reactions to, their language, gestures, or rituals. As a consequence, my analysis will usually have to proceed by indirection and inference. There are, however, all sorts of clues about the psychosexual meaning of fraternity in revolutionary symbolics, for instance, in the ordering of festivals and the choice of icons and emblems; and, on occasion, in revolutionary discourse itself—for example, in the debates on women's clubs or in the newspaper accounts of the killing of the king. The psychosymbolics of the

---

23. My account of the conscious meaning of fraternity is taken from Marcel David, *Fraternité et Révolution française, 1789–1799* (Paris, 1987); the quotations are from pp. 58, 145, 205, 244. David provides an indispensable guide to the usages of the term before and especially during the Revolution. He argues that the slogan "la fraternité ou la mort" was not meant to be as menacing as it sounds.

revolutionary political imagination are also apparent, however, in less conventional sources for historical analysis: in novels, in paintings, and especially in political pornography. All of them are examples of genres in which family romances can be dramatically enacted.

In what follows, I offer a necessarily selective but I hope not arbitrary reading of a wide range of sources, from laws about the family to pornographic novels. My subjects will include such diverse topics as the rise of portraiture in 1791, the regularization of inheritance for illegitimate children in 1793, and the vogue of novels about orphans after 1795, as well as the more obvious topics such as the killings of the king and the queen. Although the iconography of the Revolution has of late attracted considerable attention, especially as it is expressed in graphic form, much less has been done as yet with revolutionary painting and literature.[24] The revolutionary decade has been considered unworthy of attention by most literary critics and art historians because it produced little in the way of great literature or painting, apart from works by Jacques-Louis David. Until very recently, scholars continued to assume that the Revolution had had little positive impact on "high" art beyond the "vandalization" of national treasures that occurred during the radical period of late 1793 and early 1794.[25] Literary histories of the Revolution, for instance, still begin with considerations of political speeches and newspapers, just as they did in the nineteenth century.[26] It is obvious that no one scholar can hope to offer a survey of all the relevant cultural and political expressions of the period in the search for their underlying patterns of familial imagery. I certainly

24. See, for example, the essays in *French Caricature and the French Revolution, 1789–1799,* catalogue for an exhibition coorganized by the University of California, Los Angeles, and the Bibliothèque nationale de France (Los Angeles, 1988). For a useful general discussion of revolutionary art forms see Emmet Kennedy, *A Cultural History of the French Revolution* (New Haven, 1989).

25. Serge Bianchi, "Le 'Vandalisme révolutionnaire' ou la naissance d'un mythe," in *La Légende de la Révolution,* actes du colloque international de Clermont-Ferrand, juin 1986 (Clermont-Ferrand, 1988), pp. 189–199. In his excellent study of revolutionary painting William Olander remarks on the denigration of revolutionary art: "Too often, the decade of the 1790s has been seen merely as a continuation of art and policies pursued under the *ancien régime,* or as a simple, but unrealized prelude to the era of Napoleon and beyond." *"Pour transmettre à la postérité:* French Painting and the Revolution, 1774–1795" (Ph.D. diss., New York University, 1983), p. 11.

26. See, for example, the useful overview by Béatrice Didier, *La Littérature de la Révolution française* (Paris, 1988).

do not claim to account for every engraving, painting, or novel in my analysis, but I do hope to offer an account of the links between family images and power that will prompt others to examine their own sources in new lights.

Anyone who works on the revolutionary period knows how difficult it is to use art-historical and literary materials. Sources such as paintings, engravings, and novels are by their nature particularly rich in representations of fathers, mothers, and children, but they are not transparent representations of the imagery of power. Painters rarely painted with straightforward political purposes, even during the French Revolution, and novelists rarely wrote with the self-conscious aim of supporting a particular political order. Moreover, we know little about the specific intentions of artists or novelists of the period.

The difficulties are also technical. We do not know the press runs of most novels published at the time, and the exhibition catalogues of the revolutionary period are often limited to simple and uninformative designations of paintings such as "family scene" or "head of an individual." The example of engravings is particularly instructive. Prints required less time for production and as a consequence could be expected to follow the latest political developments more rapidly than the less obviously politicized media.[27] Revolutionary prints were not produced from a set of systematic or self-conscious themes, however; they were produced in response to a variety of demands ranging from the immediate propaganda aims of the government to the consumer market for subscription engravings that captured revolutionary history even as it unfolded.[28] There are over 30,000 prints from the French Revolution collected in various libraries and museums in the world. Most of them are not dated or signed, so drawing conclusions about their meaning is even more risky than in the case of works by well-known painters.

These problems compound the difficulty of working in a psychoanalytic perspective. I will be moving constantly between the familial

27. On the lack of revolutionary themes in French painting of the period, see James Leith, *Art as Propaganda in France, 1750–1799: A Study in the History of Ideas* (Toronto, 1965). Leith estimates that only 5 percent of French paintings exhibited in the official salons treated revolutionary themes. They were vastly outnumbered by landscapes, portraits, and genre paintings. See especially pp. 135, 145. A more nuanced view can be found in Olander, *"Pour transmettre."*
28. See *French Caricature and the French Revolution.*

and the political, on the grounds that they are interconnected; and I will be shifting back and forth through a variety of sources, on the grounds that they tell a set of interrelated stories about the founding of a new political and social order. Like the "new historicists" in art and literary criticism, I juxtapose the work of literature, painting, or other art form with other kinds of contemporaneous historical documentation. Yet in the end, my aim is different from theirs. Rather than trying to account for the work of art or literature, I want to get at the common historical and imaginative processes that animate painting, engraving, and literature—as well as political events during the French Revolution. I find that common ground in the development of family romances that both unified and threatened to unravel the revolutionary experience as a whole.

2

The Rise and Fall of the Good Father

In a speech given to the Constituent Assembly in August 1790, a little-known deputy drew the connection between tyranny in the family and tyranny in the polity:

> After having made man free and happy in public life, it remains for us to assure his liberty and his happiness in private life. You know that under the Old Regime the tyranny of parents was often as terrible as the despotism of ministers; often the prisons of state became family prisons. It is suitable therefore to draw up, after the declaration of rights of man and citizen, a declaration, so to speak, of the rights of spouses, of fathers, of sons, of parents, and so on.[1]

The Revolution opened the way to a reconsideration not only of state authority but also of authority within the family. The rights of every family member and all family relationships were now to be regulated in the interest of liberty and happiness. It is obvious from this passage that the position of the king was still very much undecided one year after the beginning of the Revolution. The despotism of ministers, rather than the tyranny of kings, was the focus of the deputy's concern. Within a year, however, both the king and his queen would become the focus of a violent, often scurrilous campaign to denigrate their authority.

The story of the king's fall from his lofty position was intimately tied up with the fortunes of the ideal of the good father. If the king was father of his people, then changes in the image of fathers would have an inescapable impact on the king's representation of himself to the public. Criticism of excessive or tyrannical paternal authority began long before 1789. The Enlightenment conviction that mankind was moving out of its political and intellectual adolescence led to increasing demands for participation in public affairs. It might be

---

1. Deputy Gossin speaking on 5 August 1790, during the discussion of judicial reorganization, *Archives parlementaires*, vol. 17 (Paris, 1884), p. 617.

said that the emergence of a new realm of public opinion in the eighteenth century implied the maturation of the king's subjects/children into autonomous men/citizens.

The general eighteenth-century trend in western Europe toward regarding children as separate individuals deserving of affection and educational concern also helped to create the ideal of the good father.[2] Rousseau and the other philosophes had taken up Locke's and Pufendorf's insistence on the limits to paternal power; the father's power was to end when the child no longer needed his help, and after that moment, father and (male) children were presumed to be equals. Rousseau explained: "The father is only the master of the child as long as his help is necessary to him; beyond that moment, they become equals and then the son, perfectly independent of the father, owes him only respect and not obedience."[3] The philosophes also subscribed to Locke's notion that paternal power could not provide a model for political power, though like Locke before them, they still insisted that fathers should be dominant within families. As Montesquieu argued, "the example of paternal power proves nothing," but "paternal authority is still very useful for the maintenance of morals."[4]

The influence of the ideal of the good father was apparent on the most self-conscious political level, as Jeffrey Merrick has shown in his study of parlementary discourse in the eighteenth century. During the rhetorical struggles between king and parlement, parlementary magistrates used filial language to express their obedience but also to make palatable their resistance to royal authority. In 1732 the magistrates asked Louis XV to show them that he was "more our father than our master." In their view, "filial respect is not at all opposed to legitimate complaints." When requesting royal action against "despotic" behavior by clergy, tax collectors, or even royal officials, the magistrates appealed to the "common father," who

2. On the ideological background, see the very brief discussion in Marcel Garaud and Romuald Szramkiewicz, *La Révolution française et la famille* (Paris, 1978), especially pp. 135–37. The classic study remains Philippe Ariès, *Centuries of Childhood: A Social History of Family Life*, trans. Robert Baldick (London, 1960). For a more recent discussion, see Jean Delumeau and Daniel Roche, eds., *Histoire des pères et de la paternité* (Paris, 1990), and Yvonne Knibiehler, *Les Pères aussi ont une histoire* (Paris, 1987).

3. *Discours sur l'origine de l'inégalité parmi les hommes*, quoted in Garaud and Szramkiewicz, *La Révolution française et la famille*, p. 136.

4. Quoted in Nadine Bérenguier, "L'Infortune des alliances: Famille et roman au dix-huitième siècle" (Ph.D. diss., Stanford University, 1988), p. 27.

would show "paternal solicitude," "paternal affection," and "paternal tenderness." They were asking the good father to curb his own powers.[5]

In countering parlementary resistance to his policies, the king used some of the same rhetoric, but to his own advantage. He knew how "to let himself be moved like a father" but also how "to make himself obeyed like a master." He was willing to respond "with the indulgence of a father," but he also required that the magistrates set an example of filial submission for the kingdom as a whole. The king and his ministers were quick to seize upon the implications of the rhetoric of the good father and to insist on their own interpretation. Faced with the challenge, the king insisted that the magistrates could not be "masters" on their own and remain loyal to him.[6]

Images of state and familial power were perhaps most closely intertwined in the controversy over lettres de cachet that developed during the eighteenth century. The king could use lettres de cachet to imprison or exile anyone who threatened public order, and lettres de cachet could be solicited by parents to incarcerate their children, without a hearing, for the sake of familial order and reputation.[7] During the eighteenth century, critics of government policy and officials of the crown alike began to doubt the wisdom of using lettres de cachet, whose very name had come to connote secrecy and arbitrary judgment. In 1770, for example, Malesherbes attacked the use of lettres de cachet on behalf of the Cour des Aides of Paris. Malesherbes complained of the abuses of power made possible by these extraordinary administrative instruments: "The orders signed by Your Majesty are often filled with obscure names of people whom Your Majesty could not possibly know. . . . The result, Sire, is that no citizen in your realm is assured of not seeing his liberty sacrificed to personal vengeance."[8]

---

5. Jeffrey Merrick, "Patriarchalism and Constitutionalism in Eighteenth-Century Parlementary Discourse," *Studies in Eighteenth-Century Culture* 20 (1990): 319, 321, 323. I am very indebted to Professor Merrick for sharing the unpublished results of his research on Old Regime patriarchalism with me.

6. Ibid., p. 326.

7. For a discussion of the actual use of lettres de cachet in the first half of the eighteenth century, see Arlette Farge and Michel Foucault, *Le Désordre des familles: Lettres de cachet des Archives de la Bastille au XVIIIe siècle* (Paris, 1982). The authors say very little about the opposition to the use of lettres de cachet.

8. Quoted in Frantz Funck-Brentano, *Les Lettres de cachet à Paris: Etude suivie d'une liste des prisonniers de la Bastille, 1659–1789* (Paris, 1903), p. xli.

The publication of memoirs written in the Bastille or other prisons by those who had suffered from the abuse of lettres de cachet drew public attention to the intertwining of despotic royal and despotic familial power. Mirabeau wrote of his father, who had had him imprisoned by lettre de cachet for causing a public scandal by his affair with a married woman, "Listening to the enemies of his son and refusing to hear him, punishing him more severely than the law required and by extrajudicial means, immolating him slowly and refusing him what a human master would not refuse his lackey—those are so many parricides."[9] While in prison in Vincennes, Mirabeau wrote an extensive denunciation, *Des Lettres de cachet et des prisons d'état* (published in 1782), which helped transform public opinion both about the powers of the monarchy and about the powers of families. Mirabeau addressed himself to public opinion and to parents with the aim of showing that "the use of lettres de cachet is *tyrannical.*"[10]

The abuse of lettres de cachet in family matters eventually attracted the attention of the king's own ministers. In 1784 Breteuil sent out a circular to all intendants and to the lieutenant general of police in Paris warning of parental severity: "Fathers and mothers are sometimes either unjust or too severe, or too easily alarmed; and I think that it is always necessary to require that at least two or three principal relatives sign the memoirs requesting orders [for lettres de cachet] along with the fathers and mothers."[11]

The efforts of the king's ministers to put a stop to misuse of lettres de cachet was part of the remaking of the king's image as good father. This image emerged in a variety of forms, sometimes in spite of official efforts. While the king's officials were commissioning paintings in the grand manner of classical and French history subjects, for instance, Louis XVI and Marie-Antoinette appeared in popular paintings, drawings, and engravings as examples of virtue and beneficence—the good parents—rather than in old-style dynastic glory.[12] Thus the public came to 1789 already prepared for the ambiguities of the reference to the king as good father: would the

9. *Lettres originales de Mirabeau. Ecrites au donjon de Vincennes, pendant les années 1777, 78, 79, et 80. Recueillies par P. Manuel, citoyen français* (Paris, 1792), vol. 3, p. 88.

10. *Oeuvres de Mirabeau*, vol. 7, *Des lettres de cachet et des prisons d'état* (Paris, 1835), pp. 10–11; Mirabeau's emphasis.

11. Quoted in Funck-Brentano, *Les Lettres de cachet*, p. xliv.

12. William Olander, "*Pour transmettre à la postérité:* French Painting and the Revolution, 1774–1795" (Ph.D. diss., New York University, 1983), p. 26.

good father give in to demands for independence from the children or resist changes in his status as detrimental to good family and political relationships?[13]

The ideal of the good father took shape in a variety of ways, ranging from tracts on education to paintings of sentimental family scenes. Perhaps the most influential source for new attitudes about both fathers and children was the novel. The rise of the novel and the emergence of interest in children and a more affective family went hand in hand. It is in fact impossible to tell which—the novel or the child-centered family—was cause and which was effect. As sensibility and individual subjectivity, even for children, came to be more and more emphasized, the role of the father was bound to change. A stern, repressive father was incompatible with the new model of the family as emotional center for the nurturing of children and the new model of the individual as an autonomous self.

Since eighteenth-century novels focused on the individual in his or her relationship to the social world and especially to family pressures, they inevitably enacted a family romance (or series of them). In the form of fiction, writers were able to explore facets of social existence usually suppressed in polite discourse: dreams of social mobility and individual self-transformation; fatal conflicts between parents and children; and the perils and allures of incest. As a consequence, the novel is an essential starting point for any consideration of the familial foundations of authority.

The increasing prominence of the novel in eighteenth-century France is in itself a sign of the growing interest in the sources of personal identity and in conflicts between the individual and the family. Novels were not limited to relations between fathers and children, of course. Joan De Jean has shown how women writers at the turn of the eighteenth century novelized their concern with the conflicts between marriage as a social contract and marriage for personal fulfillment. In these novels, the problem is not the father but the abusive husband and the support he gets from unjust laws.[14]

13. On the failure of Louis XVI as a paternalist as opposed to patriarchalist ruler, see Jeffrey Merrick, "Sexual Politics and Public Order in Late Eighteenth-Century France: The *Mémoires secrets* and the *Correspondance secrète*," *Journal of the History of Sexuality* 1 (1990): 68–84.

14. Joan De Jean, "Notorious Women: Marriage and the Novel in Crisis in France, 1690–1715," *The Yale Journal of Criticism* 4 (1991): 67–85.

Similarly, in the novels of Marie-Jeanne Riccoboni, one of the most popular novelists of the last half of the eighteenth century, it is the husband and lover, not the father, who is identified with tyrannical authority and arbitrary constraint. Men "pretend to be made to guide, sustain, and protect the *weak* and *timid* sex, but all the while it is they alone who attack, insist on her timidity, and profit from her weakness."[15] The ultimate in this tendency to efface father figures in female-authored novels may be Françoise de Graffigny's widely read *Lettres d'une Péruvienne* (1747). Her central character Zilia is an Inca priestess who is captured by the Spanish and then the French. The center of her emotional life is her "brother" Aza, whom she was slated to marry on the day of her capture. She is the model of a woman living outside of conventional family life, and she refuses to marry anyone once her brother abandons her for a nonincestuous Spanish Christian marriage.[16] It seems, then, that women writers in the eighteenth century identified the law with husbands, not fathers, and they showed little concern for paternal authority per se.

The intensity of concern with family conflicts—whether between wife and husband or between father and children—is reflected in the sheer number of novels that were produced. Eight new novels appeared in France in 1701, 52 in 1750, and 112 in 1789; the production of new works increased constantly (and then declined during the decade of revolution, a subject to which I will return).[17] There have been many explanations of the eighteenth-century explosion of the novel. Most critics seem to agree, however, that the good father only emerged in force in novels after 1750 and that even then the role of the father was often ambiguous; as the father became "good," he also carried less weight in the story line. There may be a convergence of novels written by men and those by women in this respect; fathers had not played a major role in most novels written by women, and by the end of the eighteenth century even novels written by men began to efface the father.

15. *Histoire d'Ernestine* (1765), quoted in Joan Hinde Stewart, *The Novels of Mme Riccoboni*, North Carolina Studies in the Romance Languages and Literatures, no. 165 (Chapel Hill, 1976), p. 104.

16. Janet Gurkin Altman, "Making Room for 'Peru': Graffigny's Novel Reconsidered," in Catherine Laforge, ed., *Dilemmes du roman: Essays in Honor of Georges May*, Stanford French and Italian Studies, vol. 65 (Saratoga, Calif., 1989), pp. 47–56.

17. See Jacques Rustin, *Le Vice à la mode: Etude sur le roman français du XVIIIe siècle de Manon Lescaut à l'apparition de La Nouvelle Héloïse (1731–1761)* (Paris, 1979), p. 20; and for the revolutionary period, Angus Martin, Vivienne G. Mylne, and Richard Frautschi, *Bibliographie du genre romanesque français, 1751–1800* (London, 1977).

From the 1720s onward, the French novel went through a remarkable evolution in regard to father figures. Some critics have
argued that father-son conflict was not much of an issue in the
French novel before 1725.[18] Father-son conflict was hardly new in
French literature, however; the classical theater of the seventeenth
century had given great prominence to family conflicts. In the second and third quarters of the eighteenth century, the depiction of
the family in both the novel and the theater changed decisively. The
novels of the 1730s, 1740s, and 1750s portrayed a family world in
disarray, whether in novels by women in which wives confronted the
abuses of husbands or in novels by men in which tyrannical fathers
were opposed by rebellious and sacrilegious sons.[19] Family relations
in the writings of Prévost, Voltaire, and Marivaux, for instance,
tended to be tragic or at least filled with obstacles.

In the novels and plays of the 1760s, 1770s, and 1780s, in contrast, the "bourgeois drama" with its emphasis on emotion and
good family relations became prominent; yet paradoxically, both the
drama and the novels of this later period became more insipid.
Good fathers apparently did not make for compelling drama. First,
the obstinate tyrants were domesticated as good fathers, even as
fathers made to suffer by their children. Then, almost as soon as
they were established as virtuous and emotional figures who cared
for their children in a new way, fictional fathers began to be effaced;
they were lost, absent, dead, or simply unknown. Whatever the
father's status in any particular novel, in almost all cases fathers were
ambivalent and ambiguous figures, not unlike Louis XVI himself on
the eve of 1789.

At least one critic has discerned a reorganization of "family mythology" in French literature after 1750.[20] Replacing the repressive
father of the earlier (male-authored) novels and plays is the generous and sometimes tortured father who is made to suffer by his
guilty children. The good, virtuous, and sensitive father, in Diderot's

---

18. Paul Pelckmans, *Le Sacre du père: Fiction des Lumières et historicité d'Oedipe,
1699–1775* (Amsterdam, 1983). Pelckmans's reading is primarily indebted to Girard.

19. Rustin, *Le Vice à la mode*, especially pp. 66–71, 233–46. In Rustin's view, these
family struggles served as a representation of social conflict, a convoluted expression
of the bitterness of a declining nobility. The obsessional concern with real and
metaphorical incest between brother and sister had the function in these novels, in
Rustin's view, of representing the impossibility of a successful social integration of the
upstart adventurer.

20. Pelckmans, *Le Sacre du père*, p. 322.

play *The Father of the Family* (1758), for example, is portrayed as suffering from the errors, however minor, of his son. In *The Unhappy Fathers* (1771), Diderot depicts a rebellious son who lives in misery after rejection by his father. The son's wife consoles him by evoking an image of a father who is suffering too.[21] The fathers in Baculard d'Arnaud's widely published *Tests of Sentiment* (1770–80) seem almost incapable of being anything but good. When they are harsh, they themselves suffer. The tragic image of family relations so current in the generation of Prévost thus gives way to one of two myths: the idyllic family without conflict or the family where conflicts exist only to be resolved as soon as the son (or more rarely, daughter) sees his (or her) guilt. In Marmontel's *Moral Tales* (1761), for instance, problems are never posed, and family life is portrayed as an almost continual idyll. In Baculard d'Arnaud, Oedipal struggles are easily resolved when the son admits remorse.

The father could still be a source of ambivalent feelings, especially when he vacillated between the roles of stern patriarch and loving father. The most influential example of this ambivalent father type was the Baron d'Etange in Rousseau's *Julie, ou la nouvelle Héloïse* (1761); in fact Julie's father may be the transition figure between the tyrannical and the good father. In the celebrated sixty-third letter of part 1, Julie describes to Claire how her father first berated her mother for allowing a man without station or name into their home. When Julie interrupts and tells her father to calm himself, her father strikes her in a fit of violence. Julie notes that this is the first time in her life that he has struck her, and in his fury he also hits her mother, who has tried to interpose herself between them. Over dinner, the baron tries to make up with his wife, and after dinner he pulls Julie to him and sits her on his knees. They both cry, and Julie describes this moment of reconciliation as "the

---

21. William F. Edmiston, *Diderot and the Family: A Conflict of Nature and Law*, Stanford French and Italian Studies, vol. 39 (Saratoga, Calif., 1985), pp. 73–74. Bill Edmiston alerted me to the interesting letter written by Diderot in 1758 to Marie-Jeanne Riccoboni. In it Diderot explained the structure of contemporary comedy: "What is the basis of our comedies? Always a marriage thwarted by the fathers or by the mothers, or by the relatives or by the children, or by passion or by interest, or by other incidents that you know well. Then in all these cases, what happens in our families? The father and the mother are filled with chagrin, the children are desperate, the home is full of tumult, suspicion, complaints, quarrels, fears; and as long as the obstacles last, there is hardly a smile and many tears are shed." Notice here the emphasis on chagrin. Georges Roth, ed., *Correspondance*, vol. 2, p. 101.

most delicious" in her life. Julie's father had recognized that parental severity would not work, but a soft touch would get him what he wanted: his daughter's obedience. He remains firm in his decision that she shall not marry Saint-Preux. Critics have disagreed over the meaning of this change in the father's behavior, some seeing in it the decline of the patriarchal father and others seeing instead a new manner of exercising an old structure of authority.[22]

This difference in interpretation is worth pausing over, however briefly, because it goes to the heart of the interpretive issues of my entire analysis. Literary critics seem to agree that real, biological fathers began to disappear from novels in the last half of the eighteenth century and that the fathers that were portrayed were depicted as new-model fathers relying on affection and concern rather than unquestioned authority. I view this as a major shift in the representation of fatherhood and in the meaning of all authority relations. Critics who follow a strictly Freudian interpretation insist that the absence of fathers simply enhances rather than eradicates paternal power.[23] In Freud's terms, there is no escape from the "longing for the father." I reject this view as inherently ahistorical and reductionist (everything can be interpreted as reflecting longing for the father), and I hope to demonstrate that the shift toward the good father fatally undermined absolutist royal authority. Julie's father gets what he wants, but only because Julie agrees to it; and twice in this crucial letter she describes him as filled with shame for having struck her.[24] Julie's willingness to submit to his will is the central ingredient, not his desires.

The sentimentalization of family relations in the novel and theater did not necessarily enhance the roles of daughters and mothers. The girls of Marmontel's stories, for instance, were always submissive to their parents, chaste, modest, and never responsible for any unhappiness that came their way. The good fathers of Baculard d'Arnaud were seconded by mothers who were devoted and good by

22. Bérenguier argues that this is just a new psychological means to exercise paternal authority, "L'Infortune des alliances," p. 169. Although he does not discuss this particular scene from this point of view, Tony Tanner places the novel itself at the beginning of "an irreversible decline" in the "nom du père." Tony Tanner, *Adultery in the Novel: Contract and Transgression* (Baltimore, 1979), p. 143.
23. For an explicit formulation of this view based on a very intelligent reading of Freud, Lacan, and Foucault, see Bérenguier, "L'Infortune des alliances," p. xxiii.
24. Jean-Jacques Rousseau, *Julie ou la nouvelle Héloïse* (Paris, 1960), pp. 147–53.

their very nature.[25] Daughters depended on their mothers for protection and advice in navigating the transition to marriage, and mothers relied on their daughters for companionship.[26] When this relationship failed, as in Laclos's novel *Les Liaisons dangereuses* (1782), the result was disastrous for the family's honor. For all their importance to their daughters, however, fictional mothers did not make fathers good. Fathers, like the Baron d'Etange, had to become good on their own.

Whatever the merit of the novels and plays about virtuous families, the publication of so many popular novels and plays on this theme reflected the growing French interest, apparent in America and England too, in fatherhood as a vocation.[27] Jacques-Pierre Brissot defended his interest in Mesmerism in the 1780s, for example, by saying, "We unfortunate fathers, caught up in our business affairs, are practically nothing to our children. By mesmerism, we become fathers once again."[28] Good fathers were by eighteenth-century definition interested in their children.

The emphasis on fathers' interest in their children paralleled an increasing attention to children in fiction in the eighteenth century. In Marmontel's and Baculard's widely read works, for example, children played important roles, but they still functioned primarily as metaphors for something else; pathetic children evoked a world of hypersentimentality.[29] Children stood for innocence, emotion, and simplicity, and the family rather than childhood itself is the focus of the action. In virtually none of the novels of the eighteenth century did the years of childhood themselves feature in any important way in the plot.[30] The children in conflict with their fathers are always grown, though they are not yet married.

25. Gilbert van de Louw, *Baculard d'Arnaud: Romancier ou vulgarisateur: Essai de sociologie littéraire* (Paris, 1972), pp. 80–83, and S. Lenel, *Marmontel: Un homme de lettres au XVIIIe siècle* (Geneva, 1970; originally published 1902), pp. 270–73.

26. For a brief discussion of the representation of mothers, see Bérenguier, "L'Infortune des alliances," pp. 175–87.

27. On the American side and its English antecedents, see Jay Fliegelman, *Prodigals and Pilgrims: The American Revolution against Patriarchal Authority, 1750–1800* (Cambridge, 1982).

28. As quoted in Robert Darnton, *Mesmerism and the End of the Enlightenment in France* (Cambridge, Mass., 1968), p. 96.

29. See the brief but pertinent remarks in Patrizia Oppici, *Bambini d'inchiostro: Personaggi infantili e "sensibilité" nella letteratura francese dell'ultimo Settecento* (Pisa, 1986), pp. 40–44.

30. Adrian P. L. Kempton, "The Theme of Childhood in French Eighteenth-Century Memoir Novels," *Studies on Voltaire and the Eighteenth Century*, vol. 132 (Oxford, 1975), pp. 205–25.

After 1750, both male and female authors began to publish books written specifically for children. Typical of the new didactic genre were the sixty volumes by Madame Le Prince de Beaumont published in the 1750s, 1760s, and 1770s, and the twenty-four volumes of Arnaud Berquin's *The Children's Friend*, published in 1782–83. Yet hardly any of the children's books published before the 1780s incorporated much in the way of child psychology. Unsystematic collections of stories, dialogues, and plays are presented in a constantly moralizing tone; the children's ages and characters are depicted very vaguely; and much of the children's speech is obviously artificial. In many novels about children written after 1750, the chief aim of the author (whether Rousseau in *Emile* or Madame de Genlis in *Adèle et Théodore*) was the development of theories about education rather than exploration of children's characters from the inside. The children in these two influential novels are given hardly any physical description, for example.[31]

The first time that children appear as protagonists in their own right in French literature is in *Paul et Virginie* (1788).[32] Like Rousseau and the sentimental authors of the last half of the eighteenth century, Bernardin de Saint-Pierre also used his young characters as metaphors of innocence and simplicity, and he certainly used his novel to develop ideas about education, but the role of the children was no longer limited to these functions. Paul and Virginie are described in great detail from a young age, and their process of learning about the world is at the center of the novel. It seems likely that the popularity of such novels during the Revolution rested at least in part on this new emphasis on the development of children depicted from a child's point of view; the child is now viewed as an autonomous being.

The independent sphere of action of children was increasingly recognized in novels of the revolutionary period, and this recognition went hand in hand with a diminution of the father's traditional patriarchal role, if not with his absence altogether (as in *Paul et Virginie*). This trend was already apparent even in the novels about children's education, for almost all of them emphasized the role of a tutor or governess (in the case of *Adèle et Théodore,* of the mother),

31. In this paragraph I am summarizing the views of Adrian P. L. Kempton, "Education and the Child in Eighteenth-Century French Fiction," *Studies on Voltaire and the Eighteenth Century,* vol. 124 (Oxford, 1974), pp. 299–362.
32. This is the argument of Oppici, *Bambini d'inchiostro,* p. 35.

rather than of the child's father.[33] It might be argued that the tutor was simply a substitution figure for the father's authority, but surely it is significant that the father's authority was now being replaced. The next step—taken in the revolutionary novels—is the disappearance of the tutor and the child learning on his or her own (see chapter 6).

The effacement of the father can also be found in what the leading revolutionary politicians said about their childhoods. Fathers had no prominence, whereas maternal influence occupied a large place. Danton, Barnave, Condorcet, Marat, Barbaroux, Saint-Just and Larevellière-Lépeaux all spoke with great emotion about their mothers' imprint on them at a young age but hardly mentioned the influence of fathers (some were fatherless, of course).[34] Like the other readers of sentimental novels, these men identified the good mother with touching scenes of a happy family life. Brissot's worries about being a good father may simply have reflected a widespread sense that fathers had not yet made a successful transition into the new mores of sensibility and affection.

The literary transformations of repressive fathers into good and generous ones and the seeming effacement of the father in contrast to the more emotive mother and the increasingly interesting child all suggest that the novel as it developed in eighteenth-century France was inherently antipatriarchal. In her influential study of the origins of the novel, Marthe Robert claims that "there are but two ways of writing a novel: the way of the realistic Bastard who backs the world while fighting it head on; and the way of the Foundling who, lacking both the experience and the means to fight, avoids confrontation by flight or rejection." Neither of these options, it should be noted, has anything to do with a father's direct authority.

In Robert's view, the novel marks the emergence of the Freudian family romance from the realm of individual daydreams into the world of literature. What had been an individual fantasy that one's real parents were princes and ladies rather than the peasants or shopkeepers sitting at the family table now becomes the literary

33. "Throughout this study of children's literature and the educational novel we have observed an ever-present pedagogue figure in all the works discussed." Kempton, "Education and the Child," p. 361.

34. Pierre Trahard, *La Sensibilité révolutionnaire, 1789–1794* (Geneva, 1967), pp. 35–36.

trope of social ascension. The novel as a genre is about the foundling and the bastard making a place for themselves in the social world; they do not simply imagine a better place for themselves. This emergence from the realm of daydreams was made possible, Robert argues, by the reality of greater social mobility in the eighteenth century; dreams of social mobility now became reality and hence could be written about.[35] If the novel as a literary form was essentially about the "ideologies of independence and initiative" necessary to social mobility, then it was perhaps inevitable that many novels would be concerned with children living without the protection of their fathers. One of the most influential eighteenth-century French novels, Marivaux's *La Vie de Marianne*, had exploited this narrative device already in the 1730s.[36]

Bernardin de Saint-Pierre's novel *Paul et Virginie* brought together the various strands of the French novel's eighteenth-century development into one astounding popular triumph. On the very eve of the French Revolution, the author took the relatively common setting of an island paradise and wove a story around the lives of two children. Neither Paul nor Virginie have fathers in the novel, which gets its motive force precisely from the effort of their two families without fathers to confront the world outside the island paradise (see figure 3). In the very first pages of the novel, the author sets the scene by explaining the absence of the fathers, as if all else follows from this. Virginie's father, Monsieur de la Tour, had come to the Ile de France (now Mauritius) with his young wife when her family had opposed their marriage because he was not a nobleman. He died in Madagascar on an expedition to buy slaves before the action of the novel begins. Marguerite, the mother of Paul, was a peasant girl from Brittany who had been seduced, impregnated, and abandoned by her noble lover. The two women establish themselves next to each other and swear to provide their children with "the pleasures of love and the happiness of equality."[37]

A kind of metaphorical incest seems to threaten this island para-

35. Marthe Robert, *Origins of the Novel*, trans. Sacha Rabinovitch (Bloomington, Ind., 1980), pp. 37, 88–89.

36. Nancy K. Miller, *The Heroine's Text: Readings in the French and English Novel, 1722–1782* (New York, 1980). Miller provides a useful antidote to Robert's assumption that both the bastard and the foundling were male characters.

37. Bernardin de Saint-Pierre, *Paul et Virginie*, ed. Jean Ehrard (Paris, 1984), p. 119.

L'Enfance de Paul et Virginie.

3.   Engraving of the mothers with their two infants,
from Bernardin de Saint-Pierre's *Paul et Virginie* (1788).
Photo: Bibliothèque nationale.

dise in the absence of the fathers. The mothers bring up Paul and
Virginie as virtual brother and sister: "Thus these two small children, deprived of all their relatives, were filled with sentiments more
tender than those of son and daughter, of brother and sister, when
they were exchanged from one maternal breast to another by the
two friends who had given them birth."[38] At the same time, their
marriage is destined from the cradle. Virginie explains to Paul that
their love is natural: "Oh my brother! . . . You ask me why I love you;
but all things that have been raised together love one other. Look at

38. Ibid., p. 119.

our birds; they are always together like us."[39] Yet Virginie senses a problem: "The unfortunate girl felt troubled by the caresses of her brother."[40]

Thus families without fathers are presented as at once compelling and tragic; the female-oriented society animated by the two mothers is naturally beautiful and good, though poor; yet in the end, family ties pull the island community apart at its very seams. Virginie returns to France to her mother's aunt in the expectation of gaining a fortune in inheritance and returning to marry Paul and assist her island families, but she finds convent education little to her liking and is disinherited when she refuses to marry the man her great-aunt has chosen for her. She dies in a shipwreck on her way back to the island.

Published in 1788, *Paul et Virginie* was reprinted more often than any novel published during the revolutionary decade; thirty separate editions appeared between 1789 and 1799.[41] The author wrote to his cousin that "talk of my book brings me more than 500 letters a year."[42] In his long preamble to the illustrated 1806 edition, Bernardin explained that many novels, idylls, and plays had since been based on *Paul et Virginie;* parents often named their children after the two protagonists; and bracelets, buckles, and other female decorations were made with scenes from the novel on them.[43] It is not entirely clear why the novel was so popular; it combined the genres of the Robinson Crusoe tale, travelogue, and utopian fiction in a rhetoric of Rousseauean sentimentality that verged on melodrama.[44] Despite the emphasis on the pastoral idyll in the narrative, the family aspects of the novel nevertheless stand out; the fathers' absence sets the scene in the beginning, and the tragic ending depends upon a family quarrel over proper lineages (the aunt's decision to disinherit).

39. Ibid., pp. 156–57.

40. Ibid., p. 158.

41. I have based my figures and conclusions on Martin, Mylne, and Frautschi, *Bibliographie du genre romanesque français.*

42. Quoted in Jean-Michel Racault, ed., *Etudes sur Paul et Virginie et l'oeuvre de Bernardin de Saint-Pierre* (Paris, 1986), p. 13. The novel became even more popular between 1815 and 1840.

43. *Paul et Virginie*, ed. Ehrard, p. 30.

44. See the preliminary remarks in Jean-Marie Goulemot, "L'Histoire littéraire en question: L'Exemple de *Paul et Virginie*," in Racault, ed., *Etudes sur Paul et Virginie*, pp. 203–14.

Paul et Virginie was not the only novel about fatherless children in the prerevolutionary years. The first novels of François-Guillaume Ducray-Duminil, *Lolotte et Fanfan* (1788) and *Alexis* (1789), helped establish the vogue of popular novels about orphans and abandoned children that would continue throughout the decade of revolution. *Lolotte et Fanfan* appeared in ten editions between 1788 and 1810; *Alexis* appeared in seven editions between 1789 and 1818.[45] These novels put the family drama front and center. In the preface to *Alexis*, Ducray-Duminil explained that he got his taste for literature from his "enlightened" mother.[46]

In *Lolotte et Fanfan*, an English nobleman awakes on shore after a shipwreck to find two young children, brother and sister, hovering over him dressed in animal skins. Like Bernardin's novel, this one is meant to provide accurate descriptions of local customs and natural life; but the main line of development is an incredibly intricate family plot. Lolotte and Fanfan have been abandoned because of family relations gone bad, and in the end, a thousand pages, four volumes, and many astounding adventures later, their family is miraculously reconstituted along with the family of the English nobleman. *Alexis* is a darker novel, filled with mysterious letters, illegitimate children, double identities, and murder. Alexis is a teenage boy abandoned by his noble father; his story is dominated by the effort to find his father, and in the end he, like Lolotte and Fanfan, succeeds.

The contrast between Bernardin de Saint-Pierre's idyllic but tragic novel and the more gothic yet happily ending tales of Ducray-Duminil is instructive. Bernardin uses the pastoral description of the island to attack the prejudices of European civilization, especially the emphasis on rank, wealth, and useless knowledge. His trenchant criticisms are set in the context of a little society without fathers; only a society without fathers (and all they represent in terms of social placement) can be utopian, it seems. At the same time, however, the fatherless society comes to a tragic end without hope of progeny. Ducray-Duminil's novels include some social crit-

45. Martin, Mylne, and Frautschi, *Bibliographie du genre romanesque français*. For a favorable but uninformative review of *Lolotte et Fanfan*, see *Journal général de France*, no. 117, 27 September 1788.

46. *Alexis, ou la maisonnette dans les bois; Manuscrit trouvé sur les bords de l'Isere, et publié par l'Auteur de Lolotte et Fanfan* (Grenoble, 1789), vol. 1, p. ix.

icism, but despite appearances they are not utopian. Lolotte and
Fanfan and their new protector-father, Milord Welly, are eager to get
off the island in order to search for their respective families. They
return in the end, but only because they are forced into exile in the
last pages of the novel, and only when the families have been happily reunited and Lolotte and Fanfan each marry socially suitable
partners. The exile is not tragic because it is accompanied by the
restoration of the fathers and the continuation of the lineage.

Lolotte, Fanfan, and Alexis, moreover, all turn out to be nobles by
birth. In this sense, it might be said that their stories are revealing
twists on the Freudian family romance; rather than fantasizing that
their real parents are of a higher social standing than they find themselves in as children, they are in fact the sons and daughters of nobles
and the action of the novels restores them to their real status. Their
problem, then, is not the low rank of their fathers, so much as fathers
who are too ambitious for their children and insufficiently attentive
to their needs. Lolotte and Fanfan's problems can be traced back to
their grandfather, who wanted their father to marry someone of
the grandfather's choosing. Instead he married secretly against the
grandfather's wishes (a typical instance of father-son conflict in the
eighteenth-century novel) and tried to flee with his children and wife
to Charleston. He was wounded and taken off the ship before sailing,
and his wife was then forced to abandon her children on the voyage,
setting in motion the train of the action.

The English rector who explains the moral of the story blames the
father for disobeying the grandfather, but then turns to reprimand
the grandfather too: "He then criticized the ambition of the parents,
who only consulted their interests and standing when establishing
their children." The author recommends that parents become the
"confidant," "the friend" of their children: "Coldness punishes
them, friendship rewards them, and they will give way more to these
two sentiments than to menaces and fear."[47] In other words, the
novel is a brief for the good father, which is what Milord Welly
becomes when he takes on Lolotte and Fanfan as his charges after
his shipwreck.

47. *Lolotte et Fanfan ou les aventures de deux enfans abandonnés dans une isle déserte.
Rédigées et publiées sur des manuscrits anglais, par M. D** du M** (Paris, 1788), vol. 4,
pp. 171, 173.

Thus, on the eve of the Revolution, fathers are very much at issue in literature. Paul and Virginie come to a tragic end because they do not have fathers; Lolotte, Fanfan, and Alexis reach happy endings when they find their lost fathers. Whether tragic or comic in genre, these prerevolutionary novels portray families in crisis, and the crisis in each instance has been set in motion by the actions of fathers, rebelling against their fathers or abandoning their children. The popular novels of Ducray-Duminil seem to argue that fathers can be reformed and found again. The more powerful novel of Bernardin de Saint-Pierre refuses this "longing for the father," as Freud termed it, but also explores the consequences of a world without fathers. What is perhaps most remarkable, however, is how much of the action of all of these novels takes place in the absence of the father. In a sense, then, the eighteenth-century French novel predicts the fate of the king; it might even be argued that the novel produces the fate of the king in that the spread of the ideal of the good father and the father's subsequent effacement fatally undermined the absolutist foundations of the monarchical regime.

Even the minor genres on the eve of the Revolution are animated by the father's absence. The sexual education of the young nobleman depicted in the anonymous libertine novel, *Interesting Adventures of a French Orphan, or Letters of M. the Count of ***, to Madame the Baronness of ***, by M. ** * (1789), depends on the same device of the father's absence; the boy had never known his mother and expresses no emotion whatsoever about the death of his father.[48] This novel combines libertine adventures with an attack on the despotic powers of the family; much of the plot concerns the orphan's efforts to recover the fortune that is being dissipated by his high-living uncle-guardian. In a reversal of the family romance, the uncle tries to force the fourteen-year-old to serve as apprentice to a wigmaker. The boy escapes and has an affair with a marquise whom he calls "ma chère maman [my dear mama]." The affair ends precipitously with her untimely death. In the end, the orphan recovers both his fortune and his rightful place.

The possibility of incest, whether real or metaphorical as in this

---

48. *Avantures intéressantes d'un orphelin françois, ou lettres de M. le Comte de ***, à Madame la Baronne de **, par M. *** (1789), supposedly published in The Hague; the title page also lists a bookseller in Paris and Versailles, who was the bookseller of the king and queen.

instance of "ma chère maman," runs like a red thread through the eighteenth-century novel. Some have seen in the incest theme a representation of the impossibility of socially integrating the "adventurer," whether the adventurers are foundlings or bastards (the prototypical heroes of the novel), or just social parvenus more generally.[49] The threat of incest, in this view, necessarily lurks behind every attempt of the adventurer to establish social relationships, because he or she does not know his or her true origins. Whatever the possible social implications of the incest theme (and we will return to them in subsequent chapters), incest always depends on uncertainty about lineage and especially about paternity. The suggestion of incest in *Paul et Virginie*, for instance, depends on the absence of the fathers, which leads the mothers to bring up their children in excessive proximity to each other.

The incest theme is taken to its logical, literal conclusion in the 1789 epistolary novel *The Illegitimate Son*. Jules, who only discovers at age fourteen that he is not a peasant but born of noble blood (yet another version of this particular prerevolutionary family romance), is "the most miserable being, always alone, always wandering among men," because he is obsessed with discovering the secret of his birth.[50] He knows that his father died just before marrying his mother and that he was separated from his twin sister at birth. In the course of his wandering, he falls in love with an older woman only to discover just in time that she is his mother. Forced to flee in order to keep the secret of his illegitimate existence from her husband, Jules then retires to a monastery, where he falls in love with Sophie. He only realizes that she is his long-lost twin sister after they have made love and she finds herself pregnant. Once the baby is born in his monk's cell where he has hidden Sophie, the guilty couple are found out and denounced to the Inquisition, only to be saved at the last minute by their mother and Jules's steadfast friend Dormeuille. This unlikely reconstituted family then goes off together into exile in England.

As in virtually all pre-Sade novels about incest, the lovers are not guilty because they did not know of their family relationship before

49. Rustin, *Le Vice à la mode*, p. 240. Rustin remarks on the need for a study of the theme of incest, p. 240, n.50.

50. *Le Fils naturel*, erroneously attributed to Diderot, 2 vols. (Geneva, 1789), vol. 1, p. 22.

the deed was committed. In this novel, brother and sister are willing to take responsibility for their act and bring up their child together (they promise never to commit the crime of incest again). Once more, the absence of the father both motivates the child's wandering in the world and undermines the possibility of his or her establishing true social relationships, that is, relationships that bring outsiders into the family circle. Even before the beginning of the Revolution, then, novelists had begun to explore the consequences of a world without fathers.

Father figures had also become problematic in painting in the decades before the Revolution. In Jean-Baptiste Greuze's paintings of the 1750s, 1760s, and 1770s we can see an analogue to the sentimental bourgeois drama that dominated the novels and theater of the time. Children have great prominence in the paintings of Greuze, but they are there for moralizing purposes. Greuze alternately portrayed good fathers surrounded by their virtuous families (*The Father Reading the Bible to His Children*, 1755, or *The Village Bride*, 1761) and conflicts between fathers and their children. Struggles for power between father and son fascinated Greuze, who developed his paired paintings of *The Father's Curse* and *The Son Punished* (1777–78) out of earlier tinted drawings (1765), which were much admired by Diderot. In his criticism of the Salon of 1765, Diderot called Greuze the first French painter "to make art moral and to develop events in such a way as to suggest a novel."[51] The paintings based on the biblical story of the prodigal son emphasized the faults of the son, not the tyranny of the father, despite the terrible sound of the titles. The son's punishment is to return just as his father breathes his last breath in his bed. Thus it is the excessively egoistic son, not a despotic father, who threatens the harmony of the family. This is a version of Diderot's fathers who are made to suffer by their sons.[52]

51. As quoted in *Greuze et Diderot: Vie familiale et éducation dans la seconde moitié du XVIIIe siècle*, Conservation des Musées d'Art de la Ville de Clermont-Ferrand (Clermont-Ferrand, 1984), p. 13. This catalogue emphasizes Greuze's attention to education and family life.

52. A different interpretation of the father figure in Greuze and the eighteenth century more generally is given in Jean-Claude Bonnet, "La Malédiction paternelle," *Dix-huitième siècle* 12 (1980): 195–208. Bonnet emphasizes the continuing power of the father figure and its appropriation by eighteenth-century writers such as Rétif de la Bretonne.

In general, French Salon paintings in the second half of the eighteenth century seem increasingly preoccupied with figures of old men who had trouble holding onto their powers. Greuze himself painted a *Return of the Drunken Father* (1780?) and *The Death of an Unnatural Father Abandoned by His Children* (1769). Paintings of rebellious sons were appearing with great frequency, along with paintings of Oedipus as an old and blind patriarch or of the general banished by the emperor Justinian, old Belisarius, who was often shown blindly wandering and begging for alms. Such images of sympathetic but weakened old men, according to one interpretation, expressed forbidden Oedipal impulses of aggression toward fathers (and by extension all established authority), and they prepared the way for the internalization of patriarchal authority by the revolutionary sons and its transformation into a new state authority.[53] It is not necessary to subscribe to this particular Freudian reading of the pictorial trend, however, in order to accept the trend's general significance as an indicator of a growing crisis in paternal authority.

The status of fathers is particularly ambiguous in the two best-known paintings of the immediate prerevolutionary decade: Jacques-Louis David's *Oath of the Horatii* (figure 4) and *Lictors Returning to Brutus the Bodies of His Sons* (figure 5). These paintings cannot be read as straightforward attacks on paternal authority; in the *Oath* the sons swear allegiance before the father, and in *Brutus* the father has had to sacrifice the sons to the well-being of the republic. Both of the fathers in these paintings appear vigorous and austere, exemplars of male virtue.

Nevertheless, the paintings demonstrate a deep worry about the relationship between family and state obligations, which sometimes seem to be in irreconcilable conflict with each other. In the *Oath*, the brothers must ignore their attachments through marriage to their opponents (incarnated by the women on the right-hand side of the painting); in *Brutus*, the father has had to overcome his natural love for his sons in order to defend the new republic. In *Brutus*, moreover, the father exercises power as a father by destroying his own lineage, his own paternity; paternity and republicanism here seem

---

53. Carol Duncan, "Fallen Fathers: Images of Authority in Pre-Revolutionary French Art," *Art History* 4 (1981): 186–202.

4.   Jacques-Louis David, *The Oath of the Horatii* (1785). Musée du Louvre.
Photo: Réunion des musées nationaux.

incompatible. Of all the possible moments in the stories that were
available to him in these immediate prerevolutionary years, David
chose to represent just those that most called attention to fathers'
relationships with their sons within the polity.

The paintings signal as well that the sons can be imagined now as
the equals of the father, even perhaps as threats to his power.[54]
Yet despite the potential father-son conflict within the polity, these
works depict men bonding to the state through their affective rela-

54.   Thomas E. Crow notes that in the *Oath*, "the body politic appears in the form
of the sons, its chosen representatives; they stand on an equal footing with the father
as his multiplied mirror image and receive from him, in a charged and ecstatic
exchange, the instruments of power. Virtue is no longer in the exclusive keeping of
the old, but passed on to the young in a moment of triumphant celebration." *Painters
and Public Life in Eighteenth-Century Paris* (New Haven, 1985), p. 213. See as well the
analysis in Joan B. Landes, *Women and the Public Sphere in the Age of the French
Revolution* (Ithaca, N.Y., 1988), pp. 152–58. In what follows, I have relied heavily on
Crow and Landes.

5.   Jacques-Louis David, *Lictors Returning to Brutus the Bodies of His Sons* (1789). Musée du Louvre. Photo: Réunion des musées nationaux.

tions to each other and developing their bonds in distinction to ordinary mixed-gender family relationships. The gender differentiation of the two paintings quite literally divides the canvases in two in ways that foreshadow the gender differentiation of republicanism. Critics at the time drew attention to the separation into two parts; as one critic of *Brutus* remarked, this was the mark of a new "virile, severe, terrifying" style.[55] It is noteworthy that this gender differentiation appears most strikingly in paintings that foreground the relationship between political fathers and sons. In that sense the paintings seem to argue that the struggle between fathers and sons for authority will necessarily entail some redistribution of control over domestic space as well.

The painters and novelists of the prerevolutionary years put the

55. Quoted in Robert L. Herbert, *David, Voltaire, Brutus and the French Revolution: An Essay in Art and Politics* (New York, 1972), p. 41.

father's authority in question, either by showing tensions between fathers and children or by proceeding from the fact of the father's absence. These stories are fundamentally ambivalent about the father figure. After 1760, at least, there seemed to be less interest in denouncing the bad father than in either representing good ones or exploring the consequences of a world in which their authority was much weakened or absent altogether. The world without fathers frequently appeared as a problematic one, in which children wandered in search of their social place, risking along the way the perils of incest, the ultimate sign that social location was uncertain. Yet one thing seemed certain in this atmosphere of family crisis: despotic paternal authority was unacceptable.

Revolutionary legislators had grown up with the novels and paintings that described paternal authority in crisis. After 1789 they began to take measures to circumscribe the father's authority in law. Since absolutism and paternal power had been ideologically intertwined under the Old Regime, an attack on absolutism seemed to entail an attack on excessive paternal authority as well. The legal challenge to "the tyranny of parents," as the deputy had described it in 1790, took shape in a series of laws restricting paternal authority over children, establishing a family council to replace the father's sole right of action, lowering the age of majority, regularizing emancipation of children from their fathers' authority, regulating rights of inheritance to limit a father's testamentary control, and not least, establishing the principle of compulsory national education.

The Constituent Assembly began the process by confronting the issues that had aroused the most legal controversy under the Old Regime: the lettres de cachet and primogeniture. Primogeniture—the passage of all titles and most of the family's land to the eldest son—was considered an integral right of noble status; it was condemned as inherently unfair to younger children (including girls). Lettres de cachet had been widely denounced as despotic in the *cahiers de doléances* that were submitted in 1789, though some cahiers, from both the Third Estate and the nobility, expressed reservations about completely abolishing their use in family matters.[56] In March 1790 the Assembly abolished primogeniture ("Les droits

---

56. For reservations about abolition, see James F. Traer, *Marriage and the Family in Eighteenth-Century France* (Ithaca, N.Y., 1980), pp. 140–41.

d'ainesse et de masculinité à l'égard des fiefs, domaines et alleux nobles, et des partages inégaux à raison de la qualité des personnes, sont abolis") and the use of lettres de cachet.[57]

In August 1790 the new law on judicial organization established family councils or courts (tribunaux de famille) to hear disputes between parents and children up to age twenty.[58] In setting up such councils, the Assembly hoped to democratize family life, by replacing the father's sole power with that of a broader council of relatives. At this stage, early in the Revolution, the state kept out of most family matters, leaving problems to be resolved by a council made up of family members. The deputies in the Constituent Assembly hoped to reform the family, removing its despotic and aristocratic characteristics, while leaving it in place as the bedrock of society. As one further element in this reform of the family, in April 1791 the Assembly decreed the equality of division of properties in all intestate successions ("Toute inégalité ci-devant, résultant, entre les héritiers *ab intestat*, des qualités d'aîné, de puiné, de la distinction des sexes et des exclusions coutumières, soit en ligne directe, soit en ligne collatérale, est abolie").[59]

The Legislative Assembly continued the work of dismantling paternal prerogatives and made it part of the effort to establish contractual relations between individuals and between individuals and the state. At issue was the definition of the individual, including the age at which a child became an adult. In a discussion of July 1792 about the age of majority, a voice was heard in the Legislative Assembly exclaiming, "A father ought to be more flattered by the respect of a free child than by the regard of a slave."[60] In August 1792, adults were declared no longer subject to paternal authority, and in September the age of majority was lowered to twenty-one.

One of the last acts of the Legislative Assembly was the law of 20 September 1792 establishing divorce.[61] It gave mothers equal

57. Emile Masson, *La Puissance paternelle et la famille sous la Révolution* (Paris, 1910), p. 255.

58. For a general treatment of family law in the Revolution, see Philippe Sagnac, *La Législation civile de la Révolution française, 1789–1804* (Paris, 1898); and Traer, *Marriage and the Family.*

59. Masson, *La Puissance paternelle*, p. 168.

60. Ibid., p. 217.

61. For a brief but useful discussion of divorce, and especially of prerevolutionary separation laws, see Candice E. Proctor, *Women, Equality, and the French Revolution*, Contributions in Women's Studies, no. 115 (New York, 1990), pp. 87–101.

rights with fathers in control over the children after divorce; in marriage, however, the mother's rights were still subordinate to the father's. Divorce followed from the declaration that marriage was a civil contract, and hence breakable under regulated conditions. The statute stated that the ability to divorce "follows from individual liberty, which would be lost in any indissoluble commitment."[62] If men and women were freely contracting individuals, then they had to have the right to break their marriage contract under certain conditions defined by law. The contractual association of free individuals was now supposed to replace the patriarchal family despotically controlled by the father as the fundamental unit of the new polity.

Two different kinds of issues were raised by this model of the freely contracting individual: how far did freedom of contract reach, and how much did it include women? If contractual notions established the freedom of property, for example, then how could the government justify restraints on the freedom of the testator by insisting on equality of inheritance (for the moment, limited to intestate successions)? Should equality have precedence over liberty? In this case, the deputies insisted that the law must prevent any despotic tendencies in the father's control over inheritance.[63]

Such tensions were inherent in the ambiguity of the revolutionary idea of the individual; individuals were imagined as free (especially if adult, male, and not economically dependent), but they were also imagined as subject to the general will. Revolutionary legislators continually wrestled with the problem of bridging this gap between the individual and the general will.[64] They would also have to confront the vexed issue of the status of women; did women have the same freedom or not? The emphasis on the equality of individuals under contracts led the legislators of the early assemblies to equalize inheritance for girls and boys and to grant women equal status in suing for divorce. They were not willing, however, to grant women equal status as citizens.

62. Quoted in Francis Ronsin, *Le Contrat sentimental: Débats sur le mariage, l'amour, le divorce, de l'Ancien Régime à la Restauration* (Paris, 1990), p. 110. Ronsin analyzes all of the debates on the question of divorce and provides many useful documents.
63. Traer, *Marriage and the Family*, p. 159.
64. On this tension more generally, see Elisabeth Guibert-Sledziewski, "L'Invention de l'individu dans le droit révolutionnaire," in *La Révolution et l'ordre juridique privé: Rationalité ou scandale*, actes du colloque d'Orléans, 11–13 septembre 1986, vol. 1 (Orléans, 1988), pp. 141–49.

Women were by definition citizens since they were not slaves, but they could not vote or hold office. In these early years of the Revolution, nonetheless, the question of the status of women was still an open one. In 1790 Condorcet could argue that excluding women would fatally undermine the principle of equality of rights: "Either no individual of the human race has true rights, or all of them have the same ones; and he who votes against the right of another, whatever his religion, his color, or his sex, has from that moment abjured his own rights."[65] The question of women's status was not resolved in definitive fashion until the great debates of 1793 (see chapter 4).

Revolutionary legislation and its attendant debates reveal only what the deputies were willing to say in formal settings about the legal powers of fathers and the new model of politics. The legislators constantly reiterated their conviction about the importance of good fathers for the social order, and their legislation was designed to eliminate or contain "bad" fathers. They did not intend to eliminate the power of fathers altogether. Similarly, they did not envision eliminating all the power of the king in those early years of the Revolution. They hoped that the king would agree to become a good father too.

In iconographic sources, in particular, it is possible to trace the vicissitudes of the image of the king as good father.[66] Until 1794 at least, engravings and caricatures represented changes in paternal and fraternal imagery much more quickly than did paintings or novels, if only because they took less time for production. During the first two or three years of the Revolution, most occasional imagery of political fatherhood focused on the king, and it was marked by

65. Quoted in Dominique Godineau, *Citoyennes tricoteuses: Les Femmes du peuple à Paris pendant la Révolution française* (Aix-en-Provence, 1988), p. 271.

66. Preliminary versions of my argument from iconography were published as "The Political Psychology of Revolutionary Caricatures," in *French Caricature and the French Revolution, 1789–1799*, catalogue for an exhibition coorganized by the University of California, Los Angeles, and the Bibliothèque nationale de France (Los Angeles, 1988); "Family Narrative and Political Discourse in Revolutionary France and America," in *Quaderno 2: The Language of Revolution*, ed. Loretta Valtz Mannucci (Milan, 1989), pp. 161–76; and "Discourses of Patriarchalism and Anti-patriarchalism in the French Revolution," in John Renwick, ed., *Language and Rhetoric of the Revolution* (Edinburgh, 1990), pp. 25–41. I have benefited from the comments of many people who listened to these papers in Los Angeles, Milan, and Edinburgh before publication.

the hope of finding the good father. This might be termed the conflict over the comic father.

In his now classic analysis of comedy, Northrop Frye provides a description that includes many elements of family romance. The movement of comedy, according to Frye, is usually a movement from one society to another: "What normally happens is that a young man wants a young woman, that his desire is resisted by some opposition, usually paternal, and that near the end of the play some twist in the plot enables the hero to have his will." In the end, a new society crystallizes around the hero, and its appearance is "frequently signalized by some kind of party or festive ritual." Rather than being repudiated altogether, the "blocking characters," usually including the arbitrary and conventional father, are most often reconciled with the son or sons.[67]

An engraving of Louis XVI helping to prepare the Champ de Mars for the Festival of Federation in July 1790 (figure 6) is typical of the comic genre as defined by Frye. Here the father is reconciled in classic comic fashion to the demands of the sons. Louis is now ready to join his family as an equal rather than as a patriarch, he works rather than standing idly by in a posture of superiority, and he participates in the preparation of a festival; festivals often celebrate just this kind of reconciliation between fathers and sons in comedy. This is the good father prefigured by eighteenth-century parlementary rhetoric and by such novelists as Ducray-Duminil.

I read this image as more than a representation of a specific event—the preparations for the Festival of Federation in 1790—and more than a sign of conscious political struggles, such as the effort to establish a constitutional monarchy. The engraved image includes within the representation a narrative of a family romance, a narrative about what the French expected of a father-king in these early years of the Revolution. There are many other engravings of Louis XVI as the good father, dispensing alms to the poor, or watching the preparations for the Festival of Federation with Marie-Antoinette and his young son.[68]

Surprisingly, though, few ordinary family scenes appear in the

---

67. Northrop Frye, *Anatomy of Criticism: Four Essays* (Princeton, 1957), p. 163.
68. For a brief analysis of the "roi-père" and the "bon roi retrouvé" of 1789, see Antoine de Baecque, *La Caricature révolutionnaire* (Paris, 1988), p. 176.

Le Roi, piochant au champ de Mars.

6. Engraving of the king digging at the Champ de Mars (1790).
Frontispiece to *Révolutions de France et de Brabant*, no. 36. Photo:
Maclure Collection, Special Collections, Van Pelt-Dietrich
Library, University of Pennsylvania.

engravings of the Festival of Federation. There are scenes of children with their mothers and even depictions of children with their
fathers, but most often the engravings present large masses of
adults, who are not grouped in families.[69] If children appear, it is

69. These observations are based on my study of the engravings presented in the
videodisc *Images de la Révolution française / Images of the French Revolution*, coproduc-
tion Bibliothèque nationale et Pergamon Press (Paris, Oxford, 1990).

frequently on the edges of the great gatherings of adults (see figure 7). The engravings of the Festival of Federation thus portray the new individual-state relationship envisioned by the liberal ideology that was taking root through the legislation of the Constituent Assembly; individuals relate to the state as individuals, through contracts (in this case oaths of allegiance, which were the centerpiece of the ceremony). The family is still essential to society, but its status as political building block is now in some doubt. The fathers as fathers are politically absent.

The public exhibition of art in the Salon of 1791 shows similar tendencies. The prints of the Salon focused on contemporary scenes of oath taking, from the Tennis Court Oath of June 1789 to the Festival of Federation of July 1790. The prints depicting the festival showed, as one prospectus for a print explained, "all the inhabitants," "French people of every station and every part of the kingdom . . . with the qualities of free and equal men," in short, virtually atomistic individuals linked to the nation through their oaths rather than by their families or other particular ties.

The other major innovation of the Salon of 1791 was the rise of portrait painting. Not only did the number of portraits entered increase, from 45 in 1789 to 210 in 1791, but the clientele also shifted as a result of the emigration of many leading nobles. Half of the individuals in the portraits were unidentified ("head of a man"), and the identified ones were often deputies, officials, or other individuals moving in the public sphere, that is, the world outside of family and corporate ties.[70] Thus the vogue of prints about oath taking and the rise of portraiture both reinforced an emphasis on the public individual rather than the private family man/father. Almost always, when specific public individuals were represented, they were men, not women.

These new trends toward the representation of unaffiliated individuals coexisted uneasily with the continuing effort to represent the king as good father. In one of its last acts, the Constituent Assembly asked the king for a portrait of himself giving the constitution to the Dauphin.[71] One of the most prolific portrait painters of the time, Adélaïde Labille-Guiard, was commissioned to paint the

70. I have followed the account of the Salon of 1791 given in Olander, "*Pour transmettre*," pp. 196–222; the quotation is from p. 203.
71. Ibid., pp. 222–36.

Rue de Paris. PACTE FÉDÉRATIF DES FRANÇAIS LE 14 JUILLET 1790 *N: 53. Pag. 1*

Cette Fête vraiment Nationale, s'est passée dans le Champ de Mars près Paris, sur un terrain de 400 toises de long, sur 160 de large; les Fédérés étoient au nombre d'environ 18000; l'enceinte Contenoit au moin 300 mille spectateurs sans compter la garde Nationale Parisienne qui faisoit le service.

7. Festival of Federation, July 1790. Frontispiece to *Révolutions de France et de Brabant*, no. 34. Photo: Maclure Collection, Special Collections, Van Pelt-Dietrich Library, University of Pennsylvania.

picture; but in early 1792, newspapers reported that David had been asked to undertake the same commission. Neither of them ever finished a painting on the subject, but David did several drawings which showed the virtuous father Louis XVI teaching his son the principles of the Revolution. By the spring of 1792, no doubt, such images, "resonant with *ancien régime* moralizing" about the family, no longer seemed appropriate.[72]

Some of the old proponents of the good father in sentimental fiction continued to publish works with this theme during the early years of the Revolution. Between 1790 and 1792, for example, Marmontel published his *New Moral Tales* in the *Mercure de France*. Included among them was a long story titled "L'Erreur d'un bon père [The Error of a Good Father]," which recounted the sad tale of Monsieur de Vaneville, who had been too busy with his business to see that his second wife was systematically alienating his son by his first marriage. The son, Alexis, runs away and becomes a shepherd. He is taken in by a man who sees him reading Virgil, and through the usual remarkable set of coincidences, Alexis is finally reunited with his father, who recognizes his error.

As if to warn fathers of the consequences of their inattention and lack of emotion, Monsieur de Vaneville explains how he had alienated his son: "I ended by pushing him away, and then he became really sullen."[73] Marmontel, the prophet of family harmony in the 1760s, now recognizes that problems must be confronted or the sons will revolt. In Marmontel's vision of the world, fathers (and kings?) still have time to repent and win back their sons. When the king himself is mentioned in the novels of the early years of the Revolution, he is often referred to as the good father; for example, "le père le plus tendre [the most tender father]." As a fishwife explains in François Marchant's 1792 novel *The Good Deeds of the National Assembly*, "Si not' bon Roi, qu'est la justice même, avoit z'été instruit dans le temps des injustices qui se commettiont [*sic*], il y auroit bien mis ordre" ("If our good king, who is justice itself, had been informed at

---

72. Ibid., p. 231. Olander does not emphasize the issue of individualism versus familial imagery, but I have found his comments on the paintings and prints invaluable.

73. *Nouveaux contes moraux* par M. Marmontel (Liège, 1792), vol. 2, p. 93. It is interesting to note that Marmontel had to publish the complete version of his tales outside France. After August 1792, royalist presses were largely shut down inside France.

8.   Engraving of the royal family as pigs (1791?). Photo:
Bibliothèque nationale.

the time of the injustices that were being committed, he would have
put them right").[74]

The comic image of the political father of 1789–92 was steadily
eroded not only by the force of political circumstances but also by an
increasing number of engravings that were devoted to denigrating
the royal family (see figure 8). In these prints we see the hope of the
good father disappointed and the father now being rejected.[75] The
mother too is being rejected and held in some way accountable for
the failure of the father, as in the pornographic engraving of the

74. Quoted in Malcolm C. Cook, "Politics in the Fiction of the French Revolution,
1789–1794," *Studies on Voltaire and the Eighteenth Century,* vol. 201 (Oxford, 1982),
p. 246.
75. For an extended analysis of similar prints, see Annie Duprat, "La Dégradation
de l'image royale dans la caricature révolutionnaire," in Michel Vovelle, ed., *Les
Images de la Révolution française* (Paris, 1988), pp. 167–76.

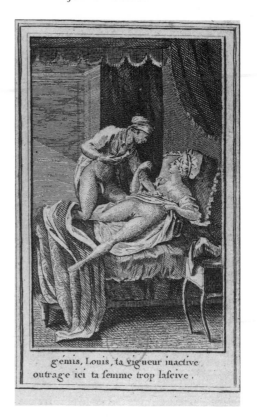

gémis, Louis, ta vigueur inactive
outrage ici ta femme trop lascive.

9.   Engraving of Louis XVI impotent in bed
with Marie-Antoinette. From *Vie privée, libertine, et
scandaleuse de Marie-Antoinette d'Autriche* (1793).
Photo: Bibliothèque nationale.

king impotent in bed with Marie-Antoinette (see figure 9). The text
below the print blames Louis for his lack of vigor but also accuses the
queen of being too lascivious. A fundamentally new family romance
of politics could take shape only if both the romance of patriarchal
kingship and that of the king as good father were destroyed. All
possibility of reconciliation with the father is implicitly denied in
such prints, and the distance between father and sons is obliterated
as the king becomes an animal, lower even than his human subjects,
or a pathetic ordinary man incapable of establishing his own succession.

The flight to Varennes in June 1791, the return from which is caricatured in figure 8, marked the turning point in representations of the king-father. According to one royalist commentator, many such engravings were sold at the time. He condemned another, similar engraving as

> the abominable caricature that the factious distributed with the greatest profusion during this deplorable time. It provides great illumination to the *sentimental* historian because it proves to him that the French in revolt had lost all feeling of humanity. . . . A being can be found that has the sacrilegious audacity to represent a wagon filled with straw and each of the members of this august family in the form of that animal which is still the most vile of all.[76]

The meaning of the representation of the royal family as pigs—or as other animals considered low—escaped no one. It was a direct means of vilification, since the pig was the most vile of all animals. At least fifteen different prints of the king as pig were printed, and Camille Desmoulins brought the metaphor to everyone's attention in his newspaper: "The citizens are warned that a fat pig has escaped from the Tuileries; those who run into it are asked to bring it back to its pen."[77]

In late 1791 and 1792, the flood of caricatures denigrating the king and the royal family overwhelmed those depicting the good father. From engravings such as *L'Idole renversée* (The overthrown idol) depicting a national guardsman, two soldiers, a veteran, an ordinary man, and a boy celebrating the destruction of a bust of Louis XVI, to pornographic attacks on the queen (described in detail in chapter 4), the aim was the same. The royalist critic quoted earlier put it in factional terms, but his language was significant: "The republican faction made the greatest efforts . . . to push a new Clement to plunge a parricidal sword into the sacred flanks of the king. . . . There is no manner of insult, no manner of horror and atrocity that the pen and the engraving tool have not traced during this memorable event [the flight to Varennes]."[78] In the view of the royalist critic, such engravings did nothing less than prepare the way for the destruction of kingship and political fatherhood, for the

76. Boyer de Nîmes [J. M. Boyer-Brun], *Histoire des caricatures de la révolte des Français* (Paris, 1792), vol. 1, pp. 203, 317–18.
77. *Les Révolutions de France et de Brabant,* quoted in de Baecque, *La Caricature révolutionnaire,* p. 184.
78. Boyer de Nîmes, *Histoire des caricatures,* vol. 1, p. 87.

murder of the father with "a parricidal sword." The critic was not explaining an event that had already occurred, however; his book was published in 1792, before the trial and execution of the king.

Like Burke before him, this royalist commentator was tracing a desacralization of monarchy, in this case through the medium of print rather than in more palpable political actions. The king no longer seemed an august, patriarchal figure far removed from the lives of ordinary mortals. In a sense, the king had already lost one of his two bodies; he still had his mortal body like all other men, but the immortal body that represented the office of kingship had been seriously undermined.

One very important step in this process had been the gradual transformation of the king into a good father. By the time Louis XVI became king in 1774, the transformation was already well under way, as the rhetorical back and forth between king and parlement had shown. By 1790 it was complete, and the fortunes of the French monarchy steadily declined thereafter. In this sense, then, the murder of the tyrannical father had already taken place before the king himself was killed. As the novels and paintings of the prerevolutionary period demonstrated, it was already possible to imagine a world without fathers. Issues about the fate of the women liberated from the control of the father (and the accompanying possibility of incest) had already been raised in these imaginary forms. They would become even more pressing, however, when the deed itself was done.

3

The Band of Brothers

Kingship was officially abolished on 21 September 1792. Deputy Henri Grégoire explained, "It is necessary to destroy this word *king*, which is still a talisman whose magical force can serve to stupefy many men."[1] In January 1793 the man Louis Capet himself was executed. The killing of the political father enacted a ritual sacrifice and opened the way to the band of brothers. Between 1792 and the middle of 1794, radical iconography instantiated a new family romance of fraternity: brothers and sisters appeared frequently in this iconographic outpouring, mothers rarely, and fathers almost never. The literal effacement of the political father was the subject of a systematic, official campaign in which images of the kings of France, as well as images of royalty, aristocracy, and feudalism, were destroyed. Local and national officials took steps in this direction immediately after 10 August 1792 and then accelerated their activities in the summer of 1793 (see figure 10).

The killing of the king may seem predetermined in hindsight, but the deputies of the newly elected National Convention only backed into it step by hesitant step. The Convention was elected after the uprising against the monarchy on 10 August 1792, and the deputies first met on 21 September 1792 to begin deliberations about a new form for French government. The abolition of the monarchy was quickly accomplished; disposing of the former king, who had been "sacred and inviolable" under the constitution of 1791, raised difficult questions.[2] Could he be tried at all, given his protected status under the constitution of 1791? Would he be tried as king or as an ordinary citizen? Who would try him? How would a verdict be reached?

1. *Moniteur universel*, no. 266, 22 September 1792, recounting the session of the National Convention on 21 September 1792.
2. The indispensable guide is David P. Jordan, *The King's Trial: The French Revolution vs. Louis XVI* (Berkeley, 1979).

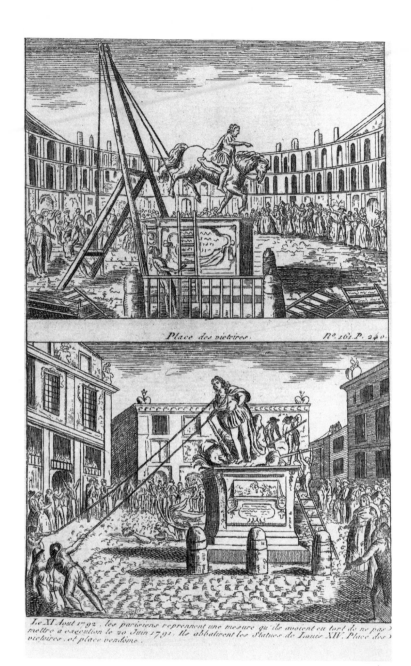

Place des victoires.   No. 161.P. 240.

Le XI Aout 1792, les parisiens reprennent une mesure qu'ils avoient eu tort de ne pas
mettre a execution le 20 Juin 1791. Ils abbatirent les Statues de Louis XIV. Place des
victoires, et place vendôme.

10. Engraving of the destruction of statues of Louis XIV in the
Place Vendôme and the Place des Victoires, ordered 11 August 1792.
From *Révolutions de Paris*, no. 161, 4–11 August 1792. Photo: Maclure
Collection, Special Collections, Van Pelt-Dietrich
Library, University of Pennsylvania.

In the weeks that followed the opening of the National Convention, the Jacobins opposed a trial and argued for a military-style execution. The young deputy and future member of the Committee of Public Safety, Louis-Antoine Saint-Just, argued, "This man must reign or die." Since "no man can reign innocently," and since the king "had no part in the contract which united the French people," he should be treated simply as a "rebel," a "usurper," and "an enemy alien."[3] The Jacobin view did not carry the day, however, and on 3 December 1792 the Convention decided to try Louis, with the Convention itself sitting as his court of judgment. A simple majority was required for a verdict.

During the trial in December and January, the deputies never referred to the king as father of his people. The commission named to draw up an act of accusation against the former king charged him as "a tyrant who constantly applied himself to obstructing or retarding the progress of liberty, and even to annihilating it by persistently sustained and renewed assaults."[4] This sounds more like a distant and perverse tyrant than like a good father gone wrong. The deputies apparently felt the need to distance themselves from Louis in order to make judging him more palatable.

At the same time, they insisted on treating him like an ordinary accused man. The back and forth of the trial helped push even further the desacralization of the monarchy. Louis appeared in person before his judges, the elected representatives of the nation; and unlike Charles I of England, he chose to respond to his accusers by denying any intention of criminal wrongdoing. To each charge, he responded with "I had no intention of spilling blood," "I do not remember what happened at that time," "I know nothing about it."[5] All sense of majesty was fast disappearing.

In the minds of the deputies, there was no doubt that the king was guilty of betraying the nation. Not one deputy voted "no" in the roll

---

3. From his speech of 13 November 1792, in Michael Walzer, ed., *Regicide and Revolution: Speeches at the Trial of Louis XVI* (Cambridge, 1974), pp. 120–27. In his analysis of the trial and execution, Walzer argues that "revolution marks the end of political fatherhood. No great commitment to psychoanalytic theory is required to describe it as the successful struggle of the 'brethren' against the father, and after it is over, the brethren are alone, without a political father" (p. 26).

4. *Moniteur universel*, no. 348, 13 December 1792, recounting the session of the National Convention on 10 December 1792.

5. Ibid., session of 11 December 1792.

call on the king's guilt. Yet they did disagree about his punishment: should he be killed or banished or imprisoned? Should the people be consulted first? Should a reprieve be offered? By a narrow majority they voted on 16 and 17 January 1793 to execute him. On 19 and 20 January they voted by a larger majority to reject a reprieve. The execution was ordered for the next day, 21 January 1793.

At the scaffold, Louis tried to speak in terms of sacrifice: "I pardon my enemies and I hope that my blood will be useful to the French, that it will appease God's anger." At that point, he was interrupted by the rolling of drums, and the executioners quickly strapped him down and slid him through the window of the guillotine. Once the guillotine had done its work, the crowd responded to the sight of the severed royal head held high by the executioner with cries of "Long live the Republic! Long live Liberty! Long live Equality!"[6]

The momentous event was greeted by remarkably restrained commentary in revolutionary France.[7] On the day of the execution, one of the regicide deputies spoke on the occasion in the Jacobin Club of Paris. He said simply, "Today he [Louis] has paid his debt; let us speak of it no longer, let us be human; all of our resentment must expire with him." Then he and the rest of the club members turned instead to a discussion of the assassination of Deputy Michel Lepeletier by a royalist.[8] In the Convention, discussion on the day of the execution concerned the assassination of Lepeletier and rumors of plots against other deputies. Danton echoed the sentiments of many deputies when he suggested, "Now that the tyrant is no longer, let us turn all of our energy, all of our excitement, toward the war."[9]

The press could not ignore the execution, of course, but in Paris and the provinces the reports on it were very much the same. Many papers simply reproduced official proclamations and reports under the usual rubric of "news from Paris," "city of Paris," and the like.[10]

6. Jordan, *The King's Trial*, p. 220.

7. A preliminary version of some of the ideas presented in these pages can be found in my essay, "The Sacred and the French Revolution," in Jeffrey Alexander, ed., *Durkheimian Sociology* (Cambridge, 1988), pp. 25–43.

8. Deputy Bourdon, in F. A. Aulard, ed., *La Société des Jacobins: Recueil de documents pour l'histoire du club des Jacobins de Paris*, vol. 4, *Juin 1792 à janvier 1793* (Paris, 1892), p. 689.

9. *Moniteur universel*, no. 25, 25 January 1793, reporting on the session of the National Convention on 21 January 1793.

10. I base this observation on my reading of the *Journal du département de l'Oise, Abréviateur universel, Courrier de Strasbourg*, and *Journal de Paris national*, among

The *Moniteur universel* called for leaving Louis under his shroud: "A victim of the law has something sacred about him for the moral and sensitive man; it is toward the future that all of the good citizens must turn their wishes."[11] The persistent sense that the French should turn away from the killing toward something else permeated all these reactions. They seem to support the contention of René Girard that the sacrificial process requires a certain degree of misunderstanding: as Girard argues, "the celebrants do not and must not comprehend the true role of the sacrificial act."[12]

Only the most radical newspaper editors provided any extended commentary on the meaning of the king's death. Marat, who editorialized freely on every subject, gave a rather solemn account: "The head of the tyrant has just fallen under the blade of the law; the same stroke has overturned the foundations of monarchy among us; I believe finally in the republic." Marat went on to compare the execution to a "religious festival" animated by feelings of fraternity: "One would have said that [the people] had just attended a religious festival; delivered from the burden of oppression that weighed on them for such a long time and pierced by the sentiment of fraternity, all hearts gave themselves over to the hope of a happier future." The final punishment of Louis was a world-historical event, in Marat's view, an event which would have a "prodigious" influence on the other despots of Europe and on the peoples who had not yet broken the irons of slavery. It would "terrorize" the Revolution's enemies both within and outside France. It would energize the nation. Marat then cited with approval the statement of another deputy: "We have finally landed on the island of liberty, and we have burned the boat that brought us to it." The monarchy could take the nation only so far, and then they had to destroy it in order to proceed further.[13]

In subsequent days, Marat celebrated again the enormity of the event. That Monday was a day forever memorable: "Goodbye then

---

others. Not surprisingly, the Girondin papers were particularly reticent; see, for example, *Chronique de Paris*. See also Alphonse Aulard, "L'Exécution de Louis XVI et la presse française," *La Révolution française* 82 (1929): 65–76. Aulard does not remark on the formulaic qualities of most reports.

11. *Moniteur universel*, no. 23, 23 January 1793.

12. René Girard, *Violence and the Sacred*, trans. Patrick Gregory (Baltimore, 1977), p. 7.

13. *Journal de la République française* (one of the many variations on *L'Ami du peuple*), 23 January 1793.

to the splendor of thrones, the prestige of worldly grandeurs, the talisman of celestial powers; goodbye to all human respect for constituted authorities themselves, when they do not command by virtue, when they displease the people, when they assert any tendency to elevate themselves above the common level." Only a great stroke could have accomplished all this. A monarchy of thirteen centuries was proscribed in a day; a monarch adored for fifteen years was punished as a tyrant. Who could have predicted this outcome? Marat asked. In his analysis, he expressed the radicals' hope that the execution would desacralize power itself and thus make power more accessible to the people. The execution of one of Europe's leading kings had destroyed the magical powers of thrones, but it had also served as a warning to every kind of authority; you had to please the people from now on, and you could not appear to be superior to them.[14]

Like Marat, Louis Prudhomme of the paper *Révolutions de Paris* (which I quoted extensively in chapter 1), saw the religious and ritual aspects of the killing. The king had to be desacralized in order for the nation to be resacralized as a republic; the king had to be the greatest of all criminals in order to take on himself all the guilt of the nation. "For more than thirteen centuries the first nation of Europe has been the most servile," declared Prudhomme. He regretted that the execution did not take place on the national altar first used in the Festival of Federation, for such an act required a large audience: "The vast expanse of the field would have permitted an even greater number of witnesses to be present at this memorable event, which could not have too many witnesses."[15] In Freud's interpretation of the murder of the father, the sense of guilt felt by the band of brothers "can only be allayed by the solidarity of all the participants."[16] Although Prudhomme would never have subscribed to any feelings of guilt about executing the king (on the contrary, it erased the guilt of willing servitude), his wish for more participation inadvertently bears out Freud's remark.

14. Ibid., 26 January and 27 January 1793.

15. "Mort de Louis XVI, dernier roi de France." *Révolutions de Paris*, no. 185, 19–26 January 1793. This is by far the longest commentary in a newspaper on the killing of the king; it extends over thirty pages.

16. *Totem and Taboo*, in vol. 13 of *The Standard Edition of the Complete Psychological Works of Sigmund Freud*, trans. James Strachey (London, 1958), p. 147.

When describing the scene at the scaffold after the execution and the benediction of the "brothers" with the king's blood, Prudhomme recounted the complaint of a witness, who feared the assimilation of the scene with cannibalism: "My friends, what are we doing? All of this is going to be reported; they are going to paint us abroad as a ferocious and bloodthirsty mob." A defiant voice responded:

> Yes, thirsty for the blood of a despot; let them go retell it, if you like, to everyone on earth; for too long the French people have given proof of their patience; it is the weakness of a nation that emboldens the tyrants. . . . The day of justice is shining finally; it must be as terrible as the crimes have been serious.[17]

In his defense of the act, Prudhomme found himself constantly reverting to the imagery of sacrifice; the king was being metaphorically devoured (the people were "thirsty for the blood of a despot") in order to transform the French from servile slaves of tyranny into brave republicans. The killing was not cannibalism because it was ritualized. The act of terrible communion was with the victim of sacrifice himself. Only by killing him could they overcome their own weaknesses; only by eliminating a great criminal could they purify the community; only by eating the king could the people become sovereign themselves.

Republicans were divided between the desire to celebrate the act and to forget it. Yet even the radicals who wanted to keep the memory of the deed alive harped on the theme of the king's own guilt rather than the consequences of the act for themselves. Jacques-René Hébert wrote in his newspaper *Le Père Duchesne*, as if in response to the deputy who had advised letting go of all feeling of resentment toward the king, "I would not say like certain dawdlers, 'Let us speak of it no longer' [the exact words of the deputy]. On the contrary, let us talk about it in order to remind ourselves of all of his crimes and to inspire in all men the horror that they ought to have for kings."[18]

The radical insistence on keeping alive the memory of the event was echoed in a few pamphlets and engravings published immediately after the execution. The twenty-three-page pamphlet titled

17. "Mort de Louis XVI."
18. "Oraison funèbre de Louis Capet, dernier roi des Français, prononcé par le père Duchesne . . . ," *Le Père Duchesne*, no. 212

The Arrival of Louis Capet in Hell included an engraving of Louis holding his head at his judgment in hell. The mythological figures in hell discuss eating a quarter of "roasted pope" ("pape à la broche"). At the end of his trial in hell, Louis is condemned to have his heart torn to pieces by a vulture, and to perpetuate his agony, his heart will be reborn each day.[19] The most radical writers and engravers thus did not shy away from the most terrifying aspect of the execution—the sight of the king's severed head with its connotations of cannibalism—and they insisted precisely on its capacity to terrify. The best known of the engravings that celebrated the execution was Villeneuve's rendition of the severed head (figure 11). The reproduction of the king's severed head must have aroused ambivalent reactions in many quarters. The decapitation was supposed to serve as a warning to other kings, but it also had a larger resonance of murder of the father, cannibalism, and potential anarchy.[20]

In fact, however, very few engravings of the execution were published in France immediately after the event. Most representations of the execution were printed outside France and were meant to serve the cause of counterrevolution. During 1793 and 1794 no commemorative medals of the execution were struck in France, though this was a very common way to memorialize important revolutionary events.[21] One of the few engravings of the execution printed immediately afterward accompanied an eight-page pamphlet which admitted that many of the spectators present at the execution had questioned the wisdom of killing the king. Many people said that the former king "being sacred, men had no right to touch him."

The author of the pamphlet claimed in response that the act was desired by all those who understood the "price of liberty." The execution was the revenge of the entire human race.[22] The radicals could only reject the sacredness of the king by killing him and taking on that sacredness for the people as a whole. Ritual sacrifice and the

19. *Arrivée de Louis Capet aux Enters* (Paris, 1793). Attributed to Villeneuve by Maurice Tourneux, *Bibliographie de l'histoire de Paris pendant la Révolution française* (Paris, 1890), vol. 1, p. 337.

20. For a Freudian analysis of this engraving which relates it to the Medusa's head and threats of castration, see Neil Hertz, "Medusa's Head: Male Hysteria under Political Pressure," *Representations* 4 (1988): 27–54, especially pp. 47–48.

21. See Michel Hennin, *Histoire numismatique de la Révolution française*, 2 vols. (Paris, 1826).

22. *Décret définitif de la Convention nationale, qui condamne Louis Capet, le Traître, le Patricide, à la peine de mort . . . suivi des réflexions d'un Républicain* (Paris, n.d.).

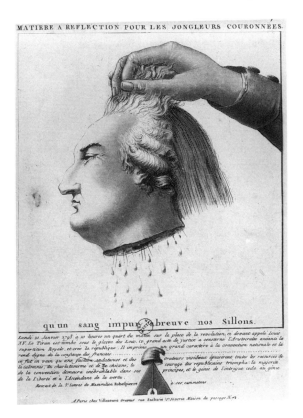

11. Villeneuve's engraving, "Food for Thought for the Crowned Jugglers" (1793). Photo: Bibliothèque nationale.

? where is this?

metaphorical eating of the king's body were the essential means of effecting this transformation. The radicals wanted to commemorate the event in order to remind the people of their necessary complicity in the act.

Five years later, one of the deputies who had voted against the death penalty gave his own version of the execution. Louis-Sébastien Mercier insisted that Paris had not been reduced to silent stupefaction by the deed. He also underlined the ritual aspects of the killing. When Louis's blood began to run, the eighty thousand armed men present cried out with joy. Several observers ran forward

to dip their fingers, pens, or pieces of paper into the blood; one tasted it and said, "it is horribly salty!" At the edge of the scaffold, an executioner was selling little packets of his hair . . . everyone tried to take away a small fragment of his clothing or a bloody reminder of this tragic scene. I saw all the people marching arm in arm, laughing, talking familiarly, as if they were coming back from a festival.

Mercier went on to claim, however, that as the days passed, "further reflection and a kind of anxious fear about the future cast a cloud over every social gathering." The deputies who had voted the death of the king began to feel afraid: "They were feeling a kind of interior dread which in some cases resembled repentance."[23] In his view, many of the deputies definitely felt guilt.

The tension between forgetting and commemorating, between feeling guilty and rejecting guilt, would continue as the Revolution proceeded. Most remarkable in this regard was the first anniversary of the killing of the king, in January 1794. No plans for any kind of celebration were made until the meeting of the Jacobin Club of Paris on 20 January 1794. The fact that no plans had been made ahead of time shows how ambivalent the deputies were about remembering their deed. One club member proposed a solution of typical displacement: a public reading of the Declaration of the Rights of Man and a memorial reading of the story of Lepeletier's assassination. A more zealous member asked for a parade of the effigies of all the kings currently at war with France, followed by their symbolic beheading. Finally, the club voted to present itself en masse to the Convention the next day to congratulate the deputies on the courage that they had shown in the trial of the king.[24] On the day of the anniversary itself, in response to the visit from the Jacobins, the Convention voted to hold an improvised festival and left as a group for the Place de la Révolution, site of the execution of the king. There they found themselves, to the distress of many, witnessing the day's executions.

The same deputy who had encouraged the Jacobins a year earlier to speak no longer of the king now complained bitterly in the Convention about the masquerade to which the deputies had been subjected. Why were four criminals taken to be executed at the same time as the visit of the deputies? he asked. Why were the deputies polluted with their blood? This was a conspiracy to make the depu-

23. Louis-Sébastien Mercier, *Le Nouveau Paris* (Paris, an VII [1799]), vol. 3, pp. 4–7.

24. Aulard, ed., *La Société des Jacobins*, vol. 5, pp. 615–66.

ties look like "cannibals": "We were going to celebrate the death of a king, the punishment of an eater of men; but we did not want to defile our attention with such a disgusting and hideous spectacle."[25] The deputies did not want to become like the king they had denounced as a "mangeur d'hommes." The violence of the Revolution threatened to undo the ritual sacrifice itself. If the situation could not be controlled, the sacrificial crisis would not end, and cannibalism and anarchy would menace the community's continuing existence.

Popular reactions to the "festival" varied from glee to disinterest. One police agent reported that women in a cabaret expressed particular satisfaction at the sight of the guillotine in operation during the festivities: "If the guillotine had not been in action, the festival would not have been so beautiful." Another agent reported, however, that people were revolted at the sight of deputies attending an ordinary execution. Some people blamed this on the city government of Paris, which was rumored to have arranged the coincidence of the four executions taking place as the deputies came to the square to celebrate the death of Louis XVI. At the central market, several people were seen carrying figures made of straw without heads as reminders of the fate of Louis. One of the other agents reported that people thought the very idea of a celebration was inappropriate because the French ought to forget the king altogether.[26]

In other parts of France, hastily organized, carnivalesque festivals picked up on the theme of the straw men without heads. Many people, and especially the popular classes, apparently wanted tangible reminders for their celebrations. In Grenoble, figures of Louis, the pope, and the nobility were smashed by two men dressed as Hercules. In Lyon, a carnival king dressed in a tiger skin sat on a throne, attended by the nobility in the guise of a wolf and the clergy in that of a fox. A dragon then set the scene on fire. As news of such celebrations spread, other towns and cities rushed to set up their own festivals. Performances of revolutionary plays, illuminations of

25. *Moniteur universel*, no. 23, 4 pluviôse an II (23 January 1794), reporting on the session of the National Convention of 3 pluviôse (22 January 1794) and the speech by Bourdon.

26. Pierre Caron, ed., *Rapports des agents secrets du ministre de l'Intérieur*, vol. 3, *28 nivôse an II– 20 pluviôse an II; 17 janvier 1794– 8 février 1794* (Paris, 1943), pp. 67–99; the quotation is from p. 67.

private and public buildings, vaudevilles, popular banquets, and speeches denouncing Louis's crimes were all brought out to give the anniversary some moment.[27]

The deputies wanted no repeat of these impromptu celebrations, so they instituted a regular festival for the future, the Anniversary of the Death of the Last King of the French. The festival held in Paris in 1799 was quite typical of these organized, official celebrations. There were no manikins, no parodies, no literal representations of violence. At 10 A.M. an artillery salute inaugurated the festivities. At 11:30 A.M. the deputies gathered in their legislative costumes and, with palm leaves in hand, marched into their meeting hall to the sound of trumpets. On the tribune sat the book of the law ornamented with civic laurels. The law had presumably replaced the father-king as the emblem of authority. Central to the ceremony were speeches and oaths to hate both royalty and anarchy (the oaths varied from year to year depending on the political situation). The speech by the president of the Council of Ancients was characteristically didactic. The deputies were not there, he proclaimed, to show joy at the memory of a scaffold and punishment, but to engrave in all souls the immortal truths that had issued from that eternally memorable day. Most of the speech consisted of a capsule history of the Revolution up to Louis's death and a review of the evidence against him (again!). Thus, throughout the remainder of the revolutionary decade, officials were constantly trying to displace, contain, and dissipate violence even as they recognized the need to remember the violence which had given birth to republican history.[28]

After the death of the king, the deputies carried forward the attack on paternal prerogatives. Many deputies now went beyond the

27. Auguste Prudhomme, *Histoire de Grenoble* (Grenoble, 1888), pp. 640–41; Joseph Mathieu, *Célébration du 21 janvier depuis 1793 jusqu'à nos jours* (Marseille, 1865), pp. 54–55; *Discours prononcé dans le temple de la Raison, à Strasbourg, le décadi 20 pluviôse, 2e année de la République françoise, une et indivisible; jour auquel on a célébré l'anniversaire de la mort du tyran Capet* (n.p., n.d.); *Abréviateur universel*, no. 397, 13 pluviôse an II (1 February 1794), report on the festival in Rouen on 8 pluviôse.

28. Corps législatif, Conseil des Anciens, commission des inspecteurs de la salle, *Programme de la fête qui aura lieu le 2 pluviôse de l'an 7, dans l'intérieur du Palais des Anciens, à raison de l'anniversaire de la juste punition du dernier tyran des Français;* Corps législatif, Conseil des Anciens, *Discours prononcé par Garat, Président du Conseil des Anciens, le 2 pluviôse an 7, anniversaire du 21 janvier 1792 [sic], et du serment de haine à la royauté et à l'anarchie.* The speech included a long comparison between the case of Louis XVI and that of Charles I.

vague condemnation of the tyranny of parents to a more precise indictment of paternal authority, especially the control of fathers over their grown children. Jean-Jacques Cambacérès explained in his proposal for a civil code in August 1793, "The imperious voice of reason has made itself heard; it says, no more paternal power; it is deceiving nature to establish its rights by compulsion."[29]

The revolutionaries wanted liberty and equality to rule in the family just as they ruled in the state, though just what was meant by liberty and equality within the context of the family remained subject to continual redefinition. Revolutionary legislators were clearest about what they opposed: tyrannical power within the family. Deputy Berlier explained, "Excessive power leads to tyranny, tyranny embitters, and too often, instead of a tender father and a grateful son, there is seen only a barbarous master and a slave in revolt." In place of this tyranny, the deputies hoped to establish what Berlier aptly called "this gentle correlation of duties," "this authority of affection that the laws cannot command," in other words, friendship and mutual recognition of rights and obligations.[30] Liberty would guarantee individual autonomy, and love would provide familial solidarity.

The effort to establish a new equilibrium between parents and children always included a paradox, however; revolutionary legislation took power away from the father (and from the church) and ultimately vested a large portion of it in the state.[31] Legislators wanted to ensure the freedom of individuals, but in order to accomplish this they had to rely on state powers to curb tyrannical fathers. The Convention was most active in the area of property law, and it took earlier legislation several steps further. On 7 March 1793 the deputies declared the equality of all inheritance in the direct line of succession, thereby extending the earlier law on intestate successions. On 5 brumaire an II (26 October 1793), equality was extended

29. Emile Masson, *La Puissance paternelle et la famille sous la Révolution* (Paris, 1910), p. 227.

30. *Discours et projet de loi, sur les rapports qui doivent subsister entre les enfans et les auteurs de leurs jours, en remplacement des droits connus sous le titre usurpé de puissance paternelle, par Berlier, député de la Côte-d'Or* (Paris, 1793), pp. 4, 6.

31. On the new equilibrium, see Pierre Murat, "La Puissance paternelle et la Révolution française: Essai de régénération de l'autorité des pères," in Irène Théry and Christian Biet, eds., *La Famille, la loi, l'état de la Révolution au Code civil* (Paris, 1989), pp. 390–411. For a view that deemphasizes the paradoxical aspects of revolutionary legislation, see Philippe Sagnac, *La Législation civile de la Révolution française, 1789–1804* (Paris, 1898).

to all inheritance in collateral lines as well and made retroactive to 14 July 1789 (though owners of property could still dispose of one-tenth of their property in direct successions and one-sixth in collateral successions).

A week later, on 2 November 1793, the Convention enacted one of its most controversial laws: it granted illegitimate children equal rights of inheritance upon proof of paternity and made the provisions retroactive to 14 July 1789.[32] An exception was made for children of adulterous unions, who gained the right to only one-third of a regular portion of the inheritance. The law authorized legal proceedings by illegitimate children for establishment of paternity or maternity against parents unwilling to admit the relationship. Equality of inheritance within the family was even more rigorously enforced by the law of 17 nivôse an II (6 January 1794), which provided that the disposable portion of property had to go to someone outside of either the direct or the collateral line of succession. In essence, then, the Convention was enforcing through the law the equality within the band of brothers.

Society and the state were now asserting the superiority of their claims over the family. The attempts to give equal status to illegitimate children and the severe constraints on testamentary freedom of action have led some legal scholars to conclude that the revolutionary legislatures disorganized and nearly ruined the family.[33] The deputies in the Convention certainly did not want to ruin the family, but they did distrust it, and they were most likely to favor the rights of children over either the individual right to dispose of property or the family's right to defend its own longterm interests. The deputies defended the new law on the rights of illegitimate children, for instance, by claiming that it would help eliminate infanticide and the double standard of sexual morality: "Sound morals will have an enemy the less, and passion a brake the more . . . when, finally, it is known that no longer can a man betray the hopes of a too confiding woman."[34] The Napoleonic codes marked a great

32. The many complications of this law are discussed in Marcel Garaud and Romuald Szramkiewicz, *La Révolution française et la famille* (Paris, 1978), pp. 116–30. For an even fuller treatment, see Crane Brinton, *French Revolutionary Legislation on Illegitimacy, 1789–1804* (Cambridge, Mass., 1936).

33. Masson, *La Puissance paternelle*, p. 329.

34. Speech by Cambacérès, quoted in Brinton, *French Revolutionary Legislation*, p. 34.

departure from this revolutionary distrust of the family; the codes explicitly considered the family a natural contract fulfilling necessary functions that required state protection.[35]

Under the National Convention, in contrast, most deputies believed that the state had to intervene to protect the rights of children against the potentially tyrannical actions of fathers, families, or churches. In many cases, such as education, the state actually took for itself the role of paternal authority. On 22 frimaire an II (12 December 1793), the Convention voted to establish state-run primary schools, and a week later it made attendance obligatory in principle. Danton proclaimed in the debate on whether primary schools should be obligatory, "Children belong to society before they belong to their family." Robespierre was even more forceful: "The country has the right to raise its children; it should not entrust this to the pride of families or to the prejudices of particular individuals, which always nourish aristocracy and domestic federalism."[36] Family prerogatives, in his view, were associated with particular interests rather than the general will, and particular interests in turn were associated with aristocracy and federalism, two major sources (though quite different in character) of opposition to the Jacobin revolution.

The republic had displayed its antipatriarchal direction: the political father had been killed, and ordinary fathers had been subjected to the constraints of the law or replaced by the authority of the state. As the radical revolution proceeded, the drama of the father disappeared from center stage, to be replaced by tensions about the nature of fraternal bonds and the place of women in the new republic. Was the family romance of fraternity to be a romance in which the brothers united gloriously to fight their common enemies or a tragedy of conflict and division? Were women the trophies of victory, the dangerous harpies of division, the helpmeets in struggle, the idealized representatives of virtue, or simply to be ignored? If the father was now absent, should one or more of the sons be imagined as taking his place, or would they remain brothers?

35. Pierre Lascoumes, "L'Emergence de la famille comme intérêt protégé par le droit pénal, 1791–1810," in Théry and Biet, eds., *La Famille, la loi*, pp. 340–48.
36. Garaud and Szramkiewicz, *La Révolution française et la famille*, p. 142.

12. Engraving titled "Mathey, Worker of Lille" (1793).
Photo: Bibliothèque nationale.

One powerful answer to such questions can be seen in an engraving from August 1793 that depicts three soldiers saluting a fallen brother (figure 12). This print echoes David's *Oath of the Horatii* in the new atmosphere created by the republic at war. It evokes romance, in the literary sense, as the brothers-in-arms eagerly take up the challenge to go off and fight the forces of evil. Frye calls romance the "nearest of all literary forms to the wish-fulfillment dream." It is the projection of the ideals of an age, and it always revolves around adventure. Romances have three main stages, according to Frye: the perilous journey, the crucial struggle, and the exaltation of the hero.[37] The sequence of stages is implicit in the narrative of the print; the three young men have been through a battle and are ready to go onward to fight again and thus establish their heroism. Their united, brotherly action is the incarnation of the ideals of the republic, the realization of the dream of fraternity.

The transformation from David's earlier oath is striking. In the print we see an oath between men who are perhaps brothers of the same family but who are in any case revolutionary brothers. The army of the republic has created its own family composed entirely of brothers. The three brothers swear their fidelity to the republic in front of a man who himself is more fraternal than paternal, despite his reference to "mes chers enfants [my dear children]," and who in any case is dying and lying prone, in contrast to the father in David's *Oath*. The father is now absent or about to disappear, and the brothers are uniting to take his place. Whether the father is good or not is irrelevant because the brothers are now the focus of the story. The feminine world is now entirely outside the scene of action.

In the new family romance of fraternity, the revolutionaries seemed to hope that they would remain perpetually youthful, as the heroes of romances always were; they wanted to be permanently brothers and not founding fathers. Even the good sans-culotte family man imagined himself as a heroic young soldier.[38] In the iconography of the radical period of the French Revolution, consequently, there were virtually no emblems of fatherhood.[39] The male representation of the people in the form of Hercules was shown as a

37. Northrop Frye, *Anatomy of Criticism: Four Essays* (Princeton, 1957), pp. 186–88; the quotation is from p. 186.

38. As Antoine de Baecque explains, "Le sans-culotte s'idéalise . . . en jeune soldat héroïque, alors que l'on sait, depuis les études sociologiques effectuées sur les sans-culottes parisiens et marseillais, qu'il est en fait un père de famille boutiquier." "Le sang des héros: Figures du corps dans l'imaginaire politique de la Révolution française," *Revue d'histoire moderne et contemporaine* 34 (1987): 573–74.

39. The exception seems to be the famous Père Duchesne, the figure who adorned the masthead of Hébert's newspaper of that name. Hébert's Père Duchesne has a wife and children, but he refers to the latter very rarely. See, for example, "La soirée des rois, du Père Duchesne, ou son souper de famille avec Jean-Bar," *Le Père Duchesne*, no. 4, where the Père refers to "mes bougres enfans" (he never refers to them by name).

13.   Dupré's sketch of Hercules for the seal of the
Republic (1793). Musée Carnavalet. Photo: author.

virile brother (figure 13); we know that he is a brother because he is
shown with his sisters, liberty and equality, who cannot be imagined
as wives, much less mothers, if only because there are always two of
them.[40]

The French brothers of 1793–94 thus seemed to be refusing to
follow the Freudian script as laid out in *Totem and Taboo;* they insisted
on "the original democratic equality" of each member of the tribe
and refused to venerate those individuals who had distinguished
themselves above the rest. In Freud's terms, they were stuck in that
phase where no one was able to or was allowed to attain "the father's
supreme power."[41] In contrast to the Americans, the French did not

40. I discuss the significance of the Hercules seal in *Politics, Culture, and Class in the
French Revolution* (Berkeley, 1984), pp. 87–119.
41. Freud, *Totem and Taboo*, pp. 148–49.

mythologize a living leader (at least not until Napoleon organized his own cult). Mirabeau, Lafayette, Marat, Danton, and Robespierre all passed from the scene without establishing an enduring cult of their own persons. Moreover, they did not successfully represent themselves either collectively or individually as fathers of the country.

The contrast with American republican imagery of the time was striking. American republican rhetoric was clearly preoccupied with familial analogies; in the most self-conscious way, American leaders portrayed themselves first as Sons of Liberty and later as Founding Fathers. The notion of Founding Fathers was not invented all at once in the 1770s or 1780s. The expression "Founding Fathers" may in fact be a relatively modern one; more common in the American past were such terms as *fathers of the republic* or *forefathers*.[42]

The parent-child analogy was widely diffused in the political literature on both sides of the quarrel over American independence.[43] Both the Americans and the English referred to the Americans as children and the English as parents. As an English pamphlet published in 1766 proclaimed, the colonies should "blush" at being "found in a posture of hostility against Great Britain," since humanity has "no name of infamy half so reproachful, as that of a base and ungrateful PARRICIDE." The defenders of the American cause in England compared America to "an industrious and intelligent youth just arriving at man's estate," and they warned that tyrannical parenting would only lead to rebellion.[44] In 1776 revolutionary propagandists began to refer to George III as an "unnatural father."[45] Moreover, children played important roles, both physically and symbolically, in the rituals of the American Revolution itself. Bands of boys intimidated merchants during the nonimportation move-

42. On the relative modernity of the phrase *Founding Fathers,* see Wesley Frank Craven, *The Legend of the Founding Fathers* (New York, 1956), p. 2, n. 1. I am indebted to William R. Everdell for this reference.

43. The phrase "parent-child analogy" comes from Edwin G. Burrows and Michael Wallace, "The American Revolution: The Ideology and Psychology of National Liberation," *Perspectives in American History* 6 (1972): 167–306. See also Jay Fliegelman, *Prodigals and Pilgrims: The American Revolution against Patriarchal Authority, 1750–1800* (Cambridge, 1982). I am indebted to Linda Kerber for helpful suggestions about the American literature.

44. Quoted in Burrows and Wallace, "The American Revolution," pp. 229, 245.

45. Paul K. Longmore, *The Invention of George Washington* (Berkeley, 1988), p. 204.

ment, taunted soldiers during confrontations, and participated in riots. In crowd actions during the 1760s and 1770s, Americans almost literally made themselves into children. For the English Friends of Liberty, they substituted Sons of Liberty, Sons of Freedom, and Liberty Boys.[46]

An important transformation in the American self-image took place during the War of Independence. The children began to imagine themselves as fathers, or at least they began to imagine one of themselves as a political father. As George III came under attack as an "unnatural father," George Washington increasingly took his place as "our political Father and head of a Great People." In 1778 Washington was referred to for the first time as "the Father of His Country." In 1779 American civilians joined army officers in celebrating his birthday, thereby inaugurating a tradition that continues to this day.[47] The way to Washington's elevation had been prepared by the colonists' reverence for their own past. They routinely referred in the 1760s to "our venerable Forefathers" and important founders such as William Penn were referred to as "our Father."[48]

By mythologizing George Washington, Americans glorified the new, more understanding father of eighteenth-century educational tracts and set a moral example for themselves. John Adams remarked, "I glory in the character of a Washington because I know him to be only an exemplification of the American character. . . . If his character stood alone, I should value it very little."[49] By the 1790s, American revolutionaries had transformed themselves collectively from political children into political fathers through the mediation of the figure of Washington; the male leadership internalized for itself the role of beneficent father. The Americans were in a position, consequently, to imagine passing on their political patrimony through a contractual document such as the constitution of 1787. It may be that this psychopolitical transformation from children into founding fathers outweighs in importance the specific

46. Peter Shaw, *American Patriots and the Rituals of Revolution* (Cambridge, Mass., 1981), p. 195.
47. Longmore, *The Invention*, pp. 204–5.
48. Craven, *The Legend*, pp. 29, 40.
49. Quoted by Fliegelman, *Prodigals and Pilgrims*, p. 223. On Washington as father of his country, see ibid., p. 200.

details of disagreement between the various languages of American politics. Civic republicanism, Lockean liberalism, work-ethic Protestantism, and state-centered theories of power and sovereignty could all be accommodated by the new family romance of the understanding fathers, who ruled through wisdom rather than despotism.[50]

No one in France had Washington's kind of living mythic status, at least not until Napoleon Bonaparte captured power. It is easier to talk about the consequences of this difference between America and France than to discern its causes. French republicans were determined to maintain a collective leadership of the Revolution; for this reason the National Convention, rather than establishing a separate executive arm, set up committees with rotating membership drawn from its own deputies to serve as a kind of loosely defined executive power. When the Convention wrote a new constitution in 1795, it provided for a five-man directory elected by the legislature, rather than a single president. Throughout the Revolution, politicians of every faction expressed fear of dictatorship. Robespierre fell from power—as one of twelve equal members of the Committee of Public Safety—because he seemed to be setting himself apart from the rest of the deputies.

This insistence on maintaining what Freud called "the original democratic equality" of each member of the tribe went hand in hand with the radicalism of the French Revolution. All forms of social distinction were suspect, as were all forms of power modeled on patriarchy. If fraternity was to be the model for a government based on equality and popular sovereignty, then any suggestion of a father figure was problematic. Perhaps what this difference between American and French republicanism comes down to is a distrust of the father figure. The French king and French fathers had such extraordinary powers under the Old Regime that the position of father was itself called into question by the French Revolution. As Balzac said, "by cutting off the head of Louis XVI, the Republic cut off the head of all the fathers of families."[51]

The nearest French equivalent to Washington was not one indi-

---

50. Isaac Kramnick, "The 'Great National Discussion': The Discourse of Politics in 1787," *William and Mary Quarterly* 45 (1988): 3–32.

51. *Mémoires de deux jeunes mariées*, quoted in Yvonne Knibiehler, *Les Pères aussi ont une histoire* (Paris, 1987), p. 161.

Rev. de Paris.   *Honneurs rendus à la mémoire de le Pelletier.*   *n°. 185. P. 226*

Jeudi 24 Janvier 1793. le Corps du Martyr de la Liberté, sorti de la maison de son frere et couvert à demie sur son lit de mort, fut exposé sur le piedestal de la Statue de Louis XIV. Place des Piques ci devant Place de Vendôme.

14.   Engraving of the bier of Lepeletier. From *Révolutions de Paris*, no. 185, 19–26 January 1793. Note that the artist has depicted an audience composed exclusively of men. Photo: Maclure Collection, Special Collections, Van Pelt-Dietrich Library, University of Pennsylvania.

vidual but rather the cult of dead heroes. The first of these was Michel Lepeletier, the regicide deputy who was assassinated by a royalist on the eve of the king's execution. On the order of the Convention, the artist-deputy David organized a public exhibition of Lepeletier's body on 24 January 1793 (see figure 14). On the pedestal of the destroyed statue of Louis XIV in the Place Vendôme (see figure 10), David built a raised base with lateral steps. The upper body was exposed to show the wound, and during the ceremony the president of the Convention crowned the body with the laurels of immortality.[52] The body was then carried to the Pantheon, where revolutionary heroes were entombed.

The ceremony for Lepeletier served as a kind of answer to the

52. For a description and analysis of the ceremony, see Herbert, *David, Voltaire*, pp. 95–96.

doubts remaining about the killing of the king. It showed that the deputies who voted for the king's death were not cannibals but rather men ready to die for their country. Lepeletier's wound was the sign of his political martyrdom and hence of his sacredness; for this reason, it had to be visible to everyone. Moreover, Lepeletier's body was still whole, unlike the king's; like a saint's body, it possessed the magical power of seeming still alive. The newspaper *Révolutions de Paris* explicitly compared the rapidly decomposing body of Louis with the "apotheosis" of Lepeletier and argued that the Convention had been able to "profit from this sad episode in order to sustain public morale at a suitable level." When Bertrand Barère delivered his eulogy for Lepeletier at the ceremony, he concluded by proposing that all those present swear an oath "on the body of Lepeletier to extinguish all personal animosity and to reunite to save the country."[53] In this way, the body of the martyr was supposed to help cement union between the remaining brothers.

Observers noted that this was a new kind of spectacle because dead bodies had never before been exposed this way in public. When David presented a painting of Lepeletier on his deathbed, *Lepeletier sur son lit de mort* (a painting that was subsequently destroyed), he explained the importance of the composition of Lepeletier's body: "See how his features are serene; that's because when one dies for one's country, one has nothing with which to reproach oneself."[54] Lepeletier's body itself justified the deputies' confidence in their action; his serenity proved that they had no reason to feel guilty (itself an admission that many people thought guilt was in order).

When Jean-Paul Marat, journalist and deputy, was assassinated on 13 July 1793, his death became the subject of the most extensive cult organized around an individual political figure. His funeral prompted a major popular outpouring of grief, and in the following months and years, his death was the subject of scores of festivals, engravings, and theatrical representations.[55] After his assassination

53. *Révolutions de Paris*, no. 185, 19–26 January 1793.

54. Quoted in William Olander, *"Pour transmettre à la postérité:* French Painting and the Revolution, 1774–1795," (Ph.D. diss., New York University, 1983), p. 248. See also pp. 244–45 for reactions to the funeral.

55. Jean-Claude Bonnet, ed., *La Mort de Marat* (Paris, 1986) and Marie-Hélène Huet, *Rehearsing the Revolution: The Staging of Marat's Death, 1793–1797*, trans. Robert Hurley (Berkeley, 1982).

Marat's blood seemed to have taken on the sacrality that the king lost on 21 January. During the funeral procession on 16 July 1793 the members of the women's club called the Société des Républicaines Révolutionnaires threw flowers on the rapidly decomposing body and gathered the blood that still seemed to flow from his wounds. One of the orators cried, "Let the blood of Marat become the seed of intrepid republicans," and the women replied by swearing to "people the earth with as many Marats as they could."[56]

This vague notion that Marat's blood might engender brave republicans was the only connection of Marat with political fatherhood in the festival (a notion entirely lacking in the case of Lepeletier). For the most part he was the martyr-brother, as in David's famous painting of him in death or David's staging of the funeral procession, where Marat's body was carried on a Roman-style bier. The orators saluted him as the friend of the people (his newspaper was named *L'Ami du Peuple*), the apostle and martyr of liberty (see figure 15). Marat was immortal, courageous—in short, the tragic brother and example, much like the fallen brother in the engraving (figure 12) discussed earlier in this chapter. Or as his fellow journalist Hébert reminded his audience a few days later, Marat liked to think of himself as the Cassandra of the Revolution, certainly far removed from the image of a founding father.[57]

References to Marat as the "father of his people" only appeared after the assassination and may have been part of an effort to rehabilitate father figures that slowly took shape in late 1793 and 1794 (the subject of chapter 6). If the father was going to reappear, however, it was only as the good father, a friend to his children, rather than as a stern, forbidding figure. In the festivals organized by the Parisian sections in the fall of 1793 to celebrate the memory of Marat, one hymn referred to "our father" ("Nous avons perdu notre père!"), but in the next line it reverted to the much more common "friend of the people" ("L'ami du peuple ne vit plus!").[58] A hymn published in the year II made the same link between father and

56. Quoted in Jacques Guilhaumou, *La Mort de Marat* (Paris, 1989), p. 63. This scene is described as a ritual massacre in Bonnet, ed., *La Mort de Marat*, p. 71.

57. Guilhaumou, *La Mort de Marat*, p. 85. For a sense of the wide variety of parallels drawn between Marat and Greco-Roman, modern republican, and even Biblical heroes (Moses, Jesus), see Jean-Claude Bonnet, "Les Formes de célébration," in Bonnet, ed., *La Mort de Marat*, pp. 101–27, especially pp. 110–11.

58. Guilhaumou, *La Mort de Marat*, p. 107, civic festival organized by the Section de la Cité, 21 October 1793.

L'AMI DU PEUPLE

Il fut l'ami du Peuple; il périt sa victime.
Ecrivain véhément, observateur profond,
Marat sut réunir par un accord sublime,
L'esprit de Juvenal et l'ame de Caton.

15.   Engraving of Marat, "the Friend of the People"
(1793). Photo: Bibliothèque nationale.

friend of the people: "Of the people he was the father, the friend most ardent."[59]

Plays written about Marat after his death show the same pattern. Camaille Saint-Aubin's *L'Ami du Peuple* ended with the line: "An entire people acclaim him and call him their father." Gassier Saint-Amand's *L'Ami du Peuple, ou la mort de Marat* ended even more pointedly: "We all lose a father, a friend." Yet as Marie-Hélène Huet has argued about these lines, only Marat's death confirms his paternity, and his paternity is a fatherhood without lineage and without heirs.[60] The very memorializations that emphasized Marat's great-

59. "Stances en l'honneur de Marat," par d'Hannouville fils, *Le Chansonnier de la Montagne* (Paris, an II), quoted by Lise Andries, "Marat dans les occasionnels et les almanachs (1792–1797)," in Bonnet, ed., *La Mort de Marat*, p. 96.

60. Quoted in Huet, *Rehearsing the Revolution*, pp. 75, 79. Huet concludes (p. 83): "In the framework of the Revolution . . . there was a rupture and a discontinuity: no inheritance could be counted on, no transmission was possible: the father had children but no heirs."

16.   Jacques-Louis David, *The Death of Bara* (1794). Musée du Louvre.
Photo: Réunion des musées nationaux.

ness seemed to imply that his contribution could not be imitated.[61]

The cult of dead heroes extended to young boys who had died fighting for the republic, in itself a significant indicator that the revolutionaries were not interested in finding father figures to emulate. The young heroes were the model for the children of the republic, and they also represented the internalized self-image of the revolutionaries as young, romantic heroes. The best known of the child-heroes was Joseph Bara, a thirteen-year-old boy whose willingness to die in opposing the Vendée rebels was immortalized in an unfinished painting by David (figure 16).[62] The heroism of Bara

61. Thus the engravings of Marat that aimed to be favorable to his legacy never presented him as father, but only as martyr, as public figure, sometimes as Christ figure. Lise Andries, "Les Estampes de Marat sous la Révolution: Une Emblématique," in Bonnet, ed., *La Mort de Marat,* pp. 187–201.

62. A discussion of the place of the painting of Bara within David's work would take me too far afield, but it should be noted that the figure of the young boy is very

was brought to the attention of the Convention in December 1793 and taken up and considerably embellished by Robespierre soon after. He described the "extraordinary child" as someone who tried to satisfy both "filial love" and "love of country," but who in the end died for the latter.[63] As Robespierre himself had explained in November 1792, "the family of French legislators is the country [la patrie]; it is the entire human race, except for the tyrants and their accomplices."[64]

Bara, as many engravings on the theme explained, had worked hard to support his widowed mother with his soldier's pay. He had no father. David planned a festival for 10 thermidor (28 July 1794) to honor Bara and another young hero, Agricola Viala, an orphan from the south, who distinguished himself in fighting against the southern rebels. David's plan for the festival was published even though the festival itself was not held because of the fall of Robespierre, its chief patron, on 27 July 1794. The festival project reproduced the same absence of the fathers found in the young heroes' stories; David's plan called for two columns, one a deputation of children, the other a deputation of mothers.[65] Although the festival was not held, Bara and Viala were the subject of scores of songs and hymns and of many operas and plays.[66] Similar in thematic reference were the engravings of the young Darrudder (figure 17), a drummer boy of fourteen who, seeing his father die at his side, grabbed his pistol and shot at the enemy. In this story too, the father is dead, and it is precisely the absence of the father that makes the courage of the son so moving.

In their own self-image, then, the French revolutionaries re-

androgynous, even female. We can see here a major move away from David's prerevolutionary paintings with their emphasis on virility, toward his post-1795 works and their revalorization of femininity. For a brief discussion, see Warren Roberts, "David's *Bara* and the Burdens of the French Revolution," *Proceedings of the Consortium on Revolutionary Europe, 1750–1850* (Tallahassee, Fla., 1990), pp. 76–81.

63. On the painting and Robespierre's support for the cult, see Olander, *"Pour transmettre,"* pp. 293–302. It is tempting to make much of the androgyny of David's figure of Bara; is this an inadvertent rendering of the very blurring of sexual boundaries so feared by the revolutionaries themselves? On this theme, see chapter 4.

64. Marc Bouloiseau, Jean Dautry, Georges Lefebvre, and Albert Soboul, eds., *Oeuvres de Maximilien Robespierre*, vol. 9, *Discours, septembre 1792– 27 juillet 1793* (Paris, 1961), p. 94.

65. *Rapport sur la fête héroique pour les honneurs du Panthéon à décerner aux jeunes Barra et Viala, par David; Séance du 23 messidor, an 2 de la République* (Paris, 1794).

66. James A. Leith, "Youth Heroes of the French Revolution," *Proceedings of the Consortium on Revolutionary Europe, 1750–1850*, (Athens, Ga., 1987), pp. 127–37.

LE JEUNE DARRUDDER.

L'Action du jeune Darrudder, tambour agé de 14 ans est un trait de bravoure et un élan de piété filiale, étant a l'affaire de Fougere dans la Vendée, il vit son pere mort à son coté, lui arrache un pistolet de sa ceinture, tire sur le meurtrier, lui brule la cervelle et continue de battre la charge contre les brigands jusqu'à leur entiere déroute, ce digne emule des Viala et des Barra est offert pour modele, aux éleves de l'école de Mars, par les representans du Peuple qui l'ont admis a cette ecole et lui ont donné l'accolade fraternelle au milieu des applaudissements, et demonstrations de la joie la plus vive.

17.   Engraving of the young Darrudder (1794?). Photo:
Bibliothèque nationale.

mained brothers. They were romantic heroes willing to fight for virtue and the triumph of the republic against the forces of evil and corruption. They were prepared to become martyrs for their cause, either on the battlefield or in the line of official duties. They expected the gratitude of the nation, but their chief reward was their sense of solidarity with their brothers. They did not envision themselves as founding fathers; they did not pick out one or a few of their number as father figures. It is most striking that the heroes of the French Revolution were dead martyrs, not living leaders (until Napoleon). None of them had the aura of aging wisdom, such as characterized Washington in America. The French republicans were

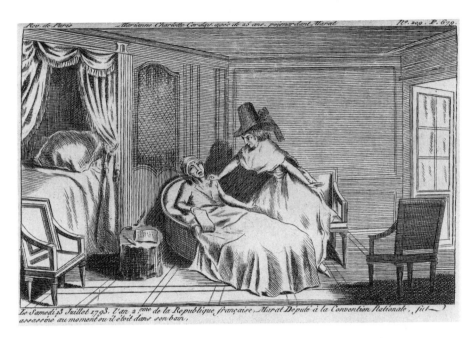

18.   Engraving of Charlotte Corday stabbing Marat. From *Révolutions de Paris*, no. 209, 6–20 July 1793. Photo: Maclure Collection, Special Collections, Van Pelt-Dietrich Library, University of Pennsylvania.

still engaged in the process of struggle, because the republic was not yet fully established. No one figure could incarnate their patrimony.

Sisters had an equivocal place in the new family romance of fraternity. Their place as inheritors from the father had been assured by revolutionary legislation, and new questions had been raised about their rights as citizens. But republican men also expressed great uneasiness about women acting in public ways. These doubts began to crystallize when Marat was assassinated by a woman. Charlotte Corday took for herself the role of the three sons in David's *Oath of the Horatii* and the role of the father in his *Brutus*. She wielded the dagger in defense of her vision of the republic (see figure 18). Corday portrayed herself as the good daughter willing to sacrifice her life to rid the republic of a tyrant. "Pardon me," she wrote to her father, "for having disposed of my existence without your permission. I avenged many innocent victims, I prevented many new disasters. The people, disabused one day, will rejoice at being delivered from a tyrant."[67]

In response to newspaper reports that were deemed too favorable to Corday, the government distributed an article that attacked her sexuality and her impertinence as a female acting politically:

> This woman, said to be very pretty, was not at all pretty; she was a virago, brawny rather than fresh, without grace, untidy, as are almost all female philosophers and eggheads. . . . Charlotte Corday was 25 years old; in our customs that is practically an old maid, especially with a masculinized bearing and boyish look. . . . Thus, it follows that this woman had thrown herself absolutely outside of her sex.[68]

As we shall see in chapter 4, this rejection of Corday's self-attributed political role soon extended to all women who wished to act politically, including the same Société des Républicaines Révolutionnaires which had been so prominent in the sacralization of Marat. Women who acted in the public sphere of politics would be described as transgressing sexual boundaries and contributing to the blurring of sexual differentiation. Their actions made them look like men; they were seen as taking on a sex not their own.

Women were not absent, however, from the iconographic family romance of the radical republic. Most representations of the republic were feminine, and they almost always showed young women, often virginal, but sometimes with very young children. Young women appear almost promiscuously in official representations, for they could be and were used to represent every imaginable political attribute such as Liberty, Reason, Wisdom, Victory, and even Force. Whenever a political message required an allegorical presentation, the allegory almost always centered on female figures.

The predominance of female figures in revolutionary iconography raises many questions. Were they present for entirely symbolic reasons or did their importance suggest something significant about women and the public sphere in revolutionary France? The reasons for the prominence of female figures are many.[69] The iconographic tradition had it that abstract qualities were best represented by

---

67. Guilhaumou, *La Mort de Marat*, p. 150.
68. Ibid., pp. 74–75.
69. For a brief and useful discussion, see Maurice Agulhon, *Marianne au combat: L'Imagerie et la symbolique républicaines de 1789 à 1880* (Paris, 1979; English version, Cambridge 1981).

female figures even when, as in the case of Fraternity or Force, for example, the representation by a female figure seemed to suggest a contradiction. This feminization of abstract qualities was reinforced by the fact that most such qualities were feminine nouns in French (and Latin and Greek) and also no doubt by the Catholic veneration of the Virgin Mary.

There were political reasons too for the apotheosis of the feminine allegory.[70] The founding of the republic required not only the destruction of every institution associated with monarchy but also a system of signs that was as distant as possible from monarchy. Since only men could rule directly in France—Salic law prevented women from succeeding to the throne—there was an obvious virtue in representing the republic by a female allegory; she could not be confused with the father/king. Moreover, French democracy operated in a manner which made any symbolic investment in individual political leaders quite problematic. If the brothers were determined to maintain what Freud called "the original democratic equality" of each member of the tribe and they refused to venerate any particular individual, then the singling out of individual male political figures as representations of the people, the nation, or the general qualities of citizenship would be unacceptable. No individual politicians appeared on French coins or paper money. Female allegories could not be associated with particular political leaders, if only because all officials were male by definition.

The presence of the female figure in iconography was not, consequently, a sign of female influence in politics. As Marina Warner has argued for the nineteenth century, the representation of liberty as female worked on a paradoxical premise: women, who did not have the vote and would be ridiculed if they wore the cap of liberty in real life, were chosen to express the ideal of freedom because of their very distance from political liberty. Liberty was figured as female because women were not imagined as political actors. Yet the embodiment of political ideals by female figures also opened the door to a different vision. As Warner remarks, "a symbolized female presence both gives and takes value and meaning in relation to actual women, and contains the potential for affirmation not only of women themselves but of the general good they might represent."[71]

70. See my discussion in *Politics, Culture, and Class*, pp. 87–119.
71. Marina Warner, *Monuments and Maidens: The Allegory of the Female Form* (New York, 1985), pp. xx, 277.

However overdetermined the choice of the female allegory might have been during the Revolution, the choice nevertheless had consequences. Women were shown as actors, and even if these women in plaster and metal were not imagined as particular women, they were still women and hence potentially threatening.[72] The constant criticism of the use of live women to represent virtues in festivals and the struggles over the female figure during the nineteenth century show that the female allegory had powerful resonances that went beyond the merely symbolic. I will try to unpack some of those resonances in the next chapters, but for now I want simply to emphasize that the female figure occupied most of the symbolic space once taken by the father/king's body.

Although there is never a father present in the official vignettes of the republic, young men, especially Hercules, did sometimes figure in tandem with their sisters. In the representations of Hercules with Liberty and Equality, the female figures often appear as trophies held in the hand of the conquering hero/brother (see figure 13, above). Thus, in iconographic terms, the incest taboo is not being very well enforced in the absence of the father. This is an iconographic family without parentage and without a lineage. The relation of the brothers and sisters to each other in this family is ambiguous and ambivalent.

Deputies, artists, or writers were hardly ever explicitly concerned with incest, but many saw a connection between the experience of the Revolution as a political and social upheaval and fundamental anxieties about family relationships. In a fragmentary manuscript written in 1792, Saint-Just argued that incest was a virtue when it was undertaken innocently: "It is virtue on the part of him who gives himself over to it in innocence and is no longer incest. . . . Observe the customs, read the laws of different peoples. The most corrupt also had the most horror of incest; innocent peoples never had a concept of it."[73] The same Saint-Just who argued so forcefully for the immediate execution of the king as a rebel here claims that the people most horrified by incest are also those who are the most politically corrupt. Incest, it might be said, was nothing but inno-

72. In my analysis of the Hercules figure, I show that the deputies chose a masculine representation when they wanted to eliminate the ambiguities created by the female allegory. *Politics, Culture, and Class,* pp. 87–119.

73. "De la nature, de l'état civil, de la cité ou les règles de l'indépendance, du gouvernement," in Louis-Antoine Saint-Just, *Oeuvres complètes,* ed. Michèle Duval (Paris, 1984), pp. 946–47.

cence about the force of the father's law, and those who were thus innocent were less likely to be contaminated by the experience of the father's despotism. As we shall see in chapter 5, such arguments were taken to a surprising conclusion by the marquis de Sade.

Incest seems to have disappeared from the novels produced during the radical revolution, and the novel itself went into decline. From a high point of 112 new novels published in 1789, the number steadily diminished from 66 in 1790 to 40 in 1792, 20 in 1793, and to the low point of 15 in 1794.[74] We do not know from direct testimony why novelists ceased producing new works, and there are many possible reasons for the decline, including a serious paper shortage.[75] Yet the production of new plays and the publication of new songs did not decrease in the same way. At least 1,500 new plays were staged between 1789 and 1799, and more than 750 were presented in the years 1792–94. Similarly, the number of new political songs rose steadily from 116 in 1789 to 701 in 1794.[76]

Apparently, the novel had come to seem suspect as a genre because it was private not public, and perhaps also because it was associated with women, both as authors and readers. By the last quarter of the eighteenth century, it was a commonplace of criticism that women were especially drawn to the novel. Laclos wrote in 1784 that he considered women especially apt for writing novels. Rousseau warned of the effect on girls of reading his own novel, and he associated novels in general with corruption. In his *Tableau de Paris* of the 1780s, Mercier concluded that novels by women were "the happiest and most agreeable luxury" of great societies.[77] If in the period 1792–94 excessive privacy, luxury, and feminine power had come to be viewed as problems—they were all explicitly attacked by the Jacobins as conducive to corruption—then it is no wonder that the novel itself might become problematic.

Those who did publish novels between 1792 and 1794 often

74. These figures are compiled from the information given in Angus Martin, Vivienne G. Mylne, and Richard Frautschi, *Bibliographie du genre romanesque français, 1751–1800* (London, 1977).

75. On the paper shortage and related matters, see Carla Hesse, *Publishing and Cultural Politics in Revolutionary Paris, 1789–1810* (Berkeley, 1991).

76. Beatrice F. Hyslop, "The Theater during a Crisis: The Parisian Theater during the Reign of the Terror," *Journal of Modern History* 17 (1945): 332–55; Robert Brécy, "La Chanson révolutionnaire de 1789 à 1799," *Annales historiques de la Révolution française* 53 (1981): 279–303.

77. Georges May, *Le Dilemme du roman au dix-huitième siècle* (Paris, 1963), especially chapter 8, "Féminisme et roman," pp. 204–46; the quotation is from p. 219.

favored the pastoral myth, apparently because it was well suited to the republic's emphasis on the didactic presentation of virtue.[78] In the pastoral tale, the heroes are pure, courageous, and generous. "Sacred duty," "simplicity" of life and love, and clear-cut distinctions between those who are good and those who are evil are the constant themes. A. T. de Rochefort's novel *Adraste et Nancy V.Y.* (1794), for example, tells the story of a French officer during the American War of Independence who is convinced of the advantages of a republic by the virtues of the Americans, especially their hospitality and generosity. The pastoral also could be adapted to contemporary settings. Dulaurent's tale *Joseph, or the Little Chimney Sweep* (1794?), presents a young boy from the Vendée region whose father is killed during the uprising against the republic. Despite being forced to leave his tranquil and happy home (the pastoral setting) by these events and having to take a job as a chimney sweep, he maintains his consistently generous character throughout. In the same vein, Ducray-Duminil wrote short stories during this period that showed that love of the countryside, love for one's fellow humans, and love for the republic were all inextricably linked. One of his best-known stories from this period, "The Oak of Liberty," centers on an old man telling tales to children whose fathers have been killed in the revolutionary wars.

As these very brief descriptions make clear, the fiction of 1792–94 is preoccupied with the deaths of fathers, and the writers favorable to the republic seem eager to demonstrate that fatherless children can be bastions of republican virtue. The children in these tales do not have particularly interesting personalities; they are simply good through and through. The fiction writers of 1792–94 thus appear uncomfortable with the ambiguities of the family romance of fraternity; they want to reassure their readers that a fatherless world poses no problems. This same insistence that everything will be alright can

---

78. In my discussion of the pastoral tale I am following the analysis of Malcolm C. Cook, "Politics in the Fiction of the French Revolution, 1789–1794," *Studies on Voltaire and the Eighteenth Century,* vol. 201 (Oxford, 1982), pp. 290–311. Henri Coulet argues that the pedagogical novel in the style of Fénelon was especially suited to moderate republicanism, whereas the heroic story situated in Rome, Greece, or the Orient was suited to patriotic Jacobinism. This may be true, but his own analysis so mixes chronology that it is hard to evaluate. "Existe-t-il un roman révolutionnaire?" in *La Légende de la Révolution,* actes du colloque international de Clermont-Ferrand, juin 1986 (Clermont-Ferrand, 1988), pp. 173–83.

be found in the one tale which directly takes up the issue of father killing. One of the pieces in P. F. Barbault-Royer's *Republican Novellas* tells the story of Démophon, who kills the tyrant Alcionaus on the urging of an oracle, only to discover that the tyrant was his father. The gods urge Démophon to reject any feeling of guilt: "When it involves the happiness of everyone, when by a divine stroke you have broken the most fierce tyrant, must you send forth lamentations? It doesn't matter that he was your father; the country and your brothers must come before everything else."[79] There is little suggestion in any of these novels and stories that the death of the father will lead to conflict between the brothers or to some form of retribution.

Similarly, the paintings of the radical period 1792–94 rarely hinted at conflict between the brothers. David's paintings of Lepeletier and Marat both showed saintly martyrs in poses of self-confident serenity. They were martyrs to the egotism, corruption, and evil designs of the counterrevolutionaries, not to the struggles between brothers within the revolutionary family. The violence of the Revolution was transcended in the composition of the paintings, which emphasized the humanity, sensibility, and generosity of the victims as well as their exemplary character for other republicans.

Painting did not diminish as an activity during the radical revolution, but most of the established names withdrew from public view. The Salon of 1793 attracted some 800 images by 350 painters and engravers, but most of the well-known names in art stayed away (including David, who exhibited his paintings in the hall of the Convention itself), and few critics wrote about the exhibition, no doubt for some of the same reasons that the novelists stayed out of print. Portraits remained an important category in the 1793 Salon, accounting for one-fourth of the images submitted. Since nearly two-thirds of the individuals in the portraits were unidentified in the catalogue of the Salon, the portraits might be seen as capturing the anonymity of the revolutionary crowd. On the other hand, portraiture by definition singles out an individual from the crowd. This tension about the role of the individual was central to revolutionary ideology; the Revolution required great individual heroism, but everyone was imagined as capable of it. By 1793 at least five collec-

79. Quoted in Cook, "Politics in the Fiction," p. 300.

tions of engravings of important figures of the Revolution had been published, but these conveyed the same message: the Revolution had been made by many individuals acting together, and it was their sheer number, not their individuality, that guaranteed success. No one great figure stood out.[80]

Killing the king/father clearly aroused great anxiety among the supporters of the Revolution. The most radical republicans denied that there were any grounds for anxiety, but their forms of denial—whether in speeches, newspaper articles, novels, engravings or paintings—usually betray the existence of nagging questions. They seemed to be answering unseen critics. The more moderate republicans hoped that the king and his death could be forgotten, or at least remembered only in a distant, orderly fashion. Neither group proved right. If the king was the scapegoat for the community's fear of its own violence in a time of great change, killing him did not work to displace or transcend that threat of violence. Thousands more victims of every social class, both men and women, proceeded to the guillotine after him.

Republicans tried hard to imagine a world for themselves in which brothers got along peacefully with each other; they even tried to ensure it in legal terms by equalizing inheritance and providing for a system of universal education. Nevertheless, competition, conflict, and violence between the brothers was an undeniable fact of life during the Revolution. To explain that continuing threat of failure to achieve liberty, equality, and fraternity, republicans looked for and found enemies everywhere. The Terror was invented as a system for forcing them into submission. Behind the real scenes of daily fear and officially instituted violence lay another kind of drama, which will be the subject of the next chapter. That drama revolved around the question of women's place and female responsibility. When the king's death failed to establish the republic on firm grounds, republicans found an even greater culprit left in their midst: the queen.

80. In this account of the Salon of 1793 I am following the analysis of Olander, *"Pour transmettre,"* pp. 254–84.

4

The Bad Mother

Once the father was dead, fraternity did not prove to be easy sailing.[1] The brothers faced two major issues: their relations with each other, and their relations with the now "liberated" women, who in Freud's analysis had previously been controlled exclusively by the father. The king of France did not directly control the destinies of all women, of course, but the legal and cultural system of the Old Regime certainly did. Once the Old Regime had been relegated to the past, some of the most pressing questions concerned the status of women: did they have equal rights in property inheritance, did they have equal rights in the family, could they participate fully in politics? In short, were they citizens in the full sense of the word? What was their role to be in the new revolutionary family?

The killing of the king/father left particularly pressing questions about one woman: the queen. Although Freud gives the mother great prominence in his Oedipal triangle, she does not figure at all in his story of the origins of political power. Moreover, in the Oedipal triangle, the mother is an object of desire (both the son's and the father's) rather than an acting subject in her own right. Similarly, queens in France had no status as actors in their own right, since women could not inherit the throne. They could act as regents for their underage sons but could not hold power in their own names. Yet French queens often attracted considerable attention—usually negative attention. As in the case of Marie-Antoinette, they were often foreign and frequently portrayed as evil influences. They never seemed to qualify as mothers of the people.

The question of Marie-Antoinette and the issue of the status of women more generally were closely connected, even though Marie-Antoinette herself probably had no interest in women's rights and

1. A version of this chapter originally appeared in Lynn Hunt, ed., *Eroticism and the Body Politic* (Baltimore, 1991), pp. 108–30.

the early French feminists had little concern for the queen. The two issues were tied together, if only unconsciously, because the queen was the most important example of a woman acting in the public sphere. Rousseau railed against the influence of women in the public sphere in his *Letter to M. d'Alembert on the Theater* (1758): "No longer wishing to tolerate separation, unable to make themselves into men, the women make us into women. . . . Whether a monarch governs men or women ought to be rather indifferent to him, provided that he be obeyed; but in a republic, men are needed."[2]

With her strategic position on the cusp between public and private, Marie-Antoinette was emblematic of the much larger problem of the relation between women and the public sphere in the eighteenth century. This issue, as Rousseau himself argued, concerned not only the specific status of women but also the grounds of sexual differentiation itself. Women in public might turn men into women, Rousseau warned ominously. Such concerns took very concrete form in the underground pamphlets published against the influence of Louis XV's mistresses, the marquise de Pompadour and especially the comtesse Du Barry. According to pamphlets such as *Les Fastes de Louis XV* (1782), the rising influence of such women on public life feminized both the king's ministers and the king himself, who was depicted as withdrawing into a "private, slothful and voluptuous life."[3]

On the eve of the Revolution, similar themes were still much in view. A newspaper review of recent novels in September 1788 reproduced, without attribution, the views expressed in the preface to Restif de la Bretonne's novel *The Unfaithful Wife*, published in 1786.[4] Restif had attacked the "gynomanes" who argued for the education of women. The "ignorance of women" had an infinite advantage, he claimed, because it contributed to subordination, to keeping women at home. Instructing them would overturn the sexual order: "In a word, making women into scholars makes men stupid and inept."

2. Jean-Jacques Rousseau, *Politics and the Arts: Letter to M. D'Alembert on the Theatre*, trans. Allan Bloom (Ithaca, N.Y., 1968), pp. 100–101.

3. Sarah Maza, "The Diamond Necklace Affair Revisited (1785–1786): The Case of the Missing Queen," in Hunt, ed., *Eroticism and the Body Politic*, pp. 63–89, especially pp. 63–69.

4. *Journal général de France*, no. 117, 27 September 1788. Thomas Beebe led me to Nicolas Restif de la Bretonne's novel *La Femme infidèle* as the source for the newspaper account.

The two sexes were unequal in nature, and destroying this natural order would have nefarious consequences: "I consider it a fact that a woman-Voltaire would only produce deformed children; I consider it a fact that a woman-Rousseau will never be able to breastfeed."[5] As we shall see, this idea of a woman-man as monster came to dominate much of the thinking by male revolutionaries about women in the public sphere.[6]

It has long been known that Marie-Antoinette was the subject of a substantial erotic and pornographic literature in the last decades of the Old Regime and during the Revolution itself. Royal figures have often been the subject of such writing, but not all royal figures at all times. When royalty's physical bodies become the focus of such interest, we can be sure that something is at issue in the body politic. As Robert Darnton has shown, for example, the sexual sensationalism of Old Regime pamphlets was a choice means of attacking the entire establishment—the court, the church, the aristocracy, the academies, the salons, and the monarchy itself.[7] Marie-Antoinette occupies a curious place in this literature; not only was she lampooned and demeaned in an increasingly ferocious pornographic outpouring, she was also tried and executed.

A few other women, such as Louis XV's notorious mistress Madame Du Barry, suffered a similar fate during the Revolution, but no other trial attracted the same attention or aired the same range of issues as that of the ill-fated queen. The king's trial, in contrast, remained entirely restricted to a consideration of his political crimes. As a consequence, the trial of the queen, especially in its strange refractions of the pornographic literature, offers a unique and fascinating perspective on the unselfconscious presumptions of the revolutionary political imagination. It makes manifest, more perhaps than any other single event of the Revolution, the underlying interconnections between pornography and politics.

5. Maribert-Courtenay [Restif de la Bretonne], *La Femme infidelle* (Neuchâtel, 1786; reprint, Geneva, 1988), vol. 1, pp. 3–10; the quotations are from pp. 8–9.

6. In what follows, it will be apparent that I am indebted in many respects to the ground-breaking analysis of Joan Landes, *Women and the Public Sphere in the Age of the French Revolution* (Ithaca, N.Y., 1988).

7. Robert Darnton, "The High Enlightenment and the Low-Life of Literature," reprinted in *The Literary Underground of the Old Regime* (Cambridge, Mass., 1982), pp. 1–40, especially p. 29.

19.   Engraving of Marie-Antoinette at her trial. From *Révolutions de Paris*,
no. 212, 3 August – 28 October 1793. Note the presence of many women in
the spectator galleries. Photo: Maclure Collection, Special Collections,
Van Pelt-Dietrich Library, University of Pennsylvania.

When Marie-Antoinette was finally brought to trial in October
1793 (see figure 19), the notorious public prosecutor Antoine-
Quentin Fouquier-Tinville delivered an accusation against her that
began with extraordinary language, even for those inflamed times:

> In the manner of the Messalinas-Brunhildes, Fredegund and Médicis,
> who were called in previous times queens of France, and whose
> names, forever odious, will not be effaced from the annals of history,
> Marie-Antoinette, widow of Louis Capet, has been during her time in
> France the scourge and the bloodsucker of the French.

The bill of indictment then went on to detail the charges: before the
Revolution, she squandered the public monies of France on her
"disorderly pleasures" and on secret contributions to the Austrian
emperor (her brother); after the Revolution, she was the animating
spirit of counterrevolutionary conspiracies at the court. Since the
former queen was a woman, it was presumed that she could only

achieve her perfidious aims through the agency of men, such as the king's brothers and Lafayette. Most threatening, of course, was her influence on the king; she was charged not only with the crime of having perverse ministers named to office but, more generally—and more significantly—with having taught the king how to dissimulate, that is, how to promise one thing in public and plan another in the shadows of the court. Finally, and to my mind most strangely, the bill of indictment specifically claimed that

> the widow Capet, immoral in every way, the new Agrippina, is so perverse and so familiar with all crimes that, forgetting her quality of mother and the demarcation prescribed by the laws of nature, she has not stopped short of indulging herself with Louis-Charles Capet, her son—and on the confession of the latter—in indecencies whose idea and name make us shudder with horror.[8]

Incest was the final crime, the very suggestion of which was cause for horror.

The trial of a queen, especially in a country whose fundamental laws specifically excluded women from ruling, must necessarily be unusual. There was not much in the way of precedent for it—the English, after all, had only tried their king, not his wife—and the relatively long gap between the trial of Louis (in December and January) and his queen ten months later even seemed to attenuate the linkage between the two trials. Unlike her husband, Marie-Antoinette was not tried by the Convention itself; she was brought before the Revolutionary Criminal Tribunal, like all other suspects in Paris, and there her fate was decided by a male jury and nine male judges.[9]

Because queens could never rule in France, except indirectly as regents for underage sons, they were not imagined as having the two bodies associated with kings. According to the "mystic fiction of the 'King's Two Bodies'" as analyzed by Ernst Kantorowicz, kings in England and France had both a visible, corporeal, mortal body and

8. I have used the account of the trial given in the *Moniteur universel*, no. 25, 16 October 1793; the quotation is from the report on the session of 14 October 1793.

9. At least that is how many judges signed the arrest warrant on 14 October 1793, according to the *Moniteur universel*, no. 25, 16 October 1793. For the workings of the revolutionary tribunal, see Luc Willette, *Le Tribunal révolutionnaire* (Paris, 1981). The revolutionary tribunal, established in March 1793, was not in existence at the time of the trial of the king.

an invisible, ideal "body politic" that never died. As the French churchman Bossuet explained in a sermon preached before Louis XIV in 1662: "You are of the gods, even if you die, your authority never dies. . . . The man dies, it is true, but the king, we say, never dies."[10] It is questionable whether this doctrine still held for French kings by 1793, but it is certain that it never held for French queens. We might, then, ask why the destruction of the queen's mortal body could have had such interest for the French. What did her decidedly nonmystical body represent? I am going to argue that it represented many things; Marie-Antoinette had, in a manner of speaking, many bodies. These many bodies—hydralike, to use one of the favorite revolutionary metaphors for counterrevolution—were each in turn attacked and destroyed because they represented the threats, conscious and unconscious, that could be posed to the republic. These were not just ordinary threats, for the queen represented not only the ultimate in counterrevolutionary conspiracy but also the menace that the feminine and the feminizing presented to republican notions of manhood and virility.

Most striking is the way in which the obsessive focus on the queen's sexualized body was carried over from political pamphlets and caricatures to the trial itself. In the trial there were frequent references to the "orgies" held at Versailles, which were dated as beginning in 1779 and continuing into 1789. In his closing statement, Fouquier-Tinville collapsed sexual and political references in telling fashion when he denounced "the perverse conduct of the former court," Marie-Antoinette's "criminal and culpable liaisons" with unfriendly foreign powers, and her "intimacies with a villainous faction."[11] Armand Herman, president of the court, then took up the baton in his summary of the charges against her: he too referred to "her intimate liaisons with infamous ministers, perfidious generals, disloyal representatives of the people." He denounced again the "orgy" at the chateau of Versailles on 1 October 1789, when the queen allegedly encouraged the royal officers present to trample on the revolutionary tricolor cockade. In short, Marie-Antoinette had used her sexual body to corrupt the body politic

10. Quoted in Ernst H. Kantorowicz, *The King's Two Bodies: A Study in Mediaeval Political Theology* (Princeton, 1957), p. 409, n.319.

11. *Moniteur universel*, no. 36, 27 October 1793, reporting on the trial session of 14 October.

either through "liaisons" or "intimacies" with criminal politicians or through her ability to act sexually upon the king, his ministers, or his soldiers.

In Herman's long denunciation, the queen's body was also held up for scrutiny for outward signs of intentions and motives. On her return from the flight to Varennes, people could observe on her face and in her movements "the most marked desire for vengeance." Even when she was incarcerated in the Temple, her jailers could "always detect in Antoinette an attitude of revolt against the sovereignty of the people."[12] Capture, imprisonment, and the prospect of execution were, it was hoped, finally tearing the veil from the queen's threatening ability to hide her true feelings from the public. Note too the way that Herman clearly juxtaposes the queen and the people as a public force; revelation of the queen's true motives and feelings came not from secrets uncovered in hidden correspondence but from the ability of the people or their representatives to "read" her body.

The attention to the queen's body continued right up to the moment of her execution. When the tribunal announced her condemnation to death, she was reported to have kept "a calm and assured countenance," just as she had during the interrogation. On the road to the scaffold, she appeared indifferent to the large gathering of armed forces (see figure 20). "One perceived neither despondency nor pride on her face."[13] More radical newspapers read a different message in her demeanor, but they showed the same attention to her every move. *Révolutions de Paris* claimed that at the feet of the statue of Liberty (where the guillotine was erected), she demonstrated her usual "character of dissimulation and pride up to the last moment" (see figure 21). On the way there, she had expressed "surprise and indignation" when she realized that she would be taken to the guillotine in a simple cart rather than in a carriage.[14]

The queen's body, then, was of interest, not because of its connection to the sacred and divine, but because it represented the opposite principle: the possible profanation of everything that the nation held sacred. But apparent too in all the concern with the queen's body was the fact that the queen could embody so much.

12. Ibid.
13. Ibid.
14. *Révolutions de Paris*, no. 212, 3 August – 28 October 1793.

Rev. de Paris.   *Exécution de la Veuve Capet.*   N.º 212. Page 95.

Le Mercredy 16.8bre 1793.(Vieux style) Marie Antoinette d'Autriche, Veuve Capet, après un Interrogatoire de trois jours Consécutifs, a subi la Peine due à ses forfaits, sur la Place de la Révolution, au pied de la statue de la Liberté.)

20.   Engraving of Marie-Antoinette being taken to the guillotine.
From *Révolutions de Paris*, no. 212, 3 August – 28 October 1793. Photo:
Maclure Collection, Special Collections, Van Pelt-Dietrich
Library, University of Pennsylvania.

The queen did not have a mystic body in the sense of the king's two bodies, but her body was mystical in the sense of being mysteriously symbolic. It could mean so much; it could signify a wide range of threats, just as the representations of Marianne, the goddess of liberty, might have several, and sometimes conflicting, inflections.

Dissimulation was consequently an especially important theme in the denunciations of the queen. The ability to conceal one's true emotions, to act one way in public and another in private, was repeatedly denounced as the chief characteristic of court life and aristocratic manners in general. These relied above all on appearances, that is, the disciplined and self-conscious use of the body as a mask. The republicans, consequently, valued transparency—the unmediated expression of the heart—above all other personal qualities. Transparency was the perfect fit between public and private;

Rév. de Paris   *La Veuve Capet à la Guillotine .*   *N.º 212 . Pag 96 .*

En montant à l'Echaffaud, Antoinette marcha par mégarde sur le pied de l'Exécuteur des Jugemens ; elle se retourna vers lui en lui disant, Monsieur, je vous demande Excuse, je ne l'ai pas fait exprés .

21.   Engraving of Marie-Antoinette at the guillotine. From *Révolutions de Paris*, no. 212, 3 August – 28 October 1793. Note the presence of women among the spectators, and the statue of Liberty on the left who oversees the scene of execution. Photo: author.

transparency was a body that told no lies and kept no secrets. It was the definition of virtue, and as such it was imagined to be critical to the future of the republic.[15] Dissimulation, in contrast, threatened to undermine the republic: it was the chief ingredient in every conspiracy; it lay at the heart of the counterrevolution. Thus, to charge Marie-Antoinette with teaching the king how to dissimulate was no minor accusation.

Dissimulation was also described in the eighteenth century as a characteristic feminine quality, not just an aristocratic one. According to both Montesquieu and Rousseau, it was women who taught

15. I develop the notion of transparency in a somewhat different context in *Politics, Culture, and Class in the French Revolution* (Berkeley, 1984), pp. 44–46 and 72–74.

men how to dissimulate, how to hide their true feelings in order to get what they wanted in the public arena.[16] The salon was the most important site of this teaching, and it was also the one place where society women could enter the public sphere. In a sense, then, women in public were (like prostitutes) synonymous with dissimulation, with the gap between public and private.

Virtue could only be restored if women returned to the private sphere.[17] Rousseau had captured this collection of attitudes most clearly in his *Letter to M. d'Alembert:*

> Meanly devoted to the wills of the sex which we ought to protect and not serve, we have learned to despise it in obeying it, to insult it by our derisive attentions; and every woman at Paris gathers in her apartment a harem of men more womanish than she, who know how to render all sorts of homage to beauty except that of the heart, which is her due.[18]

The sexuality of women, when operating in the public sphere through dissimulation, threatened to feminize men—that is, literally to transform men's bodies. Rousseau feared that "the women make us into women." In response to critics of this work, Rousseau made his position completely clear: "I am not of your opinion when you say that if we are corrupted it is not the fault of women, it is our own; my whole book is undertaken to show how it is their fault."[19]

If the queen was a dissimulator, then it is not surprising that she was also not a good mother. Fouquier-Tinville explicitly contrasted her to Paris itself—described in his closing statement as "this city, mother and conservator of liberty." The queen was the antonym of the nation, depicted by one witness at the trial as the "generous nation that nurtured her as well as her husband and her

16. On the attitudes of the philosophes toward women, see Paul Hoffmann, *La Femme dans le pensée des lumières* (Paris, 1977), especially pp. 324–446.

17. Dorinda Outram concludes that the Revolution was committed to antifeminine rhetoric because it ascribed power in the Old Regime to women. I think that this exaggerates the identification of women with power in the Old Regime, but it nonetheless leads to fruitful reflections about the ways in which male revolutionary politicians tried to escape feelings of guilt. *"Le Langage mâle de la vertu:* Women and the Discourse of the French Revolution," in Peter Burke and Roy Porter, eds., *The Social History of Language* (Cambridge, 1987), pp. 120–35, especially p. 125.

18. Rousseau, *Politics and the Arts*, p. 101.

19. Quoted in Carole Pateman, *The Sexual Contract* (Stanford, 1988), p. 99.

family."[20] The nation, Paris, and the Revolution were all good mothers; Marie-Antoinette was the bad mother. It should be noted, however, that the nation, Paris, and the Revolution were motherly in a very abstract, even nonfeminine fashion in comparison to Marie-Antoinette.

The abstractness and nonsexual nature of these political figures of the good political mother reinforces what Carole Pateman has tellingly described as the characteristic modern Western social contract:

> The story of the original contract is perhaps the greatest tale of men's creation of new political life. But this time women are already defeated and declared procreatively and politically irrelevant. Now the father comes under attack. The original contract shows how his monopoly of politically creative power is seized and shared equally among men. In civil society all men, not just fathers, can generate political life and political right. Political creativity belongs not to paternity but masculinity.[21]

Thus the nation as mother, *La Nation*, had no feminine qualities; it was not a threatening feminizing force and hence not incompatible with republicanism. *La Nation* was, in effect, a masculine mother, or a father capable of giving birth. Several satirical prints derided the "labor" of Deputy Guy Target in giving birth to the constitution of 1791 (see figure 22). They can be taken as almost inadvertent representations of the unconscious supposition that men will give birth to the new order themselves under the new regime of fraternity.[22] Marie-Antoinette's body stood in the way, quite literally, of this version of the social contract, since under the Old Regime she had given birth to the child who would be the next sovereign.[23]

Pateman is unusual among commentators on contract theory in that she takes Freud and his conception of fraternity seriously:

20. *Moniteur universel,* no. 36, 27 October 1793, and no. 27, 18 October 1793. The latter quotation is from the testimony of Roussillon, a barber-surgeon and cannoneer.

21. Pateman, *The Sexual Contract,* p. 36.

22. See the analysis of the political immaculate conception in Vivian Cameron, "Political Exposures: Sexuality and Caricature in the French Revolution," in Hunt, ed., *Eroticism and the Body Politic,* pp. 90–107 and especially pp. 98–100.

23. Chantal Thomas argues that the anti-Marie-Antoinette pamphlets became especially virulent from the moment of her first pregnancy (1777). *La Reine scélérate: Marie-Antoinette dans les pamphlets* (Paris, 1989), p. 40.

22.   Engraving of Deputy Target giving birth
to the constitution of 1791. On the right is Mlle. Théroigne
de Méricourt, a well-known democrat and frequent figure
of derision in antirevolutionary propaganda.
Photo: Bibliothèque nationale.

"Freud's stories make explicit that power over women and not only freedom is at issue before the original agreement is made, and he also makes clear that two realms [the civil, political realm and the private, sexual realm] are created through the original pact."[24] Pateman's analysis underscores the importance of the gender question to political reconstitution, but she tends to overlook how much anxiety went into the resolution of the woman question. She claims that competition between the brothers was quickly channeled into the competition of the market and the competition for women in marriage.[25] In the French Revolution, however, competition between the brothers continued to be deadly, and the problem of women was not easily resolved. The difficulty of this resolution can be seen, for example, in the persistent recurrence of the theme of incest.

24. Pateman, *The Sexual Contract*, p. 12.
25. Pateman, *The Sexual Contract*, p. 114. Pateman does not discuss the French Revolution or any other particular political event in any detail. I am not criticizing her for overlooking the Revolution, simply pointing out that attention to an event such as the Revolution would modify her theoretical position in some respects.

The charge of incest in the queen's trial was brought by the radical journalist Hébert, editor of the scabrous *Le Père Duchesne,* which was the most determinedly "popular" newspaper of the time. Hébert appeared at the trial in his capacity as assistant city attorney for Paris, but his paper had been notorious for its continuing attacks on the queen.[26] Hébert testified that he had been called to the Temple prison by Antoine Simon, the shoemaker who was assigned to look after Louis's son. Simon had surprised the eight-year-old engaging in "indecent pollutions" (i.e., masturbating), and when he questioned the young boy about where he had learned such practices, Louis-Charles replied that his mother and his aunt (the king's sister) had taught him. The boy was asked to repeat his accusations in the presence of the mayor and city attorney, which he did, claiming that the two women often made him sleep between them. Hébert concluded:

> There is reason to believe that this criminal enjoyment [*jouissance,* which has several meanings including pleasure, possession, and orgasm] was not at all dictated by pleasure, but rather by the political hope of enervating the physical health of this child, whom they continued to believe would occupy a throne, and on whom they wished, by this maneuver, to assure themselves the right of ruling afterward over his morals.

The body of the child allegedly showed the effects of this incestuousness; one of his testicles had been injured and had to be bandaged. Since being separated from his mother, Hébert reported, the child's health had become much more robust and vigorous.[27] What better emblem could there be of feminization—that effect predicted by Rousseau—than the actual deterioration of the boy's genitals?

As sensational as the charge was, the court did not pursue it much further. When directly confronted with the accusation, the former queen refused to lower herself by responding "to such a charge made against a mother."[28] But there it was in the newspapers, and even the Jacobin Club briefly noted the "shameful scenes between the mother, the aunt, and the son," and denounced "the venom that

26. For a complementary analysis of Hébert's writing about the queen, see Elizabeth Colwill, "Just Another *Citoyenne*? Marie-Antoinette on Trial, 1790–1793," *History Workshop Journal* 28 (1989): 63–87.

27. *Moniteur universel,* no. 27, 18 October 1793.

28. Ibid., no. 28, 19 October 1793.

now runs through [the boy's] veins and which perhaps carries the source of all sorts of accidents."[29] The Jacobin newspaper *Journal des hommes libres de tous les pays* carried a long editorial on the subject during the trial. It denounced Marie-Antoinette and her sister-in-law for initiating the young Capet into the "mysteries of unbridled libertinage."[30] Since it seems surprising that republican men should be so worried about the degeneration of the royal family, it is not farfetched to conclude that the incest charge had a wider, if largely unconscious, resonance.

On the most explicit level, incest was simply another sign of the criminal nature of royalty. Hébert complained rhetorically to the supporters of royalism, "You immolate your brothers, and for what? For an old whore, who has neither faith nor respect for the law, who has made more than a million men die; you are the champions of murder, brigandage, adultery, and incest."[31] Although incest can hardly be termed a major theme in revolutionary discourse, it did appear frequently in prerevolutionary novels, as we have seen, and in the political pornography of the last decades of the Old Regime and during the revolutionary decade itself.[32] Perhaps the most striking example is the pornography of the marquis de Sade, which makes much of incest between fathers and daughters and brothers and sisters (see chapter 5).

The official incest charge against the queen has to be set in the context provided by the longer history of pornographic and semi-pornographic pamphlets about the queen's private life.[33] Although the charge at the trial was based on alleged activities that took place only after the incarceration of the royal family in the Temple prison, it was made more plausible by the scores of pamphlets that had appeared since the earliest days of the Revolution and that had their origins in the political pornography of the Old Regime itself. When *Révolutions de Paris* exclaimed, "Who could forget the scandalous

29. Ibid., no. 29, 20 October 1793.

30. *Journal des hommes libres de tous les pays, ou Le Républicain*, no. 348, 15 October 1793.

31. *Le Père Duchesne*, no. 298 (October 1793?).

32. On the last half of the eighteenth century, see Hector Fleischmann, *Les Pamphlets libertins contre Marie-Antoinette* (Paris, 1908; reprint, Geneva, 1976), especially the chapter, "La France galante et libertine à la fin du XVIIIe siècle," pp. 13–36.

33. On the prerevolutionary literature about the queen, see Maza, "The Diamond Necklace Affair."

morals of her private life?" or repeated the charges about "her secret orgies with Artois [one of the king's brothers], Fersen, Coigny, etc.," the newspaper was simply recalling to readers' minds what they had long imbibed in underground publications about the queen's promiscuity.[34]

Attacks on the queen's morality had begun as early as 1774 (four years after her arrival in France) with a satirical lampoon about her early morning promenades. Louis XV paid considerable sums in the same year to buy up existing copies in London and Amsterdam of a pamphlet that detailed the sexual impotence of his grandson, the future Louis XVI.[35] Before long, the songs and "little papers" had become frankly obscene, and the first of many long, detailed pamphlets had been published clandestinely. The foremost expert on the subject found 126 pamphlets which he could classify in the genre of "Marie-Antoinette, libertine."[36] Even before the notorious Diamond Necklace Affair of 1785 and continuing long after it, the queen was the focus of an always proliferating literature of derision that was preoccupied with her sexual body.

Many of the major accusations against Marie-Antoinette were already present in the prerevolutionary pamphlets. The *Portefeuille d'un Talon Rouge* (condemned in 1783) begins in classic eighteenth-century fashion with a preface from the presumed publisher announcing that someone had found a portfolio while crossing the Palais-Royal (the notorious den of prostitution and gambling that was also the residence of the king's cousin, the duc d'Orléans, who was assumed to have paid for many of the pamphlets). In it was found a manuscript addressed to Monsieur de la H. . . of the Académie française. It began, "You are out of your mind, my dear la H. . . ! You want, they tell me, to write the history of tribades at Versailles." In the text appeared the soon to be standard allegation that Marie-Antoinette was amorously involved with the duchesse de Polignac ("her Jules") and Madame Balbi. The comte d'Artois was

34. *Révolutions de Paris*, no. 212, 3 August – 28 October 1793.
35. Fleischmann, *Les Pamphlets libertins*, pp. 103–9.
36. Hector Fleischmann, *Marie-Antoinette libertine: Bibliographie critique et analytique des pamphlets politiques, galants, et obscènes contre la reine: Précédé de la réimpression intégrale de quatre libelles rarissimes et d'une histoire des pamphlétaires du règne de Louis XVI* (Paris, 1911). For a recent interpretation of this literature, see Thomas, *La Reine scélérate*. Thomas is especially strong on the analysis of the anti-Marie-Antoinette pamphlet literature, but she has virtually nothing to say about the trial records.

supposedly the only man who interested her. These charges, as harshly delivered as they were, formed only part of the pamphlet's more general tirade against the court and ministers in general. Speaking of the courtiers, the author exclaimed, "You are an abominable race. You get everything from your character both of monkeys and of vipers."[37]

With the coming of the Revolution in 1789, the floodgates opened, and the number of pamphlets attacking the queen rapidly rose in number. These took various forms ranging from songs and fables to alleged biographies (such as the widely circulated *Essais historiques sur la vie de Marie-Antoinette,* which appeared under various titles after 1781), confessions, and plays. Sometimes, the writings were pornographic with little explicit political content; for example, the sixteen-page pamphlet in verse titled *Le Godmiché royal* (The royal dildo, 1789) told the story of Juno (the queen) and Hebe (presumably either the duchesse de Polignac or the princesse de Lamballe). Juno complains of her inability to obtain satisfaction at home, and pulls a dildo out of her bag ("Happy invention that we owe to the monastery"). Her companion promises her penises of almost unimaginably delicious size.[38]

The long 1789 edition (146 pages in the augmented French edition) of the *Essai historique sur la vie de Marie-Antoinette* already demonstrated the rising tone of personal hostility toward the queen that would characterize revolutionary pornographic pamphlets.[39] In the most detailed of all the anti-Marie-Antoinette exposés published up to that time, it purported to give the queen's own view through the first person: "My death is the object of the desires of an entire people that I oppressed with the greatest barbarism." Marie-Antoinette here describes herself as "barbarous Queen, adulterous spouse, woman without morals, polluted with crimes and debaucheries," and she details all the charges that had accumulated against her in previous pamphlets. Now her alleged lesbianism is traced back to the Austrian court, and all the stories of amorous intrigues

37. *Portefeuille d'un Talon Rouge, contenant des anecdotes galantes et secrètes de la Cour de France* (Paris, 1911). This edition is based on the edition dated "l'an 178—, De l'Imprimerie du Comte de Paradès."

38. *Le Godmiché royal* (Paris, 1789).

39. There had been many variations on the title since its first publication in 1781. For title variations, see Henri d'Almeras, *Marie-Antoinette et les pamphlets royalistes et révolutionnaires: Les Amoureux de la Reine* (Paris, 1907), pp. 399–403.

with princes and great nobles are given concreteness. Added to the charges is the new one that she herself poisoned the young heir to the throne, who died in early 1789. This pamphlet has a characteristic seen in many of the later pamphlets: a curious alternation between frankly pornographic staging—descriptions in the first person of her liaisons, complete with wildly beating hearts and barely stifled sighs of passion—and political moralizing and denunciation put in the mouth of the queen herself. The contrast with the king and his "pure, sincere love which I so often and so cruelly abused" is striking.[40] The queen may have been representative of the degenerate tendencies of the aristocracy, but she was not yet emblematic of royalty altogether.

The Marie-Antoinette pamphlets reflect a general tendency in the production of political pornography: the number of titles in this genre rose steadily from 1774 to 1788 and then took off after 1789. The queen was not the only target of hostility; a long series of "private lives" attacked the conduct of courtiers before 1789 and revolutionary politicians from Lafayette to Robespierre afterwards. Aristocrats were shown as impotent, riddled with venereal disease, and given over to debauchery. Homosexuality functioned in a manner similar to impotence in this literature; it showed the decadence of the Old Regime in the person of its priests and aristocrats. Sexual degeneration went hand in hand with political corruption.[41] This proliferation of pornographic pamphlets after 1789 shows that political pornography cannot be viewed simply as a supplement to a

40. *Essai historique sur la vie de Marie-Antoinette, Reine de France et de Navarre, Née Archiduchesse d'Autriche, le deux novembre 1755: Orné de son portrait, et rédigé sur plusieurs manuscrits de sa main* (A Versailles, Chez La Montensier [one of her supposed female lovers], Hôtel des Courtisannes, 1789), pp. 4, 8, 19–20. Some have attributed this pamphlet to Brissot, but d'Almeras and Fleischmann both dispute this. D'Almeras, *Marie-Antoinette*, p. 339; Fleischmann, *Marie-Antoinette libertine*, pp. 67–70. Fleischmann reports the view that the marquis de Sade wrote the second part of this 1789 edition (p. 68). Earlier in 1789 a shorter work titled *Essais historiques sur la vie de Marie-Antoinette d'Autriche, Reine de France; Pour servir à l'histoire de cette princesse* [London, 1789] struck a much less violent tone. It was not written in the first person and though it discussed the queen's amorous intrigues in detail, it was not particularly pornographic in style. This version was written very much in the vein of attempts to convince the queen of her errors: "Fasse le ciel cependant que ces vérités, si elles sont présentées à cette princesse, puissent la corriger, et la faire briller d'autant de vertus qu'elle l'a fait par ses étourderies" (p. 78).

41. For a general overview emphasizing the contrast between aristocratic degeneracy and republican health, see Antoine de Baecque, "Pamphlets: Libel and Political Mythology," in Robert Darnton and Daniel Roche, eds., *Revolution in Print: The Press in France, 1775–1800* (Berkeley, 1989), pp. 165–76.

political culture that lacked political participation. Once participation increased dramatically, particularly with the explosion of noncensored newspapers and pamphlets, politics did not simply take the high road.[42]

Marie-Antoinette was without question the favorite target of such attacks. Not only were there more pamphlets about her than about any other single figure, but they were also the most sustained in their viciousness. One author has claimed that the *Essais historiques* alone sold 20–30,000 copies.[43] 1789 does appear to mark a turning point not only in the number of pamphlets produced but also in their tone. The pre-1789 pamphlets tell dirty stories in secret; after 1789 the rhetoric of the pamphlets begins self-consciously to solicit a wider audience. The public no longer "hears" courtier rumors through the print medium; it now "sees" degeneracy in action. The first-person rendition of the 1789 French edition of the *Essai historique* is a good example of this technique. In the much more elaborately pornographic *Fureurs utérines de Marie-Antoinette, femme de Louis XVI* of two years later, colored engravings showed the king impotent and Artois and Polignac replacing him.

Obscene engravings with first-person captions were the most obvious form of this visualization of female debauchery. The long *Vie de Marie-Antoinette d'Autriche, femme de Louis XVI, roi des Français; Depuis la perte de son pucelage jusqu'au premier Mai 1791*, followed by volumes two and three, titled *Vie privée, libertine, et scandaleuse de Marie-Antoinette d'Autriche, ci-devant Reine des François*, was accompanied by engravings that are an interesting case in point.[44] They showed Marie-Antoinette in amorous embrace with just about everyone imaginable: her first supposed lover, a German officer; the aged Louis XV; Louis XVI impotent (see figure 9 in chapter 2); the comte d'Artois; various women (figure 23); various threesomes with two women and a man (figure 24); Cardinal de Rohan, of the

42. Here I am taking issue with the argument by Darnton in "The High Enlightenment," especially p. 33.

43. D'Almeras, *Marie-Antoinette*, p. 403. He provides no evidence for this assertion, however.

44. The three volumes are to be found in the Bibliothèque nationale, Enfer nos. 790–92. The publication data are fabricated. The first volume reads: "Paris, Chez l'auteur et ailleurs, Avec permission de la liberté" (no date). The second volume reads: "Aux Thuileries et au Temple, Et se trouve au Palais de l'Egalité, ci-devant Palais-Royal, l'an premier de la République." The third reads: "Paris, Palais de la Révolution, 1793."

Diamond Necklace Affair; Lafayette; Barnave; and others. The rhymed couplets that serve as captions are sometimes in the first person (in figure 23: "Dieux! quels transports ah! mon ame s'envole, pour l'exprimer je n'ai plus de parole [God! what rapture! Oh, my soul takes flight, I have no words to express it]"), sometimes in the third. The effect is the same: a theatricalization of the action so that the reader is made into voyeur and moral judge at the same time. The political effect of the pornography is apparent even in this most obscene of works. In volumes two and three, the pornographic engravings are interspersed with political engravings of aristocratic conspiracy (figure 25), the assault on the Tuileries palace, and even a curious print showing Louis XVI putting on a red cap of liberty and drinking to the health of the nation in front of the queen and his remaining son and heir. Such juxtapositions, which seem strange to us now, underlined the connection between sexual misbehavior and aristocratic conspiracy.

That the pamphlets succeeded in attracting a public can be seen in the repetition of formulaic expressions in nonpornographic political pamphlets, "popular" newspapers, petitions from "popular societies," and the trial record itself. The *Essai historique* of 1789 already included the soon to be standard comparison between Marie-Antoinette and Catherine de Médicis, Agrippina, and Messalina. A sixteen-page anonymous pamphlet published in 1789 developed the comparison between Marie-Antoinette and her predecessor queens in some detail. Fredegund, the evil mistress and eventual wife of Chilperic I, a Merovingian king, talks with Catherine de Médicis: "Our crimes are finally going to be forgotten. . . . Incest, adultery, and the most infamous and shameful lubricity, the overturning of the sacred order of Nature, were games for this lewd Messalina."[45]

45. *Le Petit Charles IX ou Médicis justifiée* (n.p., 1789), pp. 3, 7. The figure of Fredegund had an interesting prerevolutionary history that may well indicate the growing worry about women with public power. When Jean-François Ducis rewrote Shakespeare's *Macbeth* for the French stage in 1784, he gave Lady Macbeth the name of Frédégonde (Fredegund is the common English equivalent). Fredegund encourages her husband to murder in order to secure the throne for her son, but in the end she mistakenly kills the son in a sleepwalking scene. Macbeth accuses his own wife of pushing him to murder in terms that are reminiscent of the anti-Marie-Antoinette literature: "C'est toi, c'est toi, barbare, en empruntant ma main." E. Preston Dargun, "Shakespeare and Ducis," *Modern Philology* 10 (1912): 137–78. I am indebted to Reeve Parker for alerting me to Ducis's use of Fredegund.

23. Engraving of Marie-
Antoinette with the prin-
cesse de Guémenée. From
*Vie privée, libertine, et scanda-
leuse de Marie-Antoinette
d'Autriche* (1793). Photo:
Bibliothèque nationale.

24. Engraving of Marie-
Antoinette in embrace with
a man and a woman. From
*Vie privée, libertine, et scanda-
leuse de Marie-Antoinette
d'Autriche* (1793). Photo:
Bibliothèque nationale.

2ème Partie   22   Page 90

Votre serment assure une Vengeance
il coulera ce sang vil de la France

25.   Engraving of Marie-
Antoinette with several
courtiers taking an oath of
vengeance against France.
From *Vie privée, libertine,
et scandaleuse de Marie-
Antoinette d'Autriche* (1793).
Photo: Bibliothèque
nationale.

These comparisons were expanded at great length in a curious
political tract called *Les Crimes des reines de France* (The crimes of the
queens of France), which was written by a woman, Louise de Keralio
(though it was published under the name of the publisher, Louis
Prudhomme).[46] The development of this work over time shows how
opinion about the queen moved from questions about her virtues to
certainties about her vices. The early editions of the tract (1791,
1792) denounced the queen in somewhat conditional terms: "Does
she merit the hatred and contempt which has been shown her so
many times? We have no certain proof of everything that has been
imputed to her; we cannot act on conjectures."[47] The "corrected and

46. The correct attribution was brought to my attention by Carla Hesse. While
working on another project, I came across a denunciation that verified Keralio's
authorship. The anonymous pamphlet *Les Crimes constitutionnels de France, ou la
Désolation française, Décrétée par l'Assemblée dite Nationale Constituante, aux années 1789,
1790 et 1791. Accepté par l'esclave Louis XVI, le 14 septembre 1791* (Paris, 1792) includes
an attack on Keralio as the author of the book.
47. *Les Crimes des reines de France, depuis le commencement de la monarchie jusqu'à
Marie-Antoinette* (London, 1792), p. 325. See also the edition published in Paris in
1791.

augmented" edition dated "an II" changed tone; now all the questions were replaced by declarations of the queen's guilt.[48]

Les Crimes was not a pornographic tract; it simply referred to the "turpitudes" committed by the queen as background for its more general political charges. Keralio reviewed the history of the queens of France and emphasized in particular the theme of dissimulation. "The dangerous art of seducing and betraying, perfidious and intoxicating caresses, feigned tears, affected despair, insinuating prayers"—these were the weapons of the queens of France (which had been identified as the weapons of all women by Rousseau).[49]

When the author came to the wife of Louis Capet, she listed many of the queen's presumed lovers, male and female, but she insisted upon passing rapidly over the "private crimes" of the queen in favor of consideration of her public ones. Marie-Antoinette "was the soul of all the plots, the center of all the intrigues, the source of all these horrors." As a "political tarantula" (a phrase introduced in the later editions), the queen resembled that "impure insect, which, in the darkness, weaves on the right and left fine threads where inexperienced gnats are caught, whom she makes her prey." On the next page the queen is compared to a tigress that, once having tasted blood, can no longer be satisfied. All this to prove, as the caption on the first engraving said, that "A people is without honor and merits its chains / When it lowers itself beneath the scepter of queens."[50]

The shorter, more occasional political pamphlets picked up the themes of the pornographic literature and used them for straightforward political purposes. A series of pamphlets appeared in 1792, for example, offering lists of political enemies who deserved immediate punishment. They had as their appendices lists of all the people with whom the queen had had "relationships of debauchery." In these pamphlets, the queen was routinely referred to as "mauvaise fille, mauvaise épouse, mauvaise mère, mauvaise reine, monstre en tout [bad daughter, bad wife, bad mother, bad queen, mon-

---

48. *Les Crimes des reines de France depuis le commencement de la monarchie jusqu'à la mort de Marie-Antoinette; avec les pièces justificatives de son procès. Publié par L. Prudhomme, avec Cinq gravures. Nouvelle édition corrigée et augmentée.* (Paris, an II).

49. Ibid., p. 2.

50. Ibid., pp. 440, 445–46. Elizabeth Colwill has suggested to me that Keralio did not write the added sections in the year II version of *Les Crimes*, if indeed she wrote the book at all. It is true that the later edition incorporates a language of bestiality and a tone of declarative certainty that is missing in the earlier editions.

ster in everything]."[51] The royalist commentator Boyer-Brun, who wrote on the subject of revolutionary caricatures, railed against these pamphlets in particular. He claimed that they appeared in June 1792 and were sold openly right under the windows of the Tuileries palace. He also noted that leading revolutionary newspapers, such as the *Annales patriotiques* and the *Chronique de Paris*, were repeating the same sorts of "blasphemy."[52]

The pamphlet literature had already begun to do its work before the beginning of the political attack on the monarchy in June 1792. Speeches in the Jacobin Club were picking up on these themes as early as the spring of 1792. One speaker at the club in April 1792 called Marie-Antoinette "this impudent woman, the modern Brunhilde . . . perverse woman" and advised Louis to banish her from his presence. Boyer-Brun claimed that *Les Crimes des reines de France* of 1791 was the precursor of all the horrible writings against the queen and that "it was only done, perhaps, in order to remove from the French every vestige of pity that might be inspired by the horrible fate of the unfortunate daughter of the Caesars." The people—"the misled multitude"—now believed anything written about the queen even without any proof, according to Boyer-Brun. Newspapers carried articles calling for public whippings of the queen at the theater. Everywhere, according to the outraged royalist observer, from the local marketplaces to the terrace of the Tuileries palace itself, people were heard insulting the queen.[53]

The movement from allegations of sexual misdemeanors to bestial metaphors that was apparent in the later editions of *Les Crimes des reines de France* was characteristic of much "popular" commentary on the queen, especially in her last months. In *Le Père Duchesne* Hébert had incorporated the Fredegund and Médicis comparisons by 1791, but still in a relatively innocent context. One of his favorite devices was to portray himself as meeting in person with the queen and trying to talk sense to her.[54] By 1792 the queen had become

---

51. See, for example, *Têtes à prix, suivi de la Liste de toutes les Personnes avec lesquelles la Reine a eu des liaisons de débauches*, 2nd ed. (Paris, 1792), and the nearly identical *Liste civile suivie Des noms et qualités de ceux qui la composent, et la punition dûe à leurs crimes . . . Et la liste des affidés de la ci-devant reine* (Paris, n.d.).

52. Boyer de Nîmes [J. M. Boyer-Brun], *Histoire des caricatures de la révolte des Français* (Paris, 1792), vol. 2, pp. 8–11.

53. Ibid., vol. 1, pp. 217, 296–97, 309–11.

54. *Le Père Duchesne*, no. 36.

"madame Veto," and once the monarchy had been toppled, Hébert made frequent reference to the "ménagerie royale." In prison, the former queen was depicted as a she-monkey ("la guenon d'Autriche"), the king as a pig. In one particularly fanciful scene, Père Duchesne presents himself in the queen's cell as the duchesse de Polignac ("cette tribade"), thanks to the effect of a magic ring. The former queen throws herself into her friend's arms and reveals her fervent hopes for the success of the counterrevolution.[55] After her husband had been executed, the tone of hostility escalated, and Marie-Antoinette became the she-wolf and the tigress of Austria. At the time of her trial, Hébert suggested that she be chopped up like meat for pâté in revenge for all the bloodshed she had caused.[56]

Local militants picked up the same rhetoric. In a letter to the Convention congratulating it on the execution of the queen, the popular society of Rozoy (Seine-et-Marne department) referred to "this tigress thirsty for the blood of the French . . . this other Messalina whose corrupt heart held the fertile germ of all crimes; may her loathsome memory perish forever." The popular society of Garlin (Basses-Pyrénées department) denounced the "ferocious panther who devoured the French, the female monster whose pores sweated the purest blood of the sans-culottes."[57] Throughout these passages, it is possible to see the horrific transformations of the queen's body; the body which had once been denounced for its debauchery and disorderliness becomes in turn the dangerous beast, the cunning spider, the virtual vampire who sucks the blood of the French.

The use of bestial metaphors seems to have been particularly characteristic of denunciations aimed at a popular audience. The more restrained Jacobin newspapers—whose audience was probably constituted by Jacobin officials rather than by popular militants—avoided the explicit bestial metaphors and concentrated instead on sexual debauchery. The *Journal des hommes libres*, for example, published a long editorial celebrating the execution of the queen, which was taken up and republished by some local newspapers.[58] It denounced the crimes of Marie-Antoinette and gave

55. Ibid., no. 194.
56. Ibid., nos. 296 and 298. On bestial metaphors, see Thomas, *La Reine scélérate*, pp. 130–34.
57. Quoted in Fleischmann, *Marie-Antoinette libertine*, p. 76.
58. See, for example, *Journal révolutionnaire de Toulouse*, no. 9, 24 October 1793, which repeats the editorial in *Journal des hommes libres*, no. 350, 17 October 1793.

great prominence to "her lascivious self-satisfaction," her "lewd-ness," her adultery, her "devouring" of state funds, and her determi-nation to "bathe in the blood of the French"—without, however, an explicit comparison to a tiger or she-wolf. The paper praised her execution as a "purification" of the globe.[59]

Explicit in some of the more extreme statements and implicit in many others was a pervasive preoccupation with genealogy. For ex-ample, the post-1789 pamphlets constantly raised questions about the paternity of the king's children (they were often attributed to the king's brother, the comte d'Artois). In a fascinating twist on the charge of false genealogy, *Le Père Duchesne* denounced a supposed plot by the queen to raise a young boy who resembled the heir to the throne in order to take the heir's place.[60] The culminating charge, of course, was incest; in the trial, this was limited to the queen's son, but in the pamphlet literature the charges included incest with the king's brother, the king's grandfather Louis XV, and her own father, who taught her "the passion of incest, the dirtiest of pleasures," from which followed "hatred of the French, aversion for the duties of spouse and mother, in short, all that reduces humanity to the level of ferocious beasts." The reductio ad absurdum of these charges was the following verse, which loses most of its effect in translation:

> Ci-gît l'impudique Manon,
> Qui, dans le ventre de sa mère,
> Savait si bien placer son c. . . ,
> Qu'elle f. . . avec son père.[61]

Here lies the lewd Manon / Who, in the belly of her mother / Knew so well how to place her c. . . / That she f. . . with her father.

Bestialization and accusations of disorderly sexuality and falsifica-tion of genealogy were all linked in the most intimate way.

Promiscuity, incest, poisoning of the heir to the throne, plots to replace the heir with a pliable substitute—all of these charges reflect a fundamental anxiety about queenship as the most extreme form of

59. *Journal des hommes libres*, no. 350, 17 October 1793.
60. *Le Père Duchesne*, no. 36.
61. *Vie privée, libertine et scandaleuse*, reprinted in Fleischmann, *Marie-Antoinette libertine*, pp. 173–74. The same "Epitaphe de Manon" appeared earlier in *La Con-fédération de la nature, ou l'art de se reproduire* (London, 1790), p. 48, without any specific reference to Marie-Antoinette (and without any ellipses). This 48-page pamphlet included a variety of obscene verses, some of which were anticlerical.

the invasion of the public sphere by women. Where Rousseau had warned that the salon woman would turn her "harem of men" into women "more womanish than she," the radical militant Louise de Keralio would warn her readers that "a woman who becomes queen changes sex."[62] The queen, then, was the emblem (and sacrificial victim) for the feared disintegration of gender boundaries that accompanied the Revolution.

In his study of ritual violence, René Girard argues that a sacrificial crisis (a crisis in the community that leads to the search for a scapegoat) entails the feared loss of sexual differentiation: "One of the effects of the sacrificial crisis is a certain feminization of the men, accompanied by a masculinization of the women."[63] A scapegoat is chosen in order to reinstitute the community's sense of boundaries. Girard himself considered the queen an example of his more general theories. In his study of scapegoating and collective persecution, *Le Bouc émissaire*, he claimed that the French Revolution had all the characteristics of a great crisis that facilitates collective persecutions. Marie-Antoinette was accused of incest, according to Girard, in order to blame her for the dedifferentiation that was felt as a collective threat. The crime had to be a "dedifferentiating crime" in order to make the scapegoat an appropriate victim for the community's violence.[64] Incest is a particularly striking example of dedifferentiation because it threatens the boundaries defining difference within the family and threatens the general establishment of exogamy and the boundaries between family and society.

By invoking Girard, I do not mean to suggest that the French Revolution precisely followed his script of sacrificial crisis or scapegoating. In fact, the Revolution did not single out a particular scapegoat in the moment of crisis; it was marked instead by a constant search for new victims, as if the community did not have a distinct enough sense of itself to settle upon just one (the king or the queen, for example). Nevertheless, Girard's suggestion that an intense crisis within a community is marked by fears of dedifferentiation is very

62. *Les Crimes des reines de France*, p. vii.

63. René Girard, *Violence and the Sacred*, trans. Patrick Gregory (Baltimore, 1977), p. 141.

64. René Girard, *Le Bouc émissaire* (Paris, 1982), pp. 33–34. I am grateful to James Winchell for this reference.

fruitful, for it helps make sense of the gender charge of revolutionary events.

The charge of incest against the queen was only the most striking example of the connection of the fear of dedifferentiation with the queen's fate. The charge of lesbianism (*tribadism* was the term of the time) served the same purpose. In the pornographic pamphlets written against her, Marie-Antoinette is shown as a creature whose voracious sexuality knows no limits and no gender differentiation (or, for that matter, class differentiation). She was often denounced as a whore, that is, as a public woman whose sexuality destroyed any possibility of tracing paternity. In a violent pamphlet against prostitutes, for example, the queen was reviled as *la reine des garces*, the queen of whores (and the word *garce* itself clearly connotes gender blurring, since it has the same root as *garçon*, boy): "abominable *garce*, execrable model of incurable lewdness . . . you who by your incestuous examples, your perpetual adulteries, never cease to insult virtue."[65]

The evidence for a feared loss of sexual differentiation in the Revolution is in fact quite extensive. A fear of gender reversal can be seen in a lewd poem printed in May 1790 by the satirical royalist newspaper, *Journal général de la cour et de la ville:*

> Nous sommes transportés aux temps miraculeux.
> Tandis que d'Aiguil . . . en femme se déguise,
> Antoinette devient un homme courageux,
> Et digne d'honorer le noble sang de Guise.[66]

We have been transported to miraculous times. / While d'Aiguil . . . [the duc d'Aiguillon] disguises himself as a woman, / Antoinette becomes a courageous man [presumably an attack on her supposed tribadism], / Worthy of honoring the noble blood of Guise.

This poem is addressed to the royalist side, which is being undermined, according to the paper, by its own internal scandals.

The problem of dedifferentiation was not limited to the queen, and worries about women in politics were shared by men of every political stripe. In the early years of the Revolution, counterrevolutionaries ridiculed women who tried to take some role in politi-

65. *Jugement général de toutes les putains françoises, et de la reine des garces, Par un des envoyés du Père Eternel* (De l'Imprimerie des Séraphins, n.p., n.d.).
66. *Journal général de la cour et de la ville,* 5 May 1790.

cal discussion; Théroigne de Méricourt (her real name was Anne-Joseph Terwagne) was denounced in royalist newspapers as a "slut," an "amazon" in red, a libertine willing to sleep with any of the deputies, the fantasized image of a liberated woman who enjoyed "the rights of men."[67]

The march to Versailles in October 1789, in which women played such a prominent part, prompted cries of outrage on the right; the market women who had participated were "assassins and savages," according to one French commentator. Edmund Burke portrayed the market women in lurid terms and contrasted them explicitly with the "delightful vision" that had been the queen before the pollution of the October days:

> [The heads of two of the king's bodyguards] were stuck upon spears, and led the procession; whilst the royal captives who followed in the train were slowly moved along, amidst the horrid yells, and shrilling screams, and frantic dances, and infamous contumelies, and all the unutterable abominations of the furies of hell, in the abused shape of the vilest of women.[68]

Women acting in the public sphere—whether the market women as portrayed by Burke or Marie-Antoinette as depicted by her republican critics—were likened to beasts; they lost their femininity and with it their very humanity. If the veil of social constraints that shielded them from the public eye was rent, their dangerous and presocial nature as furies was revealed.

In February 1792 a royalist newspaper advertised an engraving that captured the fear of dedifferentiation in a satirical vein. The engraving, titled "Grand Débandement de l'Armée Anticonstitutionelle" (Great disbanding of the anticonstitutional army; figure 26), shows various aristocratic women known for their revolutionary sentiment displaying their bare bottoms to the Austrian army. They are led by Théroigne de Méricourt, who shows her "Republic" (her *res publica*, public thing) to the army, which is caught in a pose of virtual Freudian sexual fright at the sight. The Jacobins and sansculottes hide behind the row of bare bottoms and present pikes with dangling hams, sausages, and other charcuterie.[69]

67. Elisabeth Roudinesco, *Théroigne de Méricourt: Une Femme mélancolique sous la Révolution* (Paris, 1989), pp. 44–46.

68. Edmund Burke, *Reflections on the Revolution in France* (New York, 1973), p. 85.

69. For an extensive analysis of the engraving, see Cameron, "Political Exposures," pp. 90–107.

GRAND DÉBANDEMENT DE L'ARMÉE ANTICONSTITUTIONELLE.

Un détachement de principales Caillete qui ont joué un Role dans la revolution, elles se presentent aux troupes de l'Empereur pour les faire Débander, ce qui leur reussit complettement et on cesse d'etre étonné de cette Catastrophe lorsqu'on voit la demoiselle Terouya qui leur montre sa République, et Mesdames Fla.. Dondon,.. Silles..Calo..Talmouse..Condor.. leur montrent leur Villette – Ce detachement est renforcé par les sans culote et des Jaco bins qui presentent au bout de leur piques des Cervelas, des Jambons, des bouteilles des Saucisses des Andouilles &c &c....on voit dans l'armée une terrible y a-t'il a la debandade des soldats laissent tomber leur fusils et leur sabres; les drapeau baissent pendant le General Bender meme laisse tomber une de ses Boules.

26.   Engraving titled "Great Disbanding of the Anticonstitutional Army"
(1792). Photo: Bibliothèque nationale.

This engraving is filled with layers of ambiguity, but what interests me here is its expressed worry about gender roles. The gesture
of the aristocratic patriot women, for example, is both a carnivalesque expression of debasement (of the anticonstitutional army)
and a reference in this specific context to homosexuality. The
women are showing their "Villette," according to the text—a reference to the marquis de Villette, a defender of women's rights and
known homosexual and pederast. Théroigne de Méricourt carries a
rifle while also exposing herself. Her gesture, backed up by the rows
of dangling sausages and hams, clearly threatens castration along
with gender reversal (a woman carrying a rifle, the men in back
reduced to presenting the representations of their virility on their
pikes). The castration threat is underlined by the pun in the title of
the engraving; *débander* means both "to disband" and "to lose an

erection." In the engraving as in the poem quoted earlier, we can see that homosexuality and the masculinization of women are linked in a general fear of the blurring of gender boundaries. This fear animated counterrevolutionaries and revolutionaries alike.

At every critical moment during the Revolution, whenever women were prominent in some way, their participation elicited the same kinds of remarks. In the struggle between the Montagnard and Girondin deputies in May 1793 over the future direction of the Revolution, some women, in particular the members of the Société des Républicaines Révolutionnaires, played an active role in the conflicts within local assemblies. Girondin journalists denounced them as devotees of Robespierre, bacchanalian followers of Marat, and the "group of shrews." Women were said to have armed themselves because they were "excited by the furies" and drunk with the prospect of blood.[70]

After Charlotte Corday assassinated Marat in July 1793, leading Jacobins began to turn their attention to public women. One of the leaders of the Société des Républicaines Révolutionnaires, Claire Lacombe, was attacked in the newspaper *Feuille de salut public* on 24 September 1793. On 7 October she protested the assimilation of her activities with the crimes of Catherine de Médicis, Elizabeth of England, Marie-Antoinette, and Charlotte Corday: "Our sex has only produced one monster, whereas for four years we have been betrayed, assassinated by innumerable monsters produced by the masculine sex."[71]

Hostility to women's political clubs had been growing for some time. Women had formed political clubs in Paris and in at least fifty provincial towns and cities between 1791 and 1793, and they were often supported at first by local men's clubs. Although most women in the clubs proclaimed their adherence to the ideal of patriotic and republican motherhood, the very fact of their politicization eventually provoked attacks. As early as January 1793 Prudhomme in his newspaper denounced the provincial women's clubs as a "plague to the mothers of good families." Jacobins in the provinces reminded women of their natural characteristics of irrationality, credulity, and

---

70. Dominique Godineau, *Citoyennes tricoteuses: Les Femmes du peuple à Paris pendant la Révolution française* (Aix-en-Provence, 1988), p. 137.
71. Ibid., p. 179.

flightiness. They never tired of reminding women, as one Bordeaux group insisted, that "your sex is different from ours."[72]

When the Jacobins turned against women's clubs in the fall of 1793, they used the same language of denunciation first pioneered by the rightwing press. Just two weeks after the execution of the queen on 16 October 1793, the Convention discussed the participation of women in politics, in particular the Société des Républicaines Révolutionnaires. The Jacobin deputy Fabre d'Eglantine insisted that "these clubs are not composed of mothers of families, daughters of families, sisters occupied with their younger brothers or sisters, but rather of adventuresses, knights-errant, emancipated women, female grenadiers."[73]

Deputy Jean-Baptiste Amar, speaking for the Committee on General Security of the Convention, laid out the official rationale for a separation of women from the public sphere:

> The private functions to which women are destined by nature itself are related to the general order of society; this social order results from the difference between man and woman. Each sex is called to the kind of occupation which is proper for it. . . . Man is strong, robust, born with great energy, audacity and courage. . . . In general, women are not capable of elevated thoughts and serious meditations, and if, among ancient peoples, their natural timidity and modesty did not allow them to appear outside their families, then in the French Republic do you want them to be seen coming to the bar, to the tribune, and to political assemblies as men do?

To reestablish the "natural order" and prevent the emancipation of women from their familial identity, the deputies solemnly outlawed all women's clubs.[74]

In response to a deputation of women wearing red caps that appeared before the Paris city council two weeks later, the well-known radical spokesman (and city official), Pierre Chaumette, exclaimed:

72. Quotations from Suzanne Desan, "Constitutional Amazons: Jacobin Women's Clubs in the French Revolution," forthcoming in a book edited by Bryant T. Ragan, Jr., and Elizabeth Williams. I am indebted to Suzanne Desan for sharing this article and many other helpful suggestions with me.

73. *Moniteur universel*, no. 39, 9 brumaire an II (30 October 1793), reporting on the session of the National Convention of 8 brumaire (29 October 1793). For a general discussion of the Société and its suppression, see Godineau, *Citoyennes tricoteuses*, pp. 129–42, 163–77.

74. *Moniteur universel*, no. 40, 10 brumaire an II (31 October 1793), reporting on the session of the National Convention of 9 brumaire (30 October 1793).

It is contrary to all the laws of nature for a woman to want to make herself a man. The Council must recall that some time ago these denatured women, these viragos, wandered through the markets with the red cap to sully that badge of liberty. . . . Since when is it permitted to give up one's sex? Since when is it decent to see women abandoning the pious cares of their households, the cribs of their children, to come to public places, to harangues in the galleries, at the bar of the senate?

Chaumette then reminded his audience of the recent fate of the "impudent" Olympe de Gouges, author of *The Declaration of the Rights of Woman and Citizen* (1791), "who was the first to set up women's societies, who abandoned the cares of her household to get mixed up in the republic." He also denounced the "haughty" Madame Roland, "who thought herself fit to govern the republic and who rushed to her downfall."[75] Olympe de Gouges went to the guillotine on 3 November, Madame Roland on 8 November. They were held up as examples of *femmes-hommes,* "mixed beings" who transgressed the boundaries of nature.[76]

Even after these actions of repression, newspapers still complained that women were spending too much time attending meetings of popular societies and local assemblies.[77] On 19 November 1793 the *Moniteur universel* commented on the recent executions of Marie-Antoinette, Olympe de Gouges, and Madame Roland. It amalgamated them under the rubric of unnatural women. The former queen was denounced for being a "bad mother, debauched wife"; Olympe de Gouges for "wanting to be a man of state" and for "having forgotten the virtues suitable to her sex"; and Madame Roland for "having sacrificed nature by wishing to elevate herself above her station" and forgetting "the virtues of her sex." The *Feuille de salut public* advised women "never to follow the popular assemblies with the desire of speaking there."[78]

Marie-Antoinette was certainly not in alliance with the women of the Société des Républicaines Révolutionnaires, or with Madame

75. Speech of 17 November 1793, quoted in Darline Gay Levy, Harriet Branson Applewhite, and Mary Durham Johnson, eds. *Women in Revolutionary Paris, 1789–1795* (Urbana, Ill., 1979), pp. 219–20.

76. On this metaphor, see Godineau, *Citoyennes tricoteuses,* pp. 268–70.

77. Catherine Marand-Fouquet, *La Femme au temps de la Révolution* (Paris, 1989), pp. 268–69.

78. Both papers quoted in Paule-Marie Duhet, *Les Femmes et la Révolution, 1789–1794* (Paris, 1971), pp. 205–6.

Roland or Olympe de Gouges. But even political enemies, as Louise de Keralio discovered, shared similar political restrictions, if they were women. Keralio herself was accused of being dominated by those same "uterine furies" that beset the queen; by publishing, Keralio too was making herself public. Her detractors put this desire for notoriety down to her ugliness and inability to attract men:

> Mademoiselle de Keralio. Ugly and already over the hill; even before the revolution, she consoled herself for the disgrace of her gray hair and the indifference of men by the peaceful cultivation of letters. Given over since the revolution to demagogic disorders and no doubt also dominated by *uterine furies*, she married Robert. . . . Abandoned by her family, scorned by honest people, she vegetates shamefully with this miserable man . . . [and] works by the page for the infamous Prudhomme.[79]

As Dorinda Outram has argued, women who wished to participate actively in the French Revolution were caught in a double bind; virtue was a two-edged sword which bisected the sovereign into two different destinies, one male and one female. Male virtue meant participation in the public world of politics; female virtue meant withdrawal into the private world of the family. Even the most prominent female figures of the time had to acquiesce in this division. Madame Roland recognized this: "I knew what role was suitable to my sex and I never abandoned it."[80] Of course, she paid with her life because others did not think that she had in fact restrained herself from participating in the public sphere.

Read from this perspective on the difference between male and female virtue, the writings and images about the queen as well as those about other prominent women reveal fundamental anxieties about the construction of a new social order. When they executed Marie-Antoinette, republican men were not simply concerned to punish a leading counterrevolutionary. They wanted to separate mothers from any public activity, as Carole Pateman argues, and yet give birth by themselves to a new political organism. In order to accomplish this, they first had to destroy the Old Regime link between the ruling family and the body politic, between the literal

---

79. *Les Crimes constitutionnels de France.*
80. Outram, *"Le Langage mâle de la vertu,"* p. 125; the quotation is from p. 126. See also the chapter on "Women and Revolution," in Landes, *Women and the Public Sphere,* pp. 93–151.

bodies of the rulers and the mystic fiction of royalty. In short, they had to kill the patriarchal father and the mother.

Strikingly, however, the killing of the father was accompanied by little personal vilification. Hébert's references to the pig, the ogre, or the drunk were relatively isolated; calling the former king a cuckold ("tête de cocu") hardly compared to the insistent denigration of Marie-Antoinette.[81] The relative silence about Louis among the revolutionaries perhaps reflects an underlying sense that, after all, he represented the masculinity of power and sovereignty. The aim was to kill the paternal source of power and yet retain its virility in its republican replacement.

The republican ideal of virtue was based on a notion of fraternity between men in which women were relegated to the realm of domesticity. Public virtue required virility, which required in turn the violent rejection of aristocratic degeneracy and any intrusion of the feminine into the public. By attacking Marie-Antoinette and other publicly active women, republican men reinforced their bonds to each other; Marie-Antoinette in particular was the negative version of the female icon of republican liberty, the bad mother in a republic that was supposed to be shaped by the lessons of good republican mothers.

The opposing ideal of patriotic motherhood had always been implicit in revolutionary rhetoric. In June 1790, for example, a Madame Mouret presented a project to the city government of Paris for a "Confederation of Women," in which the women present would take an oath to bring up their children as good patriots.[82] In February 1791 Prudhomme laid out the soon to be standard revolutionary view in his *Révolutions de Paris*. The Revolution depends on you, Prudhomme wrote to his women readers; "without leaving your homes, you can already do much for it. The liberty of a people is based on good morals and education, and you are their guardians and their first dispensors." A few months later he insisted that things should be as in republican Rome, where "each sex was in its place . . . men made the laws . . . and women, without allowing themselves to question it, agreed in everything with the wisdom and knowledge of

81. *Le Père Duchesne*, no. 180, for example.
82. Jane Rendall, *The Origins of Modern Feminism: Women in Britain, France, and the United States, 1780–1860* (New York, 1984), p. 47.

their husbands or their parents."[83] In this vision, widely shared by women as well as men, the most important role of women was as mothers, who would educate the new generation of patriots and, after 1792, republicans.

Even the most militant women subscribed to the ideal of the republican mother. Women's clubs took oaths to "persuade on all occasions my husband, my brothers, and my children to fulfill their duties towards the country" as part of a general belief in the importance of women's functions within a family framework.[84] Women's clubs, though they fostered women's independent political activity, almost always confined themselves to the pursuit of general revolutionary and republican objectives rather than to any explicit feminist program. Yet, despite their self-imposed limitations, the clubs prompted women to demand more participation for their sex, and their very existence alarmed many, indeed most, men whatever their political leaning.

In other words, the problem that Freud saw emerging after the murder of the father—what to do with the women—proved very difficult to resolve. Republican men were no more misogynist than their predecessors, but they faced a new ideological challenge. If patriarchy, custom, and tradition were no longer adequate justifications for authority in the state or for the father's authority over his children, then just what was the justification for women's separate, different, and unequal roles in both the family and the state? In this implicit and often unconscious gender drama, the figure of Marie-Antoinette played a critical and crystallizing role.

83. Prudhomme quoted in Candice E. Proctor, *Women, Equality and the French Revolution* (New York, 1990), p. 56.
84. Ibid., p. 62.

5

Sade's Family Politics

The rise and fall of the good father, the band of brothers, Marie-Antoinette as the bad mother, and the contrasting ideal of republican motherhood were all collectively shared images. Every person, every group, every political faction did not share them in the same way, of course, yet such images, and the conflicts over them, helped to structure narratives of power and authority. Early in the Revolution, Edmund Burke articulated the relationship between family and state power and predicted the inevitable destruction of both of them. He was so horrified by the consequences of the revolutionary assault on deference that he could not see the many ways in which revolutionaries were trying to reconstruct family and state power on new grounds. In 1795, after the end of the Terror, the marquis de Sade published his novel *La Philosophie dans le boudoir* (Philosophy in the boudoir). Sade's novel gave a kind of concretion to Burke's predictions and provided an extended, if idiosyncratic, commentary on the revolutionary reconstruction of the relationship between family and state. In this chapter, I will shift my focus away from collectively configured images of power in order to look closely at this most thoroughgoing individual analysis of the revolutionary family romance.

Although the marquis de Sade has obsessed generations of the literary avant-garde in France and made recurrent appearances in feminist theory, he has been almost entirely absent from works of French history.[1] A few formulaic references to his long passages in prisons and asylums mark the only recognition that almost all of

---

1. This is not to say that the historical aspects of Sade's work have been ignored by literary critics. See, for example, the essays in Michel Camus and Philippe Roger, eds., *Sade: Écrire la crise* (Paris, 1983), especially those by Michel Delon, Jean-Claude Bonnet, and Jean-Pierre Faye. An interesting analysis informed by Freudian and feminist concepts can be found in Angela Carter, *The Sadeian Woman: An Exercise in Cultural History* (London, 1979).

Sade's work was written either just before or during the decade of revolution. Some of the best known of Sade's novels were obviously shaped by the revolutionary experience, in some cases explicitly and self-consciously so. More important, they can be read as a commentary on the revolutionary experience, a commentary that is sometimes explicit and self-conscious, sometimes implicit or unconscious, and almost always paradoxical, if not parodic. Central to Sade's commentary is his own peculiar version of the family romance.

In this chapter I will argue that *La Philosophie dans le boudoir* is one of the most revealing texts about the revolutionary political unconscious, despite the claim of at least one critic that it is "the least important of Sade's private writings."[2] By its very extremes of rationalist argument and pornographic staging, by its consistent reductio ad absurdum of Enlightenment ideals and revolutionary rhetorical practices, and especially by its revelation of the psychosexual anxieties of the new republican order, the novel uncovers meanings in the revolutionary experience—much in the manner of dreams—that would be otherwise inaccessible to us.[3]

Reading this text presents a series of fascinating and difficult problems. Little is known about the circumstances of its writing or publication. Although the book first appeared in print in 1795, much of it may have been written in the late 1780s.[4] References

2. Donald Thomas, *The Marquis de Sade* (London, 1976), p. 182.

3. Philippe Roger pointed out to me that Aldous Huxley had seen the function of reductio ad absurdum in Sade. "His books are of permanent interest and value because they contain a kind of *reductio ad absurdum* of revolutionary theory. Sade is not afraid to be a revolutionary to the bitter end. Not content with denying the particular system of values embodied in the *ancien régime*, he proceeds to deny the existence of any values, any idealism, any binding moral imperatives whatsoever. . . . De Sade is the one completely consistent and thoroughgoing revolutionary of history." Aldous Huxley, *Ends and Means: An Enquiry into the Nature of Ideals and into the Methods Employed for their Realization* (London, 1938), pp. 271–72. Huxley's remarks may be taken as part of the general reevaluation of Sade that took place in the intellectual avant-garde in the 1930s. My view differs from Huxley's in several respects: I do not see Sade as a revolutionary but rather as a particular kind of self-conscious commentator on the inner logic of revolutionary principles and of revolutionary rhetorical techniques. He was also an inadvertent commentator on the centrality of the "woman question" to revolutionary ideology and on the hidden links between revolutionary rhetorical strategies and pornographic writing.

4. The dating is discussed by Yvon Belaval in his preface to the Gallimard edition (Paris, 1976), p. 19. Page number citations given with the French quotations from the novel are to this edition. The original edition can be consulted in the reserve room of the Bibliothèque nationale under *La Philosophie dans le boudoir: Ouvrage posthume de l'Auteur de Justine*, 2 vols. (London, 1795).

within the inserted tract, "Français, encore un effort si vous voulez être républicains [Frenchmen, yet another effort if you want to be republicans]," date at least this part of the novel to late 1794 or 1795.[5] Allusions are made in the pamphlet to the overthrow of the Bastille (p. 198), to the execution of the king (p. 198), to "the infamous Robespierre" and his cult of the Supreme Being (p. 195), and to the preparation of a new code of law (p. 209)—in short, to major revolutionary events between 1789 and 1794. The surrounding dialogues, on the other hand, might well have been composed before 1789. That Sade was able to insert a tract written during the Revolution into a text that was probably composed in the 1780s shows how much his understanding of pornography anticipated some of the central issues structuring the revolutionary political imagination. Sade's pornography, which was easily adapted to revolutionary circumstances, thus anticipated developments in the revolutionary family romance just as the eighteenth-century novel more generally predicted and produced the fate of the king.

We know as little about the reader reception of Sade's text as we do about the circumstances of its writing and publication. Pornographic publications were regularly denounced in the press and in the legislature, but they were never effectively suppressed during the French Revolution. The revolutionary government exercised little control over pornography after the freeing of the presses in 1789. In July 1791 the Constituent Assembly had considered passing laws against "those who have made a criminal attempt, publicly and in outrageous fashion, on the modesty of women by dishonest action, by the exhibition and sale of obscene images, by having favored debauchery, corrupted young people of either sex, or abused them." In the discussion, Pétion and Robespierre both argued against the immediate passage of a law prohibiting obscene images, on the grounds that obscenity was not clearly defined and that further action depended upon developing a principled basis for censoring both images and writings. The enforcement of any measures against obscenity therefore passed to local authorities, and the

---

5. English translations from the French are my own. An English version of the novel is available in *The Marquis de Sade: The Complete Justine, Philosophy in the Bedroom and Other Writings*, trans. Richard Seaver and Austryn Wainhouse (New York, 1965); unfortunately, the translation is not always accurate (a *boudoir*, for example, is a lady's sitting room as well as a bedroom).

Commune of Paris did on several occasions try to force the expurgation of plays or arrest actors for having appeared in obscene plays. But for the most part, the Commune's railing against prostitution and indecency remained without any enforcement.[6]

La Philosophie dans le boudoir was first published during the period of reaction against the political and moral puritanism of the Terror. Pornographic works apparently proliferated during the late 1790s. In his *Nouveau Paris* of 1798, Mercier bemoaned the increasingly public display of obscene literature:

> They display nothing but obscene books whose titles and engravings are equally offensive to decency and to good taste. They sell these monstrosities everywhere, along the bridges, at the doors of theaters, on the boulevards. The poison is not costly; ten sous a volume. . . . One could say that these purveyors of brochures are the privileged merchants of garbage: they seem to exclude from their display any title that is not foul. Young people are able to go to these sources of every kind of vice without any obstacle or scruple. This horrible manufacture of licentious books is carried on by all the counterfeiters, pirates who will kill the publishing industry, literature, and men of letters. It is based on that unlimited liberty of the press which has been demanded by the falsest, most miserable, and blindest of men.[7]

Only under Napoleon would the French state develop a complete bureaucratic mechanism for suppressing such works. We can assume, then, that Sade's works of the late 1790s were part of a more general trend.

It might seem strange to focus in this chapter on only one text, since the previous chapters have taken a much wider purview. Although some of Sade's other works also refer, if only in passing, to revolutionary events or slogans, this one novel provides his most extended, explicit commentary on it, especially in the form of the inserted pamphlet. The pamphlet "Français, encore un effort" is presented in a form and a rhetoric similar to those of other revolutionary political pamphlets (it is not pornographic itself), but its content goes far beyond the usual, as we shall see. It is precisely

---

6. For a brief but useful discussion of these legislative efforts, see Jean-Jacques Pauvert, *Estampes érotiques révolutionnaires: La Révolution française et l'obscénité* (Paris, 1989), especially pp. 18–40.

7. Louis-Sébastien Mercier, *Le Nouveau Paris* (Paris, an VII [1799]), vol. 3, pp. 178–79.

Sade's extremity, his consistent use of the reductio ad absurdum, that makes him so interesting for my purposes. This applies to the body of the novel as well, for in the boudoir Sade enacts a fantasy of the family romance of fraternity that is also more extreme than anything suggested in popular fiction, paintings, or engravings. Sade also goes beyond the run-of-the-mill pornography of the 1790s; he is not content to ridicule clerics, aristocrats, political figures, or prostitutes. Instead, he offers a kind of theoretical overview of the place of pornography within political writing and of the role of the family in the new political order.

Because Sade's fantasies and logic are so extreme, because he takes the expressed principles of the Revolution apart and subjects them to intense scrutiny, because he is able to play with and distort the universals of the "rights of man," Sade provides a uniquely comprehensive perspective on the experience of the French Revolution. It is worth emphasizing, however, that I do not mean to argue that Sade expresses some "real truth" of the Revolution; republicans rejected his views out of hand. Sade nevertheless reveals the points of tension in revolutionary ideology: the relations between men and women, the relations between parents and children, and the tension between individual, egoistic desire and the need for social interaction. A reductio ad absurdum may be absurd in the end, but it can only work as a rhetorical strategy if it seizes upon principles that appear at first to be sound and widely shared.

It is no accident that Western pornography reached its culmination with Sade during the French Revolution. Sade pushed his analysis of the desiring, selfish ego right up to the limits of death. Murder is the final point in boudoir philosophy, where desire meets annihilation; and pornography can go no further than that. It can only repeat the same moves. Sade was able to push out against the limits of the imagination because he lived at a time when the social order was disaggregating and reforming, a moment when the conventional nature of social relations was becoming starkly evident. Sade, like Burke, was among the first to appreciate the theoretical challenges posed by this process of disaggregation and reformation.

Sade's own psychology may explain why he was sensitive in his particular way to the crisis created by the emergent "visibility" of society, that is, by the discovery that society was created from within and not by some other anterior or ulterior force.[8] Whatever his personal reasons for seeing the world the way he did, his depiction of sexual-social relations has to be read alongside those of the other great eighteenth-century commentators on the institution of the social, Rousseau and Burke. As Simone de Beauvoir said of him, "though not a consummate artist or a coherent philosopher, he deserves to be hailed as a great moralist."[9] I hope that by the end of this chapter, the comparison of Sade with the other great eighteenth-century thinkers about the social order will no longer seem absurd.

La Philosophie dans le boudoir has an unusual structure for a Sadeian novel. Presented in seven "dialogues," the book resembles a play more than a novel (but then the dialogue form, with its implication of teaching a lesson, had been favored in erotic literature throughout the seventeenth century).[10] The only real character development—if development is really the right word—is that of Eugénie Mistival, the fifteen-year-old daughter of a rich financier, who is progressively corrupted by her encounter with Madame de Saint-Ange; Madame's brother, the chevalier de Mirvel; and the evil genius of the piece, Dolmancé. As in the classical theater, all of the action takes place in the space of one day in one place. The book claims affiliation with the tradition of libertine literature from the start of its preface, which is addressed "Aux Libertins." From the very beginning, the gender ambivalences of the text are evident as the author addresses himself to "voluptueux de tous les âges et de tous les sexes [voluptuaries of all ages and of every sex]."

As in some of Sade's other works, a woman plays a central role as libertine in alliance with an always more powerful and even more libertine man. In the very first scene, Madame de Saint-Ange describes herself as "un animal amphibie; j'aime tout, je m'amuse de tout, je veux réunir tous les genres" (p. 40; "an amphibious creature: I love everything, I enjoy everything, I want to bring together all

---

8. On the visibility of society and its imaginary foundations, see Brian C. J. Singer, *Society, Theory and the French Revolution: Studies in the Revolutionary Imaginary* (New York, 1986).

9. Simone de Beauvoir, "Faut-il brûler Sade?" *Les Temps modernes*, 75 (1952): 1205.

10. On the history of erotic literary forms, see Patrick J. Kearney, *A History of Erotic Literature* (London, 1982), especially p. 29.

27.   Engraving from the 1795 edition of the
marquis de Sade's *La Philosophie dans le boudoir*.
Photo: Bibliothèque nationale.

kinds"). Throughout the action, Madame de Saint-Ange plays the
role of right-hand man to Dolmancé, sharing his philosophical positions and views of the world. We might say as well that she shares his
sexual positions when she wears a dildo to sodomize him (figure 27).
The action takes place, moreover, in her house.

The ambiguities of Sade's portrayal of Madame de Saint-Ange
reproduce many of the tensions about gender definition that we
have seen in the literature about Marie-Antoinette. In language that
resonates with Louise de Keralio's claim that "a woman who becomes queen changes sex," Madame de Saint-Ange asserts that she
is willing to "changer de sexe" with Dolmancé (p. 41; "to change
sexes" with him). Madame de Saint-Ange is never Dolmancé's equal,
of course, but she is also not simply an object of his pleasure. She is
depicted seducing Eugénie and as a sodomizer of men. So from the

28.   Engraving from the 1795 edition of the
marquis de Sade's *La Philosophie dans le boudoir*.
Photo: Bibliothèque nationale.

beginning, the role of women in the novel will oscillate, undermining all efforts to categorize this as simply another pornographic
exercise in misogyny.

Other aspects of the text likewise call attention to its consistent
tendency to destabilize the expected categories. For example, the
corruption of Eugénie in the space of a few hours is finally laugh-
able as much as it is morally vicious. The engravings that accompanied the original text have the same characteristic; they are pornographic, but also in many ways ludicrous (see figure 28). The
obvious parody of the interminable seduction scenes of Samuel
Richardson's *Clarissa* or even of Laclos's *Les Liaisons dangereuses* becomes, in the end, a parody of the pornographic genre itself as it was
being developed by Sade and other writers. The implicit criticism of
the endlessly convoluted interpersonal maneuvers of seduction in

the classic eighteenth-century novel accelerates quickly into a sexual tempo that can only be characterized as a *reductio ad absurdum* of realist and materialist techniques of presentation.[11] The seduction through letter writing and the understated interchanges in polite society are replaced by straightforward and rapid-fire initiation into the secrets of sexual pleasure that are always suggested but never enacted in the novels of Richardson or Rousseau. The scenes of sexual orgy that are used by Sade to deflate the romance of the respectable eighteenth-century novels are themselves self-deflating, however; as the writer himself recognizes with his constant interruptions of the orgy scenes, the realistic depiction of bodily pleasure loses interest when it is constantly repeated.[12]

Sade follows the classic eighteenth-century novels of love and family in their emphasis on the dangers of words, but in this area too he takes the proposition to its absurdly logical conclusion. When Madame de Saint-Ange explains to Eugénie that rape, incest, even murder and parricide are not necessarily criminal, the young girl exclaims, "Ah! cher amour, comme ces discours séducteurs enflamment ma tête et séduisent mon âme!" (p. 85; "Oh! my dear love, how these seductive words inflame my mind and captivate my soul!"). Here the words themselves, with their taboo-transgressing effect, are taken to their farthest imaginable extreme, and words alone appear to accomplish what words allied with sentiment accomplished in the eighteenth-century novel.

The noted literary critic Jean-François La Harpe attributed the Revolution's aberrations to its language; he argued that "the words, like the things, were monstrosities."[13] The power of the word in the Revolution, according to La Harpe, was the effect of *philosophie* run riot. The power of the word, both spoken and written, is one of the major themes of Sade's novel, and his analysis of the power of the word also suggests in its own way that *philosophie* has indeed run

11. On Sade's relationship to other eighteenth-century novelists, including comparisons to Jane Austen, see the suggestive remarks in R. F. Brissenden, "*La Philosophie dans le boudoir;* or, A Young Lady's Entrance into the World," *Studies in Eighteenth Century Culture* 2 (1972): 113–41.

12. On the problem of repetition in pornography, see the suggestive but undeveloped remarks by Luce Iragaray, *This Sex Which Is Not One,* trans. Catherine Porter with Carolyn Burke (Ithaca, N.Y., 1985), pp. 201–3.

13. I discuss La Harpe's views briefly in *Politics, Culture, and Class in the French Revolution* (Berkeley, 1984), p. 19.

riot.[14] Eugénie can be corrupted by the sheer force of language. Words have this power in the new order because people are discovering that society is its own source of power, that society itself has an imagined base in social convention rather than in otherwordly truths. This newly visible society seems a very fragile basis for social order.

If language is unstable, so too is sex itself, as presented by Sade. Many of the sexual tableaus of the novel go beyond the challenge of conventional morality to a kind of parody of themselves. In the penultimate staging of the fifth dialogue, for example, Madame de Saint-Ange farts into the mouth of Dolmancé, who is biting her. Although this scene is supposedly presented under the general philosophical aegis of anything goes for pleasure, it cannot help but appear carnivalesque at the same time.

The dialogue form of the novel lends itself well to a curious and similarly ridiculous alternation between erotic stagings of unending complexity and variety and philosophical discourses of mock seriousness. The tendency to parodic philosophizing reaches its apogee in the very long (one-quarter of the book) pseudorevolutionary pamphlet, "Français, encore un effort," which is inserted into the fifth dialogue. The insertion of the pamphlet, which Dolmancé claims to have bought at the Palais de l'Egalité (p. 185)—the Palais Royal of the Old Regime, notorious for its gambling dens, houses of prostitution, and clandestine pornographic pamphlets—brings the parodic self-consciousness of the novel into high relief. The reading aloud of the pamphlet seems ludicrously jarring in the midst of scenes of sexual orgy. Not surprisingly, the supposed pamphlet presents in organized, linear fashion all the notions about morality that Dolmancé and Madame de Saint-Ange have been advancing piecemeal throughout the theatrical dialogues. With its interruption of the action and its mimicry of the text's insistent, extreme materialism, the pamphlet calls our attention to the fact that the novel constantly subverts even its own literary structures as it shifts between pornography, political tract, and parody of these two forms.

Beneath this destabilization in literary structures is an insistent

14. A fascinating analysis of Sade's erotic lexicon can be found in Beatrice Fink, "La Langue de Sade," *Eroticism in French Literature*, University of South Carolina College of Humanities and Social Sciences, French Literature Series, vol. 10 (Columbia, S.C., 1983), pp. 103–12.

affiliation between the novel and contemporary political pornography. There is considerable evidence in the text itself that Sade was very familiar with the rapidly proliferating genre of political pornography and in particular with the pamphlets against the queen. In the third dialogue, for example, Madame de Saint-Ange refers to Marie-Antoinette in the same vulgar tones that the revolutionary pamphlets had taken. Explaining to Eugénie that she can teach her how to hide the impending loss of her virginity, she alludes to the queen's presumed exploits: "Eusses-tu foutu comme Antoinette . . ." (p. 86; "had you fucked like Antoinette"). The epigraph on the title page of the original 1795 edition of the book, "La mère en prescrira la lecture à sa fille [the mother will prescribe this reading to her daughter]," is an obvious play on the epigraph on the title page of one of the most pornographic attacks on the queen: "La mère en proscrira la lecture à sa fille [the mother will proscribe this reading to her daughter]" adorned the title page of *Fureurs utérines de Marie-Antoinette, femme de Louis XVI*, published in 1791.[15] A nineteenth-century bibliophile, P.-L. Jacob, suggested that Sade had written the second part of one of the best-known early pamphlets against the queen, the *Essai historique sur la vie de Marie-Antoinette* (published in 1789).[16]

The text combines the pornographic staging that was characteristic of many of the politico-pornographic pamphlets with a parody of serious political pamphlets as a genre in "Français, encore un effort." Writers of political pornography frequently used the fictional first-person confessional or the format of a play to make their point. Sade uses a seemingly similar format but his purposes are much less certain. His upper-class characters are debauched and enlightened, libertine and republican at the same time. The fundamental justification for their position is that they live in "un siècle où l'étendue et les droits de l'homme viennent d'être approfondis avec tant de soin"

15. The place of publication is given as "Au Manège. Et dans tous les bordels de Paris." The similarity in epigraphs is noted in Pascal Pia, *Les Livres de l'Enfer, du XVIe siècle à nos jours*, 2 vols. (Paris, 1978), p. 1044. The second edition of *La Philosophie dans le boudoir* changed the epigraph, for reasons unknown, to read "proscrira."

16. The full title of the pamphlet is *Essai historique sur la vie de Marie-Antoinette, reine de France et de Navarre, née archiduchesse d'Autriche, le 2 novembre 1755, orné de son portrait et rédigé sur plusieurs manuscrits de sa main.* (De l'an de la liberté française 1789, à Versailles, chez la Montansier, hôtel des Courtisanes). Jacob reported that the first part of the pamphlet was written by Brissot, but this has been questioned. For Jacob's views, see Hector Fleischmann, *Marie-Antoinette libertine* (Paris, 1911), pp. 67–68.

(p. 80; "a century in which the scope and the rights of man have just been extended with such care"). Unlike the political pornography published by republican writers, the targets of attack in Sade are not clear; his debauched aristocrats are too clever to be merely examples of Old Regime decadence, and the fifteen-year-old financier's daughter hardly seems the picture of bourgeois innocence, since her seduction is so easy and so thoroughgoing.

In Sade, as a consequence, political pornography as a genre reaches its own reductio ad absurdum. Does the pornography really serve a political purpose, as it was supposed to in the pamphlets against the queen, for instance? Or does Sade's use of the pornographic simply reveal that the supposed political purposes of the pamphlets against the queen and aristocracy were in fact excuses for pornographic writing all along? Sade's text threatens to explode the fragile ties between pornography and politics and in the process threatens republican values altogether.

The centerpiece of Sade's novel is the long pamphlet, "Français, encore un effort." The views expressed in it have aroused much commentary over the years but also great uncertainty as to Sade's intentions in inserting it.[17] The pamphlet appears to realize Burke's prophecy in *Reflections on the Revolution in France* (1790) that for the revolutionaries "regicide, and parricide, and sacrilege, are but fictions of superstition, corrupting jurisprudence by destroying its simplicity." The pamphlet moves from an attack on Christianity to a demonstration that the new republican state must tolerate theft, incest, sodomy, and murder. For Burke, such a progression in argument was the inevitable consequence of "this new conquering empire of light and reason," which was rudely tearing off "all the decent drapery of life."[18] Sade's pamphlet can be compared with Burke's earlier views because both commentators saw, in their own ways, how the empire of reason was challenging all of "the pleasing illusions, which made power gentle," as Burke himself put it.

Sade's pamphlet begins in the best libertine tradition with an all-out attack on established religion, arguing that atheism is the only system possible for people who know how to reason (p. 193). In the

17. See, for example, Brissenden, "*La Philosophie dans le boudoir.*"
18. Edmund Burke, *Reflections on the Revolution in France* (New York, 1973), pp. 89–90.

first suggestion that family values are at issue, the pamphlet denounces "the dull Nazarene impostor" and "his foul and disgusting mother, the shameless Mary" (p. 192). The republic will only be successfully established when "Christian chimeras" are replaced by the values taught in a new "national education." In the second section, the common revolutionary argument is advanced that a new government requires new mores. But these are new mores with a vengeance. A "republican state" requires fraternity but no universal laws. The author then goes on to argue, for example, that theft is not a great evil in a society whose goal is equality, for how can we expect someone who has nothing to agree to protect the property of a rich person who has everything?

After theft comes modesty. In an interesting twist on Rousseau, the pamphlet's author insists that the use of clothing is based only on the difficulties of climate and "the coquetry of women"; therefore "modesty, far from being a virtue, was but one of the first effects of corruption, one of the first expressions of the coquetry of women" (pp. 216–17). Where Rousseau would argue for greater control over women's appeals to coquetry and for the elimination of women from the public sphere in the interest of maintaining their natural modesty, Sade concludes that modesty is irrelevant. The author proposes the organization of large, hygienic, public establishments ("ce temple de Vénus," p. 223) in every town, where all sexes and all ages would be offered up "to the caprices of the libertines," and where "the most absolute subordination will be the rule of the individuals participating" (p. 218).

Sade's method of proceeding here is characteristic of the reductio ad absurdum logic of the entire novel. Although this logic applies to all moral argument in the novel, it is most strikingly apparent in those sections that have to do with women. Other authors, both in the Enlightenment and during the Revolution, used the problematic aspects of women's behavior—which are always related to their sexuality invading the public sphere—as a basis for arguing for stricter control over women and their relegation to the private sphere.[19] Sade uses the same arguments for a radically different

19. For an analysis of Enlightenment and revolutionary views on women in the public sphere, see Joan Landes, *Women and the Public Sphere in the Age of the French Revolution* (Ithaca, N.Y., 1988).

conclusion: since women cannot be trusted to maintain their private virtues—to control their sexuality—their bodies should be made public, that is, available to all men. The private-public tension is thus resolved in a very different way by Sade. This resolution is not one of anarchy, however. Sade replaces conventional law with a new order that is to be every bit as minutely regulated as the old one, and perhaps even more so; in the new public establishments, "the most absolute subordination will be the rule of the individuals participating," and, the pamphlet continues, "the slightest refusal will be instantly and arbitrarily punished by the injured party" (p. 218).

In its proposal for hygienic temples of Venus, the pamphlet takes up and extends an earlier suggestion by Restif de la Bretonne. In a curious novelistic tract significantly titled *Le Pornographe* (1769), Restif advocated the government establishment of "Parthenions," or public houses, for prostitutes. Nothing was left out in Restif's plan; conditions of entry and departure, pregnancy, hours of work, prices, medical supervision, and even names were to be regulated. Perfumes and cosmetics were forbidden. Such rules were necessary, Restif claimed, in order to counter the physical and moral ravages of prostitution, or, as the subtitle had it, "the misfortunes occasioned by the publicness of women."[20]

The prostitute came in for such regulation because she was the major type (along with the exceptional case of the queen) of the woman in public. Restif used the term *pornographe* in its Greek sense of "writer about prostitutes." Gradually in the nineteenth century, the term would come to be identified with the production of obscene literature or imagery. As in so much else, Sade seems to straddle this transformation. On the one hand, he writes out of the libertine tradition of the seventeenth and eighteenth centuries, with its emphasis on anticlericalism and intellectualized eroticism designed for cultivated upper-class men. On the other hand, his flatly declarative descriptions of sexual activity prefigure modern forms of pornography, which are designed for a mass audience of men (and perhaps women too). Sade published much of his work just at the moment when newly democratized forms of pornography with their vulgar

20. Nicolas Restif de la Bretonne, *Le Pornographe ou idées d'un honnête homme sur un projet de règlement pour les prostituées* (London, 1769); reprinted in Restif de la Bretonne, *Oeuvres érotiques* (Fayard, 1985).

attacks on political leaders were soliciting wider audiences for obscene literature and imagery.[21]

The transformation of the meaning of the term *pornography* is as yet little understood and not much studied.[22] It seems to have depended at least in part on the revolutionary reflection about women's role in a newly visible society. In the early nineteenth century, a set of parallel concerns began to occupy writers about social problems: worries about the effects of prostitution, of women acting politically, and of childhood masturbation, for example, all reflected anxieties about the bodies of those who had been excluded from the political order. All were imagined as powerful sources of disorder, confusion, and even degeneration of the race. It is not surprising, then, that the position of women (and the relationship of children with their parents) would preoccupy a pivotal figure such as Sade.

The problematic position of women in a republican social order is suggested by the brief section on modesty in Sade's inserted pamphlet, which leads into a more general consideration of women. Given the principle that "all men are born free, all are equal in rights," it follows that "no man may be excluded from possessing a woman" (p. 221). Republican government requires a community of women: "All men therefore have equal rights of enjoyment [un droit de jouissance égal] in all women" (p. 222). No man can have a unique and personal right over a woman, but all women will have to prostitute themselves. In this system, women were to have the right to any pleasures they desired as long as they were willing to give themselves over to any man who wanted them. There is a kind of sexual liberation of women implied here ("Sexe charmant, vous serez libre; vous jouirez comme les hommes de tous les plaisirs dont la nature vous fait un devoir" [p. 227; "Charming sex, you will be free; you will enjoy like men all the pleasures of which nature makes a duty"]); but this liberation comes with the special clause that women must make themselves available to men's desires (p. 225). Once again, Sade reveals the extent of the problem with women by

21. I am indebted to Sarah Maza for calling my attention to the difference between libertine literature and pornography. This is a topic that deserves more attention than I can give it here.

22. For a brief history of the term, see Walter Kendrick, *The Secret Museum: Pornography in Modern Culture* (New York, 1987).

parodying the usual solutions offered by republicans; rather than arguing that women should stay home in order to ensure the legitimacy of paternity, Sade insists that they all be publicly available. All women are to become prostitutes.

As Burke predicted, the family as a social structure was bound to be threatened by these developments. What difference did it make in a republic if children had no father, the pamphlet's author asks? None, since all individuals "ne doivent avoir d'autre mère que la patrie" (p. 225; "should have no other mother than the country"). Children must belong to the republic, as Danton and Robespierre had suggested in the debates on education. Is incest dangerous? No, because it is dictated to us by the laws of nature, found in the origin of societies, and consecrated in all the religions. After a brief ethnographic review of incest practices, the author concludes that "l'inceste devrait être la loi de tout gouvernement dont la fraternité fait la base" (p. 230; "incest ought to be the law of any government based on fraternity"). Moreover, the establishment of "the community of women" necessarily entails incest ("the community of women I am establishing necessarily leading to incest . . .", p. 230).

In this system, rape is less problematic than theft, and sodomy can no longer be considered criminal. The history of Greece and Rome shows that sodomy is more frequent in republics (p. 233). Here the author pushes even further: sodomy is useful in a republic because it strengthens the bonds between men; and moreover—taking up an argument adumbrated by Rousseau and Montesquieu—it was the weakness of despotism to attach itself to women:

> L'amour des garçons . . . donnait du courage et de la force, et . . . servait à chasser les tyrans. . . . On était certain que ces liaisons affermissaient la république, on déclamait contre les femmes, et c'était une faiblesse réservée au despotisme que de s'attacher à de telles créatures.
>
> (pp. 234–35)

> The love of boys . . . instilled courage and vigor, and it was useful in driving out the tyrants. . . . People were certain that these attachments strengthened the republic, they declaimed against women, and to attach oneself to such creatures was viewed as a weakness reserved for despotism.

By his characteristic technique of reductio ad absurdum, Sade reveals the links between three critical elements in the republican imagination: the bond between men, the ambivalent position of women, and the fear of incest. In the pamphlet, the republican bond between men becomes literally homosexual; the ambivalence about women's participation in the public sphere, which is connected explicitly to despotism, is resolved by the proposal to introduce large hygienic houses of prostitution; and the fear of incest is displaced by its celebration as a necessary concomitant to the community of women. More will be said about these central themes below.

Burke would hardly be surprised that the pamphlet then goes on to argue for the decriminalization of murder on materialist and utilitarian grounds. This passage reads as a kind of justification for the Terror: "Une nation déjà vieille et corrompue qui, courageusement, secouera le joug de son gouvernement monarchique pour en adopter un républicain, ne se maintiendra que par beaucoup de crimes" (p. 243; "an already old and corrupt nation which courageously casts off the yoke of its monarchical government in order to adopt a republican one will only maintain itself by many crimes"). The author of the pamphlet concludes, "En un mot, le meurtre est une horreur, mais une horreur souvent nécessaire, jamais criminelle, essentielle à tolérer dans un Etat républicain" (p. 249; "In a word, murder is a horror, but an often necessary horror, never criminal, which it is essential to tolerate in a republican State"). The pamphlet concludes with a kind of evacuated liberalism: "Faisons peu de lois, mais qu'elles soient bonnes" (p. 251; "Make few laws, but let them be good ones"). In true liberal fashion, the author explains his opposition to any imperialist war: stay home and revive commerce and manufacturing, and the thrones of Europe will crumble of their own weight (p. 252).

Sade's own political relationship to the pamphlet is irrelevant to my analysis. It may well be that we should be tempted as Eugénie was to see Dolmancé as the author of the pamphlet (and, by extension, the pamphlet as the expression of Sade's own views). When questioned, Dolmancé responds, "It is certain that I share a part of these reflections, and my speeches which have proved this to you even give to the reading which we have just heard the appearance of a private lesson" (p. 253). Yet Dolmancé goes no further and neither need we. What matters is that the pamphlet read alongside the novel reveals the tension points in revolutionary ideology. I do not mean to say that the revolutionary belief in fraternity and the insistence on the creation of a new man inevitably led to the justification of incest, sodomy, and murder. This conclusion is Burke's, not mine, and it would certainly have been rejected by the revolutionaries. Yet Burke and Sade both saw, in their different ways, how high the stakes could be in the revolutionary situation.

Sade grasped, no doubt for reasons of his own psychological peculiarity, the most problematic aspects of the revolutionary unconscious, especially the relationship between republicanism and the ambivalence about women. He depicts a kind of Freudian family romance, not only in the pseudorevolutionary pamphlet itself (which remains, however, a purely doctrinal and even utopian statement), but especially in its enactment in the boudoir, to which I will now turn. The boudoir is the place in which sexual relations are rendered most explicit. Like the psychosexual landscape of the republic, the boudoir is dominated by the absence of the father and a gnawing obsession with the mother. All the intricate variations in gender relations of the boudoir are worked out on this grid of the absent father and the bad mother.

In the novel, the father of Eugénie never appears, though he supposedly has given his permission for his daughter's reeducation and for the vile treatment accorded his wife; a letter to this effect arrives from the father in the sixth dialogue, almost as an afterthought. The mother appears at the very end, and she meets a fate that only Sade with his fantastic hatred of the mother could have devised. Dolmancé instructs Eugénie to use a dildo on her own mother, after which he brings in his syphilitic valet to infect Madame de Mistival. On Madame de Saint-Ange's suggestion, Eugénie then sews up her mother's vagina with red thread in order to hasten the disease's progress and, as Eugénie explains, to prevent her from giving birth to any more brothers and sisters (p. 283).

This hallucinatory scene lends itself to any number of interpretations. Pierre Klossowski, for example, diagnosed Sade as suffering from "a negative Oedipus complex," which drove him to attack everything attached to maternity.[23] What strikes me, however, is the way in which the scene depicts—again by reductio ad absurdum—a fundamental revolutionary ambivalence about genealogy and en-

23. Pierre Klossowski, *Sade, mon prochain* (Paris, 1967), pp. 177–86.

gendering and about the role of mothers. It is the reductio ad absurdum of what Carole Pateman has diagnosed as the modern masculine appropriation of politically creative power and the concomitant exclusion of women from the social contract.[24] Eugénie quite literally prevents her mother from ever giving birth again with her red thread. It is the reductio ad absurdum too of the pornographic attacks on Marie-Antoinette as the bad mother. Here the "bad" mother gets a very literal punishment just because she is Eugénie's mother; her crime is her status as mother, and her executioner is her own child. The devout and upright Madame de Mistival is made to represent the general unreliability of women. Dolmancé denounces her claim to rights over her daughter: "Quand M. de Mistival, *ou je ne sais qui*, vous lança dans le vagin les gouttes de foutre qui firent éclore Eugénie, l'aviez-vous en vue pour lors?" (p. 270, my emphasis; "When M. de Mistival, *or whoever it was,* launched into your vagina the drops of fuck that brought Eugénie into being, did you have her in view then?"). In Sade's text, the Revolution does not devour her children; the children devour the mother in a rejection of lineage and reproduction.

Sade's text is obsessed with engendering. As Madame de Saint-Ange explains to Eugénie, "Une jolie fille ne doit s'occuper que de *foutre* et jamais d'*engendrer*" (p. 57; "A pretty girl ought to concern herself only with *fucking*, and never with *engendering*"). Much of her instruction consists of advice on how to avoid pregnancy (this is the virtue of sodomy; see p. 97 for details on contraception) and on the usefulness of abortion if it happens. The connection between population and politics is explicit in the inserted pamphlet, which argues that republican government needs "a dike against population" (p. 247).

The attack on engendering is directed exclusively at mothers, not at fathers. Early on in the third dialogue, Dolmancé and Eugénie agree that they both detest their mothers and adore their fathers. Moreover, as Madame de Saint-Ange and Dolmancé insist, "Uniquement formés du sang de nos pères, nous ne devons absolument rien à nos mères" (p. 64; "formed only by the blood of our fathers, we owe absolutely nothing to our mothers"). They admit that a mixture of male and female seed is needed for conception, but

24. Carole Pateman, *The Sexual Contract* (Stanford, 1988).

argue that it is the male seed that is truly creative, that is, in Aristotelian fashion, the final cause of the new personality. Still, women are the only ones who know the real fathers of their children. As Madame de Saint-Ange explains to Eugénie in the third dialogue, "il est impossible de répondre d'une femme" (p. 88; "it is impossible to be sure of a woman"), a fact which forces Sade to the ultimate solution of giving up on the search for a certain paternity.

Where others had taken this problem as the justification for female chastity and the strict control of female morals, Sade advocates making all women available to all men. Madame de Saint-Ange explains that "la destinée de la femme est d'être comme la chienne, comme la louve: elle doit appartenir à tous ceux qui veulent d'elle" (p. 82; "woman's destiny is to be like the bitch, the she-wolf: she must belong to all who want her"). This is language that resembles in its details (the she-wolf, the bitch) the attacks on Marie-Antoinette. The result here, however, is disdain for any conception of lineage or legitimacy, or for any form of family sentiment. Dolmancé concludes to Eugénie's hapless mother, "Apprenez, madame, qu'il n'est rien de plus illusoire que les sentiments du père ou de la mère pour les enfants, et de ceux-ci pour les auteurs de leurs jours" (p. 270; "You must learn, Madame, that there is nothing more illusory than the feelings of a father or a mother for their children, and those of children for the authors of their days"). Earlier in the novel he claimed, "Nous ne devons rien à nos parents . . . parce que les droits de la naissance n'établissent rien, ne fondent rien" (p. 171; "We owe nothing to our parents . . . because the rights of birth establish nothing, found nothing").

Thus, in the absence of the father, the normal laws of legitimacy and social order do not prevail, just as Freud predicted in *Totem and Taboo*. Freud's account of the first great act of sacrifice—the killing of the father of the primal horde—is in many respects a perfect inversion of Sade's. Freud argues that sexual need separates men and thus forces the brothers to erect the incest taboo after they have killed the father. The guilt of the sons is palliated by this taboo. Thus guilt about the murder—in the present, guilt about having murderous wishes against the father—is at the heart of all social organization and religious practice. Religion, politics, society, and art all have their origins in the Oedipus complex, according to Freud.

In this account, Freud has his own problems with the mother

figure. At one point he claims that the social organizations which most closely resemble the primal horde are those tribes made up of "bands of males; these bands are composed of members with equal rights and are subject to the restrictions of the totemic system, including inheritance through the mother." For Freud, true development consists in the replacement of such matriarchal systems with patriarchal ones: "With the introduction of father-deities a fatherless society gradually changed into one organized on a patriarchal basis." He confesses some perplexity about this: "I cannot suggest at what point in this process of development a place is to be found for the great mother-goddesses, who may perhaps in general have preceded the father-gods. It seems certain, however, that the change in attitude toward the father was not restricted to the sphere of religion but that it extended in a consistent manner to that other side of human life which had been affected by the father's removal—to social organization."[25] Social organization, then, requires the reinstitution of patriarchy in a sublimated form, the form of the law.

In Sade's boudoir, incest follows from the absence of the father and the father's law, and the book is filled with an insistent casualness about it. Madame de Saint-Ange reveals that her brother was her first lover, and her sexual relations with him throughout the tableaus are presented in entirely matter-of-fact fashion. (The only form of incest that is not advocated explicitly in the novel is—not surprisingly, given Sade's hatred of mother figures—mother-son incest.) Sade refuses to draw the same conclusions as Freud about the meaning of incest. He celebrates it, and though there is much ambiguity in the text about whether sexual need unites or divides men, the novel seems to be arguing that making all women available—public—would eliminate the sexual divisions among men.

Sade also resists the idea that homosexual relations are a temporary deviation from normal sexual fulfillment (in Freud, an artifact of the sons' banishment by the all-powerful father). Or rather, it would be more accurate to say that lesbianism is treated by Sade as a deviation whereas sodomy is not. Lesbianism, though not named as such, is treated nonchalantly, but it is presented as entirely subservient to the grander sexual aims of men; Madame de Saint-Ange is

25. *Totem and Taboo*, in vol. 13 of *The Standard Edition of the Complete Works of Sigmund Freud*, trans. James Strachey (London, 1958), pp. 141, 149.

allowed her infatuation with Eugénie, but it is not to be exclusive. It serves to prepare Eugénie for her more important sexual experiences with men.

Sodomy, on the other hand, does have a special place in the Sadeian scenario, and Dolmancé devotes considerable time and energy to explicating its virtues. Whereas incest is the sign of the absence of the father's law, sodomy is the sign of the disintegration of gender boundaries (just as it was in the satirical counterrevolutionary prints and poems discussed in chapter 4). In the third dialogue, Dolmancé explains the difference between active and passive sodomy, and declares the latter the most voluptuous: "Il est si doux de changer de sexe, si délicieux de contrefaire la putain, de se livrer à un homme qui nous traite comme une femme . . . de s'avouer sa maîtresse" (p. 120; "It is so sweet to change sex, so delicious to counterfeit the whore, to give oneself to a man who treats us like a woman . . . to confess oneself his mistress"). It is also possible, Dolmancé goes on, for women to "transform" themselves into men; characteristically, however, he is very brief on this subject, confining himself to advice to Eugénie on how to get the most out of anal sex (pp. 247–48).

Pride of place is reserved for the male sodomite, whose physiognomy no longers resembles that of other men:

> Ses fesses seront plus blanches, plus potelées; pas un poil n'ombragera l'autel du plaisir, dont l'intérieur, tapissé d'une membrane plus délicate, plus sensuelle, plus chatouilleuse, se trouvera positivement du même genre que l'intérieur du vagin d'une femme; le caractère de cet homme, encore différent de celui des autres, aura plus de mollesse, plus de flexibilité; vous lui trouverez presque tous les vices et toutes les vertus des femmes.
>
> (p. 162)

> His buttocks will be whiter, plumper; not a hair will shade the altar of pleasure, whose interior, lined with a more delicate, more sensual, more sensitive membrane, will be found positively of the same kind as the interior of a woman's vagina; the character of this man, once again different from that of others, will have more softness, more pliability; in him you will find almost all the vices and all the virtues of women.

The "sodomite" and the "tribade" are not contrary to nature in Dolmancé's view; rather they serve it by refusing to propagate the species (p. 160). Thus sodomy—and the effacement of gender boundaries—are linked to Sade's rage against reproduction and lineage.

René Girard's rereading of Freud's arguments about ritual sacrifice enables us to place the Sadeian view of sodomy in a more precise context. According to Girard, a sacrificial crisis provokes a blurring of boundaries, especially gender boundaries. There seems to be no better example of this blurring of gender boundaries than Sade's paean to the feminized sodomite, which we can read, via Girard, as a recognition that the lineaments of social life itself are in question. Sodomy, like incest and the community of women, are ways of effacing the systems of signs of difference that constituted French society in the eighteenth century (and perhaps any society). By advocating them, Sade in effect demonstrates the contradictions between the ideal of fraternity, taken to its logical extreme, and the idea of society.[26] If republican fraternity requires incest, sodomy, and the community of women, then there is no concept of legitimate lineage, of clearly defined kinship relations, of marriage as a social institution, or even of the differences between men and women.

Sade's fascination with sodomy and the disintegration of gender boundaries seems to threaten to undo his new male-regulated social order with its vast temples of sexuality devoted to the libertinage of men. Hence, as if in reaction to his own lyricism about the feminized sodomite, he proceeds immediately to a development of his ideas about the egoism of desire. Sade empties out the affective content of the social order. Love is at base only desire (p. 172), and desire is at base egoistic. As Eugénie has learned, "la nature fait naître les hommes isolés, tous indépendants les uns des autres" (p. 170; "nature caused men to be born isolated, all independent from each other").

Unlike Rousseau and Burke, then, Sade refuses to recognize the necessity of establishing a truly social life. Where Rousseau had proposed a solution based on transparency of the heart and a social contract based on the general will as expressed in the law, Sade seems to urge a retreat to egoistic desire, indifference towards others, and a social order based only on the satisfaction of individual

<hr>

26. On the issue of universal siblinghood more generally, see Marc Shell, *The End of Kinship: "Measure for Measure," Incest and the Ideal of Universal Siblinghood* (Stanford, 1988).

men's desires. In the end, as a result, Sade retreats from fraternity—
"ce fil de fraternité qu'inventèrent les chrétiens dans leur siècle
d'infortune et de détresse" (p. 170; "that tie of brotherhood which
the Christians invented in their century of misfortune and distress").
There was to be nothing "sacred" among men (p. 175).

After a certain indulgence for the sexual liberation of women,
which seems to be indicated in both the tract and some of the earlier
scenes, Sade concludes with a reinscription of female inferiority. Yet
he makes clear that this inferiority cannot be based on convention;
like Locke before him, Sade is forced back onto nature as an explanation, lacking any other compelling intellectual ground. As Dolmancé explains in the fifth dialogue:

> Cette débilité où la nature condamna les femmes prouve incontes-
> tablement que son intention est que l'homme, qui jouit plus que
> jamais alors de sa puissance, l'exerce par toutes les violences que bon
> lui semblera, par des supplices même, s'il le veut. . . . Plats adorateurs
> des femmes, je les laisse, aux pieds de leur insolente dulcinée, at-
> tendre le soupir qui doit les rendre heureux, et, bassement esclaves du
> sexe qu'ils devraient dominer, je les abandonne aux vils charmes de
> porter des fers dont la nature leur donne le droit d'accabler les autres.
> (pp. 260–61)

> The debility to which nature condemned women proves incontestably
> that nature's design is for man, who [during the "act of enjoyment"]
> more than ever enjoys his power, to exercise it in whatever violent
> forms he may choose, by means of tortures, even, if he wishes. . . . I
> leave dull women-worshipers at the feet of their insolent lady-loves,
> waiting for the sigh that will make them happy, and, basely the slaves
> of the sex they ought to dominate, I abandon them to the vile delights
> of wearing the chains with which nature has given them the right to
> overwhelm others.

In this passage, Sade echoes Rousseau's denunciation of salon
women. Where Rousseau had exclaimed against those men who
were "meanly devoted to the wills of the sex which we ought to protect and not serve,"[27] Sade denounces those who are "basely the
slaves of the sex they ought to dominate." Where many of the leading republican politicians had insisted that women's nature made
them unsuitable for public affairs, Sade sees them condemned by

27. Jean-Jacques Rousseau, *Politics and the Arts: Letter to M. D'Alembert on the
Theatre*, trans. Allan Bloom (Ithaca, N.Y., 1968), pp. 100–101.

nature to suffer the violence of men. As usual, in the very extremity of his views Sade gets to the heart of the matter, showing, as Carole Pateman has argued, that the sexual contract is the foundation of the social contract, and that the sexual contract is based on force.[28] In this section Sade uses explicit political imagery for the first time, all the while denying its relevance: a man in the moment of sexual pleasure, Dolmancé claims, feels a desire for despotism: "Il domine alors, il est *tyran*" (pp. 259–60; "he dominates then, he is a *tyrant*").[29] Even here, however, Sade apparently cannot resist undermining himself, for the scene of Madame de Saint-Ange farting in Dolmance's face immediately follows, with her exclaiming, "Ma vengeance est prête . . ." (p. 262; "My vengeance is ready").

Sade's rage for a social order that is not social, that has no affective content, not even men's desire to exchange women, is the ultimate reductio ad absurdum of the revolutionary problem of passing on its own patrimony. Early on in Dolmancé's disquisitions, Madame de Saint-Ange remarks, "Savez-vous Dolmancé, qu'au moyen de ce système, vous allez jusqu'à prouver que l'extinction totale de la race humaine ne serait qu'un service rendu à la nature?" He responds, "Qui en doute, madame?" (p. 98; "Do you know, Dolmancé, that by means of this system you are going to be led to prove that the total extinction of the human race would be nothing but a service rendered to nature?" "Who doubts it, Madame?"). The nonchalance of Dolmancé's ready response makes explicit one of the most striking features of the text: the rejection of guilt. In Sade's rendition of the family romance of fraternity, the brothers feel no guilt in their society without a father; they make their own laws based only on their own desires. They do not reproduce a law that expresses their "longing" for the father, as Freud had argued they must.

Thus Sade, in remarkably thoroughgoing fashion, inscribes the utopian attempt to construct a social order without social feelings, as described by Freud or, for that matter, Claude Lévi-Strauss. In his fundamental work *The Elementary Structures of Kinship*, Lévi-Strauss concluded that society can only survive if the incest taboo ensures social reciprocity:

28. Pateman, *The Sexual Contract.*
29. In a note, Sade insists: "La pauvreté de la langue française nous contraint à employer des mots que notre heureux gouvernement réprouve aujourd'hui avec tant de raison; nous espérons que nos lecteurs éclairés nous entendront et ne confondront point l'absurde despotisme politique avec le très luxurieux despotisme des passions de libertinage" (p. 260).

The rules of kinship and marriage are not made necessary by the social state. They are the social state itself. . . . The social recognition of marriage (i.e., the transformation of the sexual encounter, with its basis in promiscuity, into a contract, ceremony or sacrament) is always an anxious venture, and we can understand how it is that society should have attempted to provide against the risks involved by the continual and almost maniacal imposition of its mark.[30]

Faced with this anxiety, Sade rejected the imposition of society's mark and tried to set up an antisociety based on the boudoir, which was by definition cut off from regular social intercourse. Lévi-Strauss explains why this could not be logically consistent and in the process offers his own rereading of Freud's *Totem and Taboo:*

The desire for the mother or the sister, the murder of the father and the son's repentance, undoubtedly do not correspond to any fact or group of facts occupying a given place in history. But perhaps they symbolically express an ancient and lasting dream. The magic of this dream . . . arises precisely from the fact that the acts it evokes have never been committed, because culture has opposed them at all times and in all places. Symbolic gratifications in which the incest urge finds its expression . . . are . . . the permanent expression of a desire for disorder, or rather counter-order. Festivals turn social life topsy-turvy, not because it was once like this but because it has never been, and can never be, any different.[31]

Lévi-Strauss's correction of Freud is convincing in many respects, but there are ways in which the French Revolution challenges even his certainties. Culture generally opposes the killing of the father, but it has not successfully done so in all times and all places—a fact which Freud, for all his defects in searching for origins, nevertheless suggests. The revolutionary order was more than a temporary festive expression of the topsy-turvy, waiting only to right itself again. Sade's analysis was not, and could not be, logically consistent, as I have tried to show: egocentrism works against social order, and the community of women does not encourage social exchange. Yet his procedure of ripping away the veils of social life and convention does expose in the harshest light the nature of convention and social order and the depth of the revolutionary challenges to them. Like Rousseau and Burke before him, Sade theorized the foundation and

---

30. Claude Lévi-Strauss, *The Elementary Structures of Kinship*, trans. James Harle Bell and John Richard von Sturmer (Boston, 1969), pp. 490, 489.
31. Ibid., p. 491.

meaning of social order. Through the medium of pornography, Sade was able to anticipate, even more than they did, the readings of such theorists as Freud and Lévi-Strauss. He may even allow us to reread them more fruitfully.

There is, after all, a kind of nostalgia for antisocial utopianism present even in Lévi-Strauss. In a brief passage near the end of the book, Lévi-Strauss insists that "woman could never become just a sign and nothing more"; but that is precisely the position toward which Sade was tending, and the position which Lévi-Strauss's own book demonstrates over and over again, contrary to his last-minute negation. In any case, women have to be signs that communicate, for as Lévi-Strauss maintains, as if to admonish Sade, the very emergence of symbolic thought required that "women, like words, should be things that were exchanged." In his very last paragraph, the anthropologist himself admits to an impossible dream:

> To this very day, mankind has always dreamed of seizing and fixing that fleeting moment when it was permissible to believe that the law of exchange could be evaded. . . . At either end of the earth and at both extremes of time, the Sumerian myth of the golden age and the Andaman myth of the future life correspond, the former placing the end of primitive happiness at a time when the confusion of languages made words into common property, the latter describing the bliss of the hereafter as a heaven where women will no longer be exchanged, i.e., removing to an equally unattainable past or future the joy, eternally denied to social man, of a world in which one might *keep to oneself.*[32] [Lévi-Strauss here, of course, thinks only of men keeping to themselves, not women.]

That is a fitting note on which to end this chapter, for it shows that the republican experiment, as translated and deformed by Sade, went to the heart of social existence itself. However problematic we may find the constructions of republican ideology, there is no denying that the very attempt to construct an ideology laid bare, for at least some to see, the deepest foundations of all social and political life.

32. Ibid., pp. 496–97; emphasis added.

6

Rehabilitating the Family

Few French republicans shared Sade's singular vision of family politics. They had found themselves advocating radical changes in family law and opening up fundamental questions about family arrangements as a consequence of their desire to break with the monarchical and aristocratic past. Yet they never imagined eliminating the family or severing the relationship between civic virtue and family obligations. The proposed constitution of 1793 insisted, "The fathers and mothers of the family are the true citizens."[1] Even before the Terror ended and the Directory regime began its rollback of some of the most radical provisions in revolutionary legislation about the family, many republican officials had begun to seek ways of rehabilitating the family as the cornerstone of a republican regime.

The reevaluation of the family did not take shape originally as a self-conscious political program. As in so much else, revolutionary officials found themselves stumbling in one direction and then in another, trying to find their way in a difficult and largely unknown terrain. Their preoccupation with the dangers of tyrannical fathers—whether in the state or in the family—may well have led them to put aside, at least until late 1793, the question of the family's place as a unit in the new order. The political regeneration of adults in the present and the education of a new generation of republican children attracted the attention of the architects of the new order, but the specific roles of mothers and fathers within the family received surprisingly little positive, prescriptive commentary before 1794.

Even the ideal of republican motherhood was largely defined in

---

1. Quoted in Joseph Goy, "La Révolution française et la famille," in Jacques Dupâquier, Alfred Sauvy, and Emmanuel Le Roy Ladurie, *Histoire de la population française* (Paris, 1988), p. 92.

negative terms. It came up for discussion whenever women's active participation in politics was at issue. Women who joined women's clubs announced their adherence to the ideal in order to justify their participation as political citizens. The women of the Section des Droits de l'Homme proclaimed in a speech to the Société des Républicaines Révolutionnaires:

> The Declaration of Rights is common to both sexes, and the difference consists in duties. . . . Men are particularly called to fulfill [public ones]. . . . Whether in the armies or the Senate or public assemblies, they occupy such positions preferentially. . . . Women, on the contrary, have as their first obligation private duties; the gentle functions of wives and mothers are entrusted to them.[2]

The women present on this occasion believed in the virtues of women's political activism, yet they framed that activism with typical eighteenth-century views about women's proper place. It was only after they had fulfilled their private functions that women would be permitted to enter the public sphere. Similarly, legislators were most likely to proclaim the virtues of republican motherhood at those moments when they were concerned to deny women more public roles.

The notion of republican motherhood raised uncomfortable issues for male leaders about the political education of women, and it may be that this discomfort kept the topic out of the limelight. How could women instruct their children if they themselves knew nothing about republican virtues? Most of the deputies originally agreed that women should be allowed to attend debates in the assemblies. Amar, one of the architects of the political exclusion of women, conceded: "It is necessary that they instruct themselves in the principles of liberty in order to make them dear to their children."[3] Just how far this instruction should go and how much women should be allowed to participate in public assemblies remained points of contention even after the outlawing of women's clubs in 1793.

Even less obvious was the role to be fashioned for republican fathers, who were now officially depicted as friendly, supportive, and interested in their children. Although the various governments

2. Quoted in Darline Gay Levy, Harriet Branson Applewhite, and Mary Durham Johnson, eds., *Women in Revolutionary Paris, 1789–1795* (Urbana, Ill., 1979), pp. 176–77 (no date is given for the speech).

3. Quoted in Dominique Godineau, *Citoyennes tricoteuses: Les Femmes du peuple à Paris pendant la Révolution française* (Aix-en-Provence, 1988), pp. 264–65.

after 1793 tried to affirm the importance of fatherhood, the figure of the father remained relatively effaced until the Napoleonic period, when paternalism was explicitly rehabilitated. Given the relative indifference to the role of parents in shaping the new order, it is perhaps not surprising that the affective center of gravity shifted toward children. The most striking family figure in French novels and plays after 1794 was the orphan, the child without a family. Thus the family still seemed a fragile unit upon which to build a new political and social order.

The turning point in republican images of women—and consequently of the family itself—seems to have occurred in the time between the suppression of women's clubs in October 1793 and the Festival of the Supreme Being in June 1794. After the ban on women's clubs, women still attended meetings of men's clubs, and they started agitations about food shortages and high prices and were often in the forefront of food riots in the difficult winter of 1794. In April 1794 two of the leaders of the outlawed Société des Républicaines Révolutionnaires, Claire Lacombe and Pauline Léon, were arrested. Léon was released four months later, but Lacombe was detained for fifteen months. When women appeared prominently in the popular uprisings against the National Convention in the spring of 1795—the last major political action by the sans-culottes of Paris—they were excluded from the galleries of the legislature and banned from attending any political meeting or from gathering in the streets in groups of more than five.[4]

Like most men, most women did not participate actively in political meetings or even in demonstrations about food. More important, therefore, than the explicit exclusion of women from the public political sphere was the subtle reorientation taking place with respect to the role of the family and of the mother within the family. Before the end of the Terror, Robespierre and other leading Jacobins took small yet significant steps to reinforce the virile image of the Revolution and downplay any association of women with active political roles. The choice of Hercules to replace the militant goddess of Liberty on the seal of state was only the most obvious of these decisions.[5]

4. See the important analysis in ibid., pp. 179–93, 319–32.
5. See Lynn Hunt, *Politics, Culture, and Class in the French Revolution* (Berkeley, 1984), 87–119.

When represented publicly, women were increasingly relegated to distinctly motherly roles. A giant statue of Nature, depicted as a female sphinx with huge breasts spouting the water of regeneration, served as one of the chief stations of the Festival of Unity in August 1793. The parades of pregnant women on festive occasions underlined the importance of the nurturing mother to republican ideology. In his long report of 18 floréal an II (7 May 1794) on the need for a new system of festivals, Robespierre argued that the people "recognizes that the best way of worshipping the Supreme Being is to do one's duties as a man." Robespierre advocated the establishment of festivals to celebrate not only the Supreme Being but also nature, the human race, patriotism, courage, love, conjugal fidelity, fatherly affection, mother-love, filial piety, childhood, youth, manhood, and old age (among others).[6] Implicit in this list was the sense that family values needed to be reinforced.

The Festival of the Supreme Being organized by David for 8 June 1794 brought these ideas to fruition. The festival was designed to counter the notorious Festivals of Reason that had been celebrated in Paris and many provincial centers in the late fall of 1793. In many places a young woman, often an actress, had played the role of Liberty or Reason in the ceremony. Commentators denounced the use of live women in these festivals as inappropriate to the message:

> The sense and the imagination of the philosophers are shocked as much by the idea of a *woman* representing *Reason* as by the youth of this woman. In women, this pure faculty is identified as it were with *weakness*, with *prejudices*, with the very *attractions* of this enchanting sex. In men, its empire is free from any error: force, energy, and severity are linked together in them. Reason is *mature*, it is *serious*, it is *austere*, and these qualities cannot be associated with a young woman.[7]

The Supreme Being in the new festival was to have no particular representation; it was to remain an abstract and sublime entity. Thus the Cult of the Supreme Being erased not only the idolatry implicit in worshipping an actual image of reason but also the association of that imagery with feminine qualities. David's program for the fes-

---

6. Central passages of this speech are translated in George Rudé, *Robespierre* (Englewood Cliffs, N.J., 1967), pp. 68–73.

7. *Annales patriotiques et littéraires*, quoted in Alphonse Aulard, *Le Culte de la Raison et le Culte de l'Être Suprême, 1793–1794: Essai historique* (Paris, 1904), pp. 88–89.

FÊTE CÉLÉBRÉE EN L'HONNEUR DE L'ÊTRE SUPRÊME.
Le 20 Prairiale l'an 2me de la Rép

Le véritable Prêtre de l'Être suprême, c'est la Nature, son temple l'Univers, son Culte la Vérité, ses fêtes la joie d'un grand Peuple rassemblé pour resserrer les doux noeuds de la Fraternité, et jurer la mort des tirans.

29.   Engraving of the Festival of the Supreme Being, June 1794.
Photo: Bibliothèque nationale.

tival took up again his earlier separation of the sexes in *The Oath of the Horatii* and *Brutus;* when they arrived at the site of the ceremony, the column of men stood on one side of the mountain, the column of women on the other.[8]

Moreover, the women in the ceremony were all spouses and mothers, according to the program: "The chaste spouse braids the hair of her cherished daughter with flowers while her nursing child presses against her breast."[9] Engravings of the festival emphasized the reconstitution of the family that was taking place (see figure 29).

8. I have benefited here from the suggestive analysis of Marie-Hélène Huet, "Le Sacre du Printemps: Essai sur le sublime et la Terreur," *Modern Language Notes,* 103 (1988): 782–99.

9. Quoted in ibid., p. 790.

In this reaffirmed family, as the engraving shows, the father is certainly not effaced, but neither is he dominant. The Supreme Being is suggested by the all-seeing eye in the triangle, a representation that is too abstract to suggest any gender. In other words, the festival underlined the importance of clear gender boundaries and of family feeling, but it stopped short of reinstituting a patriarchal family or patriarchal religion. Women had to maintain their proper place within a family that emphasized the natural sentiments of both parents for their children.

The idea of women's separate, maternally defined destiny had gained greater precision during the eighteenth century. During the seventeenth and eighteenth centuries many writers, both men and women, had quarreled about the nature of women's distinctive qualities. It was only in the last quarter of the eighteenth century, however, that doctors began to construct a coherent view of the effects of women's physiology.[10] Before then, most writers contented themselves with vague references to women's nature. Like many others with much more conservative metaphysical views, the radical materialist Julien Offroy de La Mettrie argued that women's nature was different from men's: "Among the fair sex their spirit accords with the delicacy of their temperament, hence this tenderness, this affection, this vivacity of feeling based more on passion than on reason; hence too these prejudices, these superstitions whose stronghold can hardly ever be loosened."[11] This same kind of vision of women's nature enabled Rousseau to argue in his influential *Emile* that Sophie's education had to emphasize dependence and constraint whereas Emile's encouraged freedom and independence.[12]

Medical writers insisted that women had a close relationship with nature because of their ability to give birth, and they traced woman's own nature to her physiology. The medical doctor Pierre Roussel argued in his influential treatise, *Système physique et moral de la femme*

---

10. Brief remarks to this effect can be found in Jeannette Geffriaud Rosso, *Etudes sur la féminité aux XVIIe et XVIIIe siècles* (Pisa, 1984). For a brief overview, see Yvonne Knibiehler, "La 'Science médicale' au secours de la puissance maritale," in Irène Théry and Christian Biet, eds., *La Famille, la loi, l'état de la Révolution au Code civil* (Paris, 1989), pp. 59–71.

11. Quoted in Maurice Bloch and Jean H. Bloch, "Women and the Dialectics of Nature in Eighteenth-Century French Thought," in Carol P. MacCormack and Marilyn Strathern, eds., *Nature, Culture and Gender* (Cambridge, 1980), pp. 33–34.

12. Jean-Jacques Rousseau, *Emile, or On Education* (New York, 1979).

(The physical and moral system of woman; first edition, 1775; five editions by 1809), that the particular character of women arose from the weakness of their physical organization: "Delicate and tender, the woman always retains something of the temperament proper to children; the texture of her organs never loses its original slackness." This physical organization had important intellectual and political consequences. The mobility of women's spirits made them incapable of synthetic thought; they were more suited for intuitive activities, in particular, of course, motherhood and its associated functions. Women should leave intellectual pursuits to men: "The care of children is the destiny of women; it is a task that nature has assigned to them."[13]

During the Revolution, Roussel occasionally wrote for *La Décade philosophique*, and he was an associate of the Class of Moral and Political Sciences in the new National Institute set up in 1795. His colleagues there shared his views. In 1795–96, his friend and fellow doctor Pierre-Jean-Georges Cabanis prepared several memoirs on the relationship between the physical and moral aspects of mankind. His memoir *L'Influence des sexes sur le caractère des idées et des affections morales* (The influence of the sexes on the character of moral ideas and affections) brought together the latest ideas about women's nature just at the moment when women's exclusion from the political sphere was being made definitive. Cabanis argued that careers for women would undermine the family and the entire basis of civil society. Women in his view had weaker muscular fibers and weaker cerebral pulp, and this latter produced a more volatile sensitivity, which made them unsuited for "long and profound meditations."[14] The physical constitution of women suited them for the roles of wife, mother, and nurse: "Because of her weakness, the woman, wherever the tyranny and the prejudices of men have not forced her to leave her nature, has had to remain in the interior of the home. The particular inconveniences and care of children kept her there or always brought her back there."[15]

Cabanis's disciple Jacques-Louis Moreau (de la Sarthe) provided

13. Quoted in Paul Hoffmann, *La Femme dans la pensée des lumières* (Paris, 1977), pp. 143, 146.
14. Martin S. Staum, *Cabanis: Enlightenment and Medical Philosophy in the French Revolution* (Princeton, 1980), p. 215.
15. Quoted in Hoffman, *La Femme*, p. 163.

the capstone for these views in his two-volume study *Histoire naturelle de la femme* (1803), which appeared just at the moment that Napoleon was reinstituting a version of patriarchal society in his Civil Code:

> If it is correct to state that the male is only male at certain moments, but that the female is female all her life, it is principally to this [uterine] influence that this must be attributed; it is this influence that continually recalls woman to her sex and gives all of her conditions such a pronounced physiognomy.

It follows then that "women are more disposed than men to believe in spirits and ghosts; that they adopt all superstitious practices more readily; that their prejudices are more numerous."[16] Women can never be like men in their intellectual pursuits, and any effort to force themselves in this direction can only be disastrous. Moreau depicted the female temperament as essentially pathological; because emotion dominated over reason in women, they were always likely to have exaggerated responses to outside stimuli.[17]

Between 1793 and 1804, then, male hostility toward women's political participation began to crystallize into a fully elaborated domestic ideology, in which women were scientifically "proven" to be suitable only for domestic occupations.[18] Some measure of the hardening of views of women's place can be found in a curious tract published in 1801 by the former radical republican and militant atheist Sylvain Maréchal. In the new paternalistic atmosphere of the Napoleonic regime, Maréchal addressed his *Projet d'une loi portant défense d'apprendre à lire aux femmes* (Project for a law forbidding women to learn to read) to all "fathers of families, heads of household, and husbands." He brought together all the familiar arguments about women's nature—"Reason proclaims that each sex keep its proper place"—in order to propose that women be forbidden to read, write, publish, engrave, or paint.[19] This project, which

16. Quoted in Lynn Hunt, "The Unstable Boundaries of the French Revolution," in Michelle Perrot, ed., *A History of Private Life*, vol. 4, *From the Fires of Revolution to the Great War*, trans. Arthur Goldhammer (Cambridge, Mass., 1990), p. 44.

17. On Moreau and others like him at the time, see Hoffmann, *La Femme*, pp. 166–71.

18. On the development of anatomical theories of sexual difference, see Thomas Laqueur, *Making Sex: Body and Gender from the Greeks to Freud* (Cambridge, Mass., 1990).

19. See the incisive analysis in Geneviève Fraisse, *Muse de la raison: La Démocratie exclusive et la différence des sexes* (Aix-en-Provence, 1989), pp. 13–45; the quotation is

fortunately had no legislative result, can be taken as Maréchal's own reductio ad absurdum of republican views of women; he wanted to remove from public life all traces of their possible autonomy.

Many women subscribed to notions of ideal motherhood, or at least to some sense of the necessary differentiation between the sexes. The leading female critic of Sylvain Maréchal's pamphlet argued that women should be educated, but this education was to prepare women to be better wives, mothers, and household managers.[20] Even Madame Roland, who participated actively in political circles in Paris during the early years of the Revolution, recognized the tension between her politics and her private life. Writing of her daughter's future as she faced the guillotine herself, she said, "I hope that one day she will be able to fulfill, in peace and obscurity, the touching duties of wife and mother."[21]

One of the most striking ways in which the attitudes of militant women overlapped with those of republican leaders was in the question of prostitution. In addition to supporting equality for men and women in all public spheres, improved education for women, and a more rational marriage contract, Olympe de Gouges proposed the regulation of prostitution.[22] Many of the women's clubs advocated reforms of prostitution in the name of the struggle against libertinage and debauchery. On 16 September 1793, the Société des Républicaines Révolutionnaires suggested that the Convention order the lockup of all prostitutes, not as a measure of public health but in order to assure political security (because prostitutes were likely to aid the counterrevolution). They also advocated a program of rehabilitation through national homes where former prostitutes would learn occupations suitable to their sex. Once regenerated, they could

---

from p. 21. This book provides a very full account of writings about women (by both men and women) in the period 1800–1820. Fraisse comes to a conclusion that is quite similar to mine: "Derrière l'évidence de la volonté de domination masculine, apparaît une angoisse profonde qui nous a ici occupé: la peur de la confusion entre les sexes" (p. 197). Maréchal's pamphlet was anticipated in many respects by Restif de la Bretonne's preface to his novel *La Femme infidèle* (1786). The preface title collapses "la femme infidèle," "la femme lettré," and "la femme monstre." Maribert-Courtenay [Restif de la Bretonne], *La Femme infidelle* (Neuchâtel, 1786; reprint, Geneva, 1988), vol. 1, p. 3.

20. Fraisse, *Muse de la raison*, pp. 36–41.

21. Quoted in Hunt, "The Unstable Boundaries," p. 37. On Madame Roland, see also Dorinda Outram, *The Body and the French Revolution: Sex, Class and Political Culture* (New Haven, 1989), pp. 124–52.

22. Jane Rendall, *The Origins of Modern Feminism* (New York, 1984), p. 50.

return to society and become mothers. In October 1793 and again in January 1794, prostitution was forbidden by law, and suspected prostitutes were arrested in large numbers. The trade recovered its vigor after the fall of Robespierre.[23]

The image of the good mother, who knew her proper place within the family, seems to have successfully taken root in the late 1790s. It is difficult to determine the relationship between images of the family and actual demographic changes because the uncertainties of war, emigration, and migration made the gathering of official statistics very uncertain. The birthrate itself was not increasing (it was declining over the long term), but it seems likely that more women were giving birth during the Revolution, because the number of marriages per year had increased from 239,000 per year in the first years of the reign of Louis XVI to 327,000 in 1793 and 325,000 in 1794.[24] Mercier, who denounced pornography and the theater for contributing to the degradation of morals, celebrated the emergence of a newly moralized family. In 1798 he wrote, "Wherever I look, I see children everywhere in the arms of all the women; even the men are carrying these innocent creatures. . . . Never in any other city or at any other time of my life have I been so struck by such a number of children. Maternity has become for our French women a higher degree of charm: all of them nurse, all of them feel honored to be mothers, and all of them feel that the only good nurse is the real mother." Wet nurses, he claimed perhaps too hopefully, had disappeared along with excessive severity toward children.[25]

After the fall of Robespierre and the dismantling of the radical republic, there was still profound uncertainty about which direction to follow in public affairs. The leading republicans of the Directory regime had no intention of reviving monarchy and with it patriarchalism, but they wanted to distance themselves from what were widely perceived as the horrors of the Terror and the radical republic. They wanted to reaffirm the republic's commitment to the family as the bedrock of society, but they were wary of overturning wholesale the revolutionary limitations on primogeniture, father's

23. Catherine Marand-Fouquet, *La Femme au temps de la Révolution* (Paris, 1989), pp. 328–33.

24. Jean-Paul Bertaud, *La Vie quotidienne en France au temps de la Révolution, 1789–1795* (Paris, 1983), p. 190.

25. Louis-Sébastien Mercier, *Le Nouveau Paris* (Paris, au VII [1799]), vol. 3, pp. 191–94.

rights, and especially paternal control of inheritance. As a consequence, the family romances of the 1795–99 period remained unstable in many respects. Only under Napoleon would a firm restatement of paternalistic values take place.

In the area of family legislation, the post-Thermidorian governments began to dismantle some of the most radical revolutionary provisions, but they left the substance of the major laws more or less intact. They did not remove all the restrictions on paternal authority, but they did turn away from the most thoroughgoing of their predecessors' enactments. The disposable portion of inheritable property was raised in some cases on 4 germinal an III (24 March 1795), the retroactivity of the most radical property law provisions was removed on 9 fructidor an III (26 August 1795), primary schooling was left to voluntary parental choice on 3 brumaire an IV (26 October 1795), family courts were suppressed on 9 ventôse an IV (28 February 1796), and the retroactivity of guarantees of inheritance for illegitimate children was removed on 15 thermidor an IV (1 August 1796). Nevertheless, the principle of equality of inheritance between children, whether boys or girls, illegitimate or legitimate, was maintained.

The case of divorce is a particularly telling example of post-Thermidor hesitations in the matter of family policy. After the fall of Robespierre, the Convention agreed to revise the divorce laws on the grounds that marriage had become "a business of speculation," but the legislative body disbanded before taking comprehensive action.[26] Petitions and pamphlets against divorce appeared in great numbers under the Directory regime. A pamphlet published in 1797 argued that the links between family authority and social order needed to be strengthened once again:

> Marriage prepares the government of the family and brings social order; it establishes the first degrees of subordination necessary to order. The father is the head by strength; the mother the mediator by gentleness and persuasion; the children are the subjects and become heads in their turn; here is the prototype of all governments.[27]

---

26. Even before the fall of Robespierre, on 28 December 1793 a decree of the National Convention modified the divorce law in favor of men; according to the new law, women still had to wait ten months before remarrying after divorce, but men could remarry without delay. Marand-Fouquet, *La Femme au temps de la Révolution*, p. 292.

27. J. Girard, *Considérations sur le mariage et sur le divorce* (Paris, 1797), quoted in Günther Lottes, "Le Débat sur le divorce et la formation de l'idéologie contre-

In this new atmosphere of consolidation, according to another author, "the only rights of man" should be "the rights of the father, the husband, the son, the wife, etc." which were nothing but "public functions."[28] These pamphlets against divorce were insisting as well on a move away from the earlier revolutionary celebrations of the autonomous individual toward a reinscription of the individual into family roles.

Under the pressure of such petitions and tracts, the Directory government too planned to review the divorce law, and the lower house (the Council of Five Hundred) set up a commission for that purpose.[29] Nevertheless, no substantial revisions were introduced until the Napoleonic regime. The Napoleonic Civil Code of 1804 retained divorce, including divorce by mutual consent, but made it much more difficult to obtain, especially for women. The husband could seek divorce on the basis of his wife's adultery, but the wife could sue for divorce against her husband's wishes only if he kept his concubine in the family house![30] Divorce was abolished altogether in 1816, under the restored monarchy.

This is not the place for a full-scale discussion of the efforts of the Napoleonic regime to reconsecrate paternal powers, but the main characteristics of these efforts should be noted. Women's rights, especially married women's rights, were severely curtailed by the new Civil Code of 1804. One of the architects of the code explained, "It is not the laws but rather nature itself that has determined the fate of each [sex]. The woman needs protection because she is weaker; the man is free because he is stronger."[31] Wives were now declared the complete dependents of their husbands. Paternal powers were not entirely restored, but they were defended as necessary to "the conservation of morals and the maintenance of public tranquillity." Although fathers' rights to disinherit were still limited, the portion of inheritance at the disposal of the testator and his ability to name inheritors was extended on the grounds that without paternal

révolutionnaire," in *La Révolution et l'ordre juridique privé: Rationalité ou scandale?*, actes du colloque d'Orléans, 11–13 septembre 1986 (Orléans, 1988), vol. 1, p. 324.

28. Quoted in Lottes, "Le Débat sur le divorce," p. 325.

29. On divorce after the fall of Robespierre, see Marcel Garaud and Romuald Szramkiewicz, *La Révolution française et la famille* (Paris, 1978), pp. 83–87.

30. See the discussion in Hunt, "The Unstable Boundaries," p. 33.

31. Jean Portalis, quoted in Garaud and Szramkiewicz, *La Révolution française et la famille*, p. 173.

authority "there are no morals, no family, no law, no society." Inheritance rights of illegitimate children were not abolished completely, but they were severely curtailed.[32]

The Thermidor and Directory regimes that followed upon the fall of Robespierre may have pointed the way toward this Napoleonic legislation, but they were hesitant to move all the way in the direction of a paternalist regime. They wanted to institute a pro-family regime without the elements of patriarchalism they had opposed in Old Regime arrangements. The festive calendar established by the Directory regime made the message clear. In the national system prescribed by the law of 3 brumaire an IV (25 October 1795), three of the seven annual festivals celebrated the family: the festivals of Youth, Old Age, and Spouses (the two other "moral" festivals celebrated Thanksgiving and Agriculture). Even the festivals of Old Age showed the progress of the rehabilitation of fatherhood. The Festival of Old Age in Paris in 1798, for example, included a presentation of Jean-François Ducis's reinterpretation of *Oedipus at Colonus,* which was described by the theater administrators as "a play where the authority of fathers is presented in a very respectable light." The ballet given for the festivities featured a young girl who "would pay homage with her crown to her father."[33]

The new festival system made explicit the undercurrent of distrust of bachelors. The constitution of 1795 (an III) celebrated family life and emphasized the male role: "We want to naturalize the family spirit in France. . . . No one is a good citizen if he is not a good son, good father, good husband."[34] The framers of the constitution of 1795 reacted against the prominence of bachelors in the radical republic—Robespierre and Saint-Just, for example—by requiring that all deputies in the upper house (Council of Ancients) be either married or widowed.[35] The new regime also levied a special sur-

---

32. For a very general overview, see Jean-Philippe Lévy, "L'Evolution du droit familial français de 1789 au Code Napoléon," in Théry and Biet, eds., *La Famille, la loi,* pp. 507–13; the quotations are from p. 511. On the question of married women's rights, see Bernard Schnapper, "Liberté, égalité, autorité: La famille devant les assemblées révolutionnaires, 1790–1800," in Marie-Françoise Lévy, ed., *L'Enfant, la famille, et la Révolution française* (Paris, 1990), pp. 325–40.

33. Quoted in David G. Troyansky, *Old Age in the Old Regime: Image and Experience in Eighteenth-Century France* (Ithaca, N.Y., 1989), p. 209.

34. Quoted in Goy, "La Révolution française et la famille," p. 93.

35. The constitutional commission originally proposed that unmarried men be excluded from both councils. In a speech on 4 August 1795, Deputy Gossuin opposed

charge on the taxes paid by men and women over thirty years old who were unmarried.[36]

The brief legislative debate about the constitutional article concerning the age and marital status of deputies to the Council of Ancients shows how important fathers and the family had become to liberal republicanism. Louis-Marie de La Révellière-Lépeaux spoke against an amendment that would loosen the requirement that all deputies to the Ancients be either married or widowed by admitting those who had adopted children. He linked family sentiment—"the love of parents for their children, filial piety, fraternal tenderness, memories of the paternal home . . . [in short], the sweet name of father"—to patriotism, whereas under the Old Regime it was linked to willingness to obey the king. He concluded, "It is only . . . by concentrating in the heart of man all of the family affections that, following the expression of the citizen of Geneva [Rousseau], you will give him this exclusive passion for the fatherland."[37] La Révellière-Lépeaux's paean to the family emphasized the memory of good fathers and concerned parents—"the sweet name of father"—not the venerable, august, or righteous attributes of the father.

Fathers were being rehabilitated, but only as good fathers. Their growing importance, but also the ambiguity of their position in the post-Thermidor republic, was explored in interesting ways in the arts. A comparison of exhibition lists for the Salons of 1793 and 1799, for instance, shows a doubling in the proportion of paintings devoted to family scenes.[38] Hardly any pictures of fathers appeared

---

this measure and suggested that it be applied only to the Council of Ancients. Among his grounds were the objection that men who had served in the armies would be excluded, as well as philosophers, artists, and scientists who might have adopted a child but not married. Moreover, he reminded his audience, "les plus grands hommes de l'antiquité, ceux qui, par leurs ouvrages, ont éclairés les siècles, vivaient dans le célibat." *Moniteur universel*, no. 322, 22 thermidor an III (9 August 1795), report on the session of 17 thermidor (4 August 1795). In the session of 13 August 1795, his suggestion was approved. See *Moniteur universel*, no. 333, 3 fructidor an III (20 August 1795), report on the session of 26 thermidor.

36. "Les hommes et femmes, âgés de plus de trente ans, et non mariés, seront tenus de payer un quart en sus de toutes leurs contributions personnelles et taxes somptuaires." Article IV, Décret sur la contribution personnelle, sur le célibat et sur des objets de luxe, 7 thermidor an III, as reported in *Moniteur universel*, no. 329, 29 thermidor an III (16 August 1795).

37. *Moniteur universel*, no. 306, 6 thermidor an III (24 July 1795), reporting on the session of 1 thermidor an III (19 July 1795).

38. This is based on my review of Jules-Joseph Guiffrey, ed., *Collection des livrets des anciennes expositions depuis 1673 jusqu'en 1800*, 43 vols. (Paris, 1869–72). I compared the *livrets* for the salons of 1793 and 1799. It is impossible to measure precisely

in the 1793 Salon besides the one based on David's *Oath* by Petit-Coupray titled *Departure for the Frontiers,* which showed two young brothers taking an oath to their father to defend the fatherland. One of the more dramatic paintings of that year was *A Spartan Woman* by Jean-Claude Naigeon, which depicted a woman who upon seeing her son die at her feet calls on his brother to replace him. Fraternity clearly inspired many of the works of 1793.

More fathers appeared in the paintings of 1799, but they were often fathers of fragile, even partially destroyed families. Louis-Pierre Baltard's painting *Cincinnatus Driving the Plough* portrayed Cincinnatus at his plow after having been abandoned by his son (according to the accompanying legend). Brutus appears in another picture at the moment of having to leave his wife. In a painting by Pierre-Narcisse Guérin, Marcus Sextus returns from exile to find his daughter in tears at the deathbed of his wife (figure 30). Fleury's *Fury of Athamas* was based on the story of a prince who crushed his son against a wall in fury and then pursued his wife, who threw herself and her son into the sea.

In many paintings, children were featured as representations of innocence, charity, and the ability to begin again. In an allegorical painting by François-Nicolas Mouchet titled *The Ninth of Thermidor, or the Triumph of Justice,* for instance, innocence is represented by a child, who sits on the knees of justice. In the corner, a little genie waters the ground to revive the buds that the passage of the Terror has dried out (according to the catalogue description). The family will be the hope of the future, perhaps, but it still has to pass through a difficult period of torment.

One of the most striking examples of the ambiguity of the rehabilitation of the father figure is the trend in representations of Oedipus during the Revolution. We have already seen how Oedipus figured in prerevolutionary painting as a figure of pathos and lost authority. He may have represented a weakened paternal authority, but he did figure as a depiction of fatherhood nonetheless. In contrast, there were very few paintings of Oedipus between 1789 and 1794.[39] Plays and operas based on Sophocles's *Oedipus at Colonus* had

---

the changes in representations of the family because the *livrets* often lumped pictures together or gave only cursory descriptions of their contents.

39. Much of the material in this and succeeding paragraphs comes from James Henry Rubin, "Oedipus, Antigone and Exile in Post-Revolutionary French Painting,"

30.   Pierre-Narcisse Guérin, *The Return of Marcus Sextus* (1799).
Musée du Louvre. Photo: Réunion des musées nationaux.

been denounced during the radical years of the Revolution as counterrevolutionary because they portrayed a deposed king sympathetically. One theater journal remarked, in explaining the distaste for the theme, "It is time finally to forget these old chimeras of our fathers."[40]

The Art Quarterly 36 (1973): 141–71. My interpretation of the material differs from Rubin's, however, in that I do not emphasize the possible allusion to the émigrés in these paintings. Although I think that Rubin is right in general about the paucity of Oedipus paintings between 1789 and 1794, his list is not complete. The Salon list of 1793 includes an *Oedipe à Colonne* by Chancourtois.
40. Quoted in Rubin, "Oedipus, Antigone and Exile," p. 148.

In 1795, after the end of the radical phase of the Revolution, the first of many new paintings on the Oedipus theme appeared in the Salon. The Oedipus paintings of the late 1790s showed Oedipus blind, being guided by his daughter Antigone, after having been exiled by his son Polynices. A family romance is explicit here: father and son have been engaged in mortal conflict, the daughter remains dutiful, the father's authority is uncertain, and the family seems a most fragile unit. In the catalogue the legend for Charles Thévenin's 1798 painting *Oedipus and Antigone* read: "The fugitive proscribed by his son wanders during a violent storm in an arid and savage countryside. . . . His daughter makes an effort to calm him."[41] The father returns, in other words, but he is still a weakened figure.

Nicolas Guillard's opera *Oedipus at Colonus,* first performed in 1785, was revived in 1796 for the Festival of Old Age. We have already seen that Ducis's play on the same theme (first created in 1778 and revised in 1797) was produced at the Festival of Old Age in 1798. Guillard and Ducis added their own interpretations to the Sophocles drama. In Sophocles, Polynices comes to seek his father's forgiveness only to be cursed and chased away. In the Ducis version, Oedipus is depicted at times as bordering on madness, and Antigone intercedes with her father and obtains his pardon for her brother. Thus Oedipus in the Ducis version—largely taken over by Guillard in his opera—is both more pathetic and more willing to be reconciled with his son. He is a father who has lost his power and now depends on his children, yet his reconciliation is considered vital enough to figure prominently in the revised story. Theater critics explicitly praised Ducis's 1797 version for its emphasis on the pardon scene.[42]

One other aspect of this new family romance bears emphasis: the dutiful, protective daughter, who intervenes to calm disputes between men. Women who maintained their loyalty to the family could, like Antigone, mitigate the effects of masculine conflict. David's dramatic painting *The Intervention of the Sabine Women,* completed in 1799 but begun in 1794 while he was in prison during the post-Robespierre reaction, drives home the same theme (figure 31). In the painting the central female figure, Hersilia, leads a group of

41. Quoted in ibid., p. 164.
42. Ibid., p. 144.

31. Jacques-Louis David, *The Intervention of the Sabine Women* (1799).
Musée du Louvre. Photo: Réunion des musées nationaux.

Sabine women who put their own bodies between the Romans and
the Sabines, forcing them to give up the fight. David chose to
represent this moment of female-engendered reconciliation rather
than the traditional subject of the rape of the Sabine women by
the Romans, which chronologically preceded the moment depicted
here.

The gender separation so prominent in David's history paintings
of the 1780s has collapsed; women, who had been the objects of
struggle between men, now try to restore harmony themselves. By
this time David himself apparently considered his earlier paintings
such as the *Oath* to be "theatrical" and "grimacing."[43] In composi-
tional terms, the women in *The Sabine Women* are pushing through
the space occupied by the men. Many of them hold children as signs

43. Quoted in Warren Roberts, *Jacques-Louis David, Revolutionary Artist: Art, Politics, and the French Revolution* (Chapel Hill, N.C., 1989), p. 112. I have followed the
main lines of Roberts's analysis of this painting.

of their new family identities; once Sabines, they are now Romans too. In his preparatory studies, David worked specifically on ways to emphasize the men's response to the women. It is worth noting that the men are responding to women whose appeal is based on their maternity, an appeal which had no effective force in David's earlier history paintings. An art critic of the time understood the political stakes implied in the painting: "Frenchmen of different parties ready to cut each other's throats with their own hands, and the mother country rising up and throwing herself between them, crying 'Stop.'" The playwright Ducis remarked on the kinship between his Antigone and David's figure of Hersilia.[44]

We know very little about women's explicit responses to the refashioning of roles for mothers and fathers. Sophie Cottin's popular novel, *Claire d'Albe*, gives us one woman's view of the changes that had taken place. Published in 1799, *Claire d'Albe* was deeply influenced by Rousseau's *La Nouvelle Héloïse*, but it tells an even more ambivalent story. There is no father-daughter conflict here, just the interior struggles of the heroine of the novel. Claire is twenty-two years old, the mother of two children, and married since the age of fifteen to a sixty-year-old manufacturer. Cottin's novel, like many of the novels written by women in the eighteenth century, is primarily concerned with love and marriage, rather than the relations between parents and children.

In her letters to her best friend Elise, Claire recounts the arrival of Frédéric, the nineteen-year-old adopted son of her husband. He is the model of the new man: interested in children, untrained in the false ways of the world, capable of "noble and grand passions," which alone push one to "glory and virtue." He is the prototype of the nineteenth-century romantic figure who combines the new emphasis on emotional sensitivity with "a new character which has not yet been blunted by the chafing of custom."[45] Claire soon falls in love with Frédéric, and tragedy results from this essentially incestuous passion. Claire tries to maintain her virtue, but when Frédéric is sent away through the intervention of her husband and her friend Elise, she goes into fatal decline. Frédéric returns in time to make love to her, and she dies in shame.

44. Rubin, "Oedipus, Antigone and Exile," p. 151; the quotation is from the same page. For an analysis that emphasizes the continuities in David's approach to the "domestication" of women, see Erica Rand, "Depoliticizing Women: Female Agency, the French Revolution, and the Art of Boucher and David," *Genders* 7 (1990): 47–68.

45. Sophie Cottin, *Claire d'Albe* (1799; reprint, Paris, 1976), p. 33.

Like Rousseau's Julie, Claire dies after a deathbed scene with her husband and friend. Claire asks Elise to instruct her daughter on the causes of her death in order to warn her about vice and its penalties. Yet the novel does not paint Claire as a weak woman who has succumbed to passion but rather as a tragic victim of the incompatibility between the demands of a conventional marriage and the impulses of a generous and true passion. Her description of her husband's business seems to resemble her marriage: "a thing purely mechanical, an exact surveillance, arid calculations."[46] In some sense, it is Elise and Monsieur d'Albe who have caused Claire's death, for they colluded in convincing Claire that Frédéric no longer loved her.

Claire appears to accept the role designed for women in the new order. In an early scene, Frédéric criticizes her indifference to politics. Claire responds with a justification of her position: "The good that a woman can do for her country comes not from her concern for what is happening nor from giving her opinion on what is being done, but from practicing the most virtue that she can." Her husband interrupts their conversation to support her with a line of argument that echoes Amar's speech to the Convention:

> Men are suited for great and vast conceptions; they are made to create government and laws; it is for women to help them by limiting themselves strictly to the cares that concern them. Their task is easy, for whatever the political order, as long as it is based on virtue and justice, they will be sure of contributing to its durability by never leaving the circle which nature has traced around them; for in order to make everything work well, it is essential that each part stays in its place.[47]

Can it be that this conventional view with its emphasis on the circumscription of women's lives was itself part of the cause of the tragedy? The author gives no hint that a tragic outcome could have been averted, and though Claire feels remorse for her adultery, no other path clearly presents itself. This was not a very cheerful view of the destiny of women.

This brief review of a variety of sources has shown, I hope, that it is possible to tease out more or less coherent images of the roles of

46. Ibid.
47. Ibid., pp. 39–40.

mothers and fathers in the post-Thermidor republic. Women were supposed to return to the home and their positions within the family, yet at the same time these roles (as daughter and mother, especially) were more highly valued than before. The brothers were now to become fathers, who would be restored to their rightful place as greatest among equals, at the very least. Yet fathers were also expected to be more loving, more affectionate, "sweeter," and less inclined to despotic assertion of their will.

What was the proper place of children in this new alignment of the family? Were they to be treated as "subjects" as one of the prominent antidivorce writers insisted? Had male children abandoned their fathers, as many paintings implied? Or were they the real republican heroes, as depicted in the cults inaugurated by Robespierre and David? What was the fate of the daughters of the Claires of the 1790s? For all their supposed interest in education, officials said little about how the psychology or personality of children figured in the republican order, imagining them as entirely malleable material.

Consequently, for some sense of their place we must turn to the one source where they were indisputably prominent: the plays and novels of the late 1790s. Playwrights and novelists were increasingly preoccupied with children. Their interest in children coincided with an explosion in the publication of novels, an explosion so remarkable that critics refer to the late 1790s as the beginnings of the popular novel in French. From a low point of 15 new novels in 1794, the publication of novels shot up to 44 in 1795, 62 in 1796, 77 in 1797, 97 in 1798, and an astounding 177 in 1799.[48] Notable in this new production was the vogue for stories centered on children.

One contemporary novelist explained the situation in 1799 in memorable terms:

> "Children are a great success this year," my bookseller tells me, "and you should write me one." . . .
> "Do you have a new child?" the booksellers . . . write to me every day. "Our female readers want them at any price; write them one, and you will have the advantage of seeing it on all the dressing tables . . . and in the pocket and at the bedside of every young girl."[49]

48. These figures are compiled from the information given in Angus Martin, Vivienne G. Mylne, and Richard Frautschi, *Bibliographie du genre romanesque français, 1751–1800* (London, 1977).

49. Quoted in Patrizia Oppici, *Bambini d'inchiostro: Personaggi infantili e "sensibilité"*

The revival of the novel, then, went hand in hand with the proliferation of novels about children, which were assumed to be particularly attractive to female readers. Novels about children helped to expand the audience for the novel, and at the same time, in a closely related development, novels about children began to be adapted for a new genre in the popular theater, the melodrama. Thus, as we shall see, the place of the child in the family romance of the post-1795 period was entwined with the democratization of literature and of the theater (and perhaps with their feminization as well).

Two figures appear prominently in all accounts of the origins of the popular novel: Pigault-Lebrun and Ducray-Duminil.[50] We have met the latter already. During the Revolution he worked as a theater critic for a Parisian newspaper. After reading the gothic novels of the English writer Anne Radcliffe, Ducray-Duminil incorporated many of the standard features of that genre into his own work (these aspects were already apparent in his *Alexis,* published in 1789). His novels *Victor ou l'Enfant de la forêt* (Victor, or the child of the forest; 1797) and *Coelina ou l'Enfant du mystère* (Coelina, or the child of mystery; 1798) were great commercial successes; they were leading examples of the "child" novel.

Charles Pigault de l'Epinoy, known as Pigault-Lebrun, was more responsible than any other French writer of the time for the transformation of novel writing into a money-making enterprise that attracted a popular audience.[51] His own career was a picturesque version of the bad father–rebellious son romance of the late eighteenth century. His father, a leading provincial royal official, had him imprisoned for disorderly behavior, including an elopement with the girl he loved, whom his father refused to let him marry. His father disinherited him and had his death officially registered when he married the girl anyway (an act which prompted the young man to change his name to Pigault-Lebrun). After a mediocre career as a dramatist and a stint in the revolutionary army, he launched his

---

nella letteratura francese dell'ultimo Settecento (Pisa, 1986), pp. 19–20. My account of the novels and plays of the Directory period is taken from this useful little monograph.

50. See, for example, the brief account in André Le Breton, "Les Origines du roman populaire: Pigault-Lebrun et Ducray-Duminil," *La Revue de Paris* (1901): 814–28.

51. Oppici, *Bambini d'inchiostro,* p. 21.

novelistic career with *L'Enfant du carnaval* (1796), the prototype of the post-Thermidorian child novel. It appeared in seventeen editions within thirty years. From 1796 onward, Pigault-Lebrun turned out potboilers one after another right through the 1820s.

A comparison between one of Pigault-Lebrun's failed plays and his first successful novel (both of which were written about the same time) illuminates some of the central characteristics of the latter. In November 1795 the author presented a play, *Le Blanc et le noir* (The white and the black), which by his own admission aroused only a "desperate silence," and he withdrew it after three performances at a Parisian theater.[52] The play told the story of a father and son who were rich colonists in Saint-Domingue. The son explains in the first act, "I am dependent on a father whose principles are not mine." The son is outraged by slavery, while the father is resigned to what he sees as the necessary evils of the system from which he and his family benefit. The father is not a tyrant, however. In the manner of late-eighteenth-century representations of the good father, the father insists on his friendship and openness to his son. Nevertheless, when the son uses money from his father to free two of his favorite slaves who love each other, the father foils the plan and gets the money back. He complains of his son's attitude: "Are you forgetting that you are speaking to your father? The love of humanity should not teach you to overlook the rights of nature. . . . You disdain my authority."[53]

When the male slave whom he had tried to free plans a revolt, the son is caught between loyalty to his father and loyalty to the slave. The slave exhorts him to join his side: "Leave aside personal considerations. The true parricide is the one which kills the liberty of nations. Consult your integrity, the rights of man, eternal justice." The father enjoins him, in contrast, to "reestablish the peace in a home which your violence and my severity might perhaps destroy irrevocably." After inadvertently revealing the plot, the son joins the revolt. In the final act, the father reappears disheveled and weary after the battle, which has been lost to the slaves. The female slave—like Antigone and Hersilia—steps in to prevent her lover, the leader

52. *Le Blanc et le noir. Drame en quatre actes et en prose, par Pigault-Lebrun. Représenté et tombé sur le Théâtre de la Cité, le 14 brumaire de l'an IV* (n.p., n.d.).

53. Ibid., pp. 2, 54.

of the revolt, the favorite of the son, from killing the father. She is moved by the father's expression of regret and concludes that "sensibility therefore has its own conquests."[54]

The novel *L'Enfant du carnaval* presents a very different family romance. The story is told from the point of view of the protagonist, who is a virtual orphan, like almost all the hero-children of these novels. The title of the novel comes from the fact that the hero was conceived on the Sunday before Mardi Gras, when a Capuchin friar seduced the housekeeper of a respectable gentleman in the latter's kitchen. In one of the many anticlerical and burlesque moments of the book, the friar/father is described as "ignorant like his saintly founder, dirty like him, a gourmand like all of the Capuchins of the Christian world, egotistical and thoughtless like them, and on the whole honest enough for a monk."[55] So much for the father figure, who never acts as a father in the story.

Emetics having failed to produce an abortion, the young infant is sent out to an evil wet nurse for six years and then rescued and put to work in the monastery kitchen. At age ten he runs away and fortuitously lands himself a position as the valet to an English lord, who names him Happy (in English) when he shows great pleasure learning how to read and write. After falling in love with the lord's daughter and going through an amazing number of adventures that culminate in his being saved from the guillotine by the fall of Robespierre, Happy ends up in London, rich and married to the daughter of the English lord.

It is hard to imagine two pieces of literature more diverse in tone than these two works by the same author. The play is sentimental and didactic, a kind of bourgeois drama updated by revolutionary ideology. The novel combines anticlerical satire (evil monks appear at various points) with a seemingly haphazard patchwork of elements from the libertine, sentimental, burlesque, adventure, and gothic types of novel. As a result, not surprisingly, there is a lack of psychological coherence in the presentation of the protagonist.[56] Although the novel is told from Happy's point of view, little narra-

54. Ibid., pp. 70–71, 87.
55. Pigault-Lebrun, *L'Enfant du carnaval,* in Oeuvres complètes (Paris, n.d.), p. 5.
56. Oppici, *Bambini d'inchiostro,* pp. 22–24.

tive weight is invested in his psychological development. The attraction of the story seems to be almost entirely centered on the romance of an illegitimate child making his way in the new world. Happy himself is not at all politically motivated, but his rise to success continually comes up against the realities of revolutionary France. His actions and his insertion into events, rather than his thoughts, are the focus of the story.

Both the play and the novel are fundamentally concerned with family romances. We can almost see Pigault-Lebrun at his desk in 1795 trying to dream up the family romance that will sell, that will resonate with the concerns of his audience. The politically correct romance of the rebellious son imbued with revolutionary ideals, confronting the conflict between his "natural" feelings for his father and his reasoned convictions about liberty, fails. The audience cried, the author reports, but it never applauded. The more unpredictable and unstable story about a boy without a recognizable father, who finally establishes his own family on his own terms, is the romance that attracts an audience. In the novel, the Revolution provides a backdrop, a canvas of uncertainty, rather than, as in the play, a kind of final cause of the action.

I have concentrated on Pigault-Lebrun's first successful novel because it was so influential, and consequently typical of a certain genre. At least twenty-three other explicitly titled child novels were published between 1796 and 1800, including two or three in translation from other languages.[57] Since many novelists were also playwrights, like Pigault-Lebrun, it is not surprising that child plays soon appeared on the stage in great numbers too. Some of them, though not all, were adaptations of the novels. I am not claiming that the child novel or play entirely dominated the production of new novels and dramas, but contemporaries seemed to be convinced that it was the striking new element on the literary landscape.

In some respects, of course, the new child novel of the late 1790s took up where the prerevolutionary novel left off. Children and their struggles to make their way in a shifting world are the center of interest in both. These children, like Paul and Virginie before them, are almost always without fathers: they are illegitimate, foundlings,

57. See the list in ibid., pp. 85–87.

orphans, or like Happy, virtually so.[58] Yet the joyful family reunion scenes so characteristic of the early novels of Ducray-Duminil and of other eighteenth-century sentimental writers have now disappeared.

What distinguished the child novels of the late 1790s from their predecessors was the way they mixed genres.[59] The relatively few novels published during the Terror tended to be didactic, pastoral and/or allegorical in presentation. The post-1795 child novel, in contrast, displayed a dizzying pastiche of the sentimental, the gothic, the burlesque, and even on occasion the pornographic. There was a *Children of Pleasure* (1796? and 1799), a *Child of the Brothel* (1800) that was attributed, perhaps erroneously, to Pigault-Lebrun himself, and a *Child of Mardi Gras* (1802). Just as Sade in *La Philosophie dans le boudoir* played with the types of the sentimental novel and the libertine novel and thereby undermined them both, so too the popular child novels of the post-1795 period juxtaposed all the current genres against each other and in so doing raised questions about the forms of representation appropriate to post-Thermidorian literature.

The distinctiveness of generic oscillation in the child novel can be seen in a comparison of two works by the ever adaptable Ducray-Duminil. His novel *Les Soirées de la chaumière, ou les leçons du vieux père* (Evenings in the cottage, or lessons of the old father; 1795) was not a child novel but rather a didactic piece similar in tone to his stories published during the Terror, except that it takes up the typical post-Thermidor family themes and even uses examples of post-Thermidorian political language. When the narrator's son asks forgiveness in one episode, he says that he is not a "bloodthirsty tiger" who would bring shame upon his father. "Ce tigre altéré de sang [this bloodthirsty tiger]" was a typical post-Thermidorian reference to the Jacobins.

In this novel Ducray-Duminil extolls the good father, the very figure being rehabilitated at the time. The father Palamère is a peasant farmer who has lost his wife and now has charge of their four children. He aims to devote himself to creating "three virtuous

58. Ibid., p. 21.
59. The observations I offer here are necessarily preliminary and suggestive; it was beyond my capacities to read and analyze all 457 new novels published between 1795 and 1799.

citizens and a mother of a family, an example for her sex." As if to echo the painter David or the playwright Ducis, or even Freud himself, he advocates harmony to his brood, which also includes an adopted son: "My children, my friends, always be united! Do not allow any rivalry to trouble the charm of your touching affection for each other." His stories invariably emphasize the need for parents to educate their children in virtue and responsibility and the obligation of children to respect their fathers. The father, he reminds them, is "your teacher and your friend. . . . He is the image of God on earth." He also underlines the need for fraternal reconciliation: "The bond of brothers is as sweet as the one which unites fathers and children." Girls figure rarely in the stories, which focus almost exclusively on fathers and sons.[60]

In his much more successful child novel of 1797, *Victor, ou l'Enfant de la forêt*, Ducray-Duminil tells the story of eighteen-year-old Victor, who was abandoned as a child in a forest in Bohemia and is now being raised by the baron of Fritzierne. The story is set in central Europe at the end of the seventeenth century, but the family romance embedded in it is typical of late-eighteenth-century concerns. Victor is in love with the daughter of his protector, but she thinks she simply loves a brother. One day Victor saves a woman and child from robbers in the forest and finds himself compelled almost by inner necessity to serve as the protector and educator of this newly found child. The woman he has saved has a portrait with her of a woman that exactly matches the portrait left with Victor in the forest many years before.

This coincidence leads to the discovery that Victor is the son of Roger, the leader of the forest robbers. Once Victor's terrible lineage is revealed, the baron will not permit Victor to marry his daughter. After many adventures, Victor meets his natural father, fails to convert him to an honest life, and eventually is fortuitously saved from a mistakenly ordered execution. In the end, Victor marries his true love. Although his family background was tainted (his father killed his unmarried mother), Victor is able to become a useful citizen on his own.

Child psychology was not very well developed in either of these

---

60. François-Guillaume Ducray-Duminil, *Les Soirées de la chaumière, ou les leçons du vieux père* (Paris, an III [1795]), vol. 1, pp. 6–7, 16, 43, 211; vol. 2, p. 62.

novels, or for that matter in any of the others in the genre. Nevertheless, Victor is the unique hero and focus of the novel, as was Pigault-Lebrun's Happy. In *Les Soirées de la chaumière*, in contrast, the father is the storyteller and the affective center of the piece. The stories told by the father are about children, but like those of Marmontel and Baculard d'Arnaud earlier in the eighteenth century, the father's stories are exclusively didactic and moralizing; they are stories meant for children's improvement, and they are infused with what Freud called the longing for the father. The stories of Victor and Happy, in contrast, are not stories about good children; they are stories about children who grow up almost independently to become resourceful adults. They have to overcome their parents in order to make their way in the world.

In the child novels—which seem to focus on young people more than on the years of childhood themselves—children were important as social experiments. Like Paul and Virginie before them, Happy and Victor represented human nature in the laboratory, that is, human nature when shorn of regular family relationships. They were, in short, a way of thinking about the problem of regenerating society, precisely the experiment which Rousseau had outlined in his *Emile*, and which Sade detailed in a different register in his novels, an experiment which the French as adults had just lived. These were children in search of their identities, having to rely largely on themselves and not on their families, often having to traverse the perils of possible incest that are associated with unknown lineage; in short, representing a version of the formation of the social contract.

Novels about children could be written by writers with very different sorts of political views. One of the best-known émigré novels was written by Stéphanie de Genlis, a leading liberal aristocrat and prolific author. Her novel *Les Petits émigrés, ou correspondance de quelques enfans* (The little émigrés, or correspondence of some children; 1798) was written with much more explicit political purposes than those of Ducray-Duminil or Pigault-Lebrun.[61] In her preface to her grandchildren, Madame de Genlis explained that she developed her characters to show that young people should avoid political discussion: "I hope, my children, that one day you will imitate this praiseworthy modesty and that at eighteen or twenty years of age, always

61. The subtitle is significant: *Ouvrage fait pour servir à l'éducation de la jeunesse.*

entirely devoted to your country and submissive to its laws, you will have enough intelligence not to hold forth on the different forms of government, not to hold yourself up as legislators."[62]

The novel itself consists of an exchange of letters that begins in May 1793 in Switzerland. The central character, Edouard d'Armilly, is twelve years old, the son of a noble émigré. Unlike the characters in the revolutionary child novel, Edouard still has his father, to whom he writes with his political opinions: "When I reflect on the horrors being committed in France, I am completedly disgusted with life, and if I did not have a family that is dear to me, I would be sorry to have been born." His father responds with a lesson on relations between fathers and sons; he insists that he is Edouard's "best and tenderest friend." The only thing that can wound a sensitive parent is lack of confidence, "because complete confidence is the unique proof of a true and solid friendship."

From this example of the good aristocratic father, the author constructs a distinctive political model. The just man reveres his parents and his teachers, he faithfully observes the laws, he serves his country with zeal, and he prides himself on his utility to others. "The people" is not ungrateful but it is dangerously ignorant and lacking in instruction; it therefore cannot be counted on and yet should never be despised. As for political opinions, the father professes uncertainty: "We are no more advanced in politics than at the time of the first legislators of antiquity. . . . I've learned never to despise someone for their political opinions."[63]

An encounter with an effete and mindlessly reactionary young aristocrat teaches Edouard that good education is essential and that aristocratic opinions are not always based on careful thought. The young Gustave cannot really read and write, he rarely exercises, and he knows no foreign languages—all essential skills for survival in the world of polite society. Only when he learns these from a clergyman after Edouard's gentle prodding does he begin to assume his proper role. Yet excessively democratic opinions are also dangerous, as one of the female characters writes to a young woman friend:

> One of the greatest evils caused by the revolution is, in my view, this spirit of independence and this ridiculous presumption that it has

62. *Les Petits émigrés*, vol. 1, p. iv.
63. Ibid., pp. 15–24.

given to so many young people. Modern philosophy had started to loosen the sacred bonds of filial respect; after reading a few bad pamphlets, a young man becomes a freethinker, despising morals and a religious father's principles.[64]

The virtuous characters in the book all advocate a careful balance between excessively democratic and narrowly aristocratic opinions. Respect for family values and an educated restraint on youthful enthusiasms are the keys to the successful operation of both familial and political authority.

Only in the last part of the novel are the common themes of the popular novel taken up. Edouard has been separated from his twin sister Adélaide, and her efforts to find her family form the story of the second volume. In a kind of aristocratic rewriting of *Paul et Virginie*, the author sends Adélaide off to Portugal in search of her family, in the company of the dangerous and deceitful Monsieur Godwin (the name may be a reference to the English radical and novelist William Godwin, who had married Mary Wollstonecraft in 1797 after a notorious affair). Adélaide is saved from his evil clutches by an émigré priest on board the ship, only to be thrown overboard in a shipwreck. Unlike Virginie, she is saved, and she is reunited with her family in London in 1796. She marries Lord Selby, who had fallen in love with her on the basis of stories told by Edouard. The marriage only takes place, however, after Adélaide has spent a year completing her education under the direction of Lord Selby's mother. A final letter from her own mother warns Adélaide not to become a lady of fashion but instead to concentrate on combining a beautiful demeanor with education and talent. Thus the novel combines in Rousseauesque fashion the education of a young boy and a young girl, but unlike Rousseau, Madame de Genlis insists on the virtually equal importance of the education of girls.

Les Petits émigrés is clearly a response, by a veteran of Old Regime novel writing, to the popular child novel. Madame de Genlis does not present children as a kind of laboratory of human nature. She argues instead for the necessity of their insertion into the family; only wise and kind parents can ensure their development into just and virtuous adults. In the child novels, in contrast, the heroes,

64. Ibid., p. 227.

usually but not always boys, make themselves into successful adults. The family either is not available or is a positive obstacle (in the case of Victor, for example). The young heroes of the child novels surmount both their lack of family and their, usually associated, lack of social standing.

The other new genre of the late 1790s, the melodrama, was closely linked to the child novel; writers of melodrama began by adapting the child novels for the stage. The term *mélodrame* (or *mélo-drame*) was first used by Rousseau to refer to his own efforts to present spoken prose in alternation with music rather than presenting them together, as in the opera. By the end of the 1790s *mélodrame* had lost its association with opera altogether and was increasingly identified with a separate genre of popular theater accompanied by music and ballets. By 1810 the term was exclusively identified with the new genre of popular theater, though the French Academy did not consecrate this usage until 1835. The most successful author of melodramas in French, René-Charles Guilbert de Pixerécourt, called his first efforts "spectacular prose dramas." After 1802 (he continued to write into the 1840s), he regularly called his plays melodramas. Theater critics began to call such works melodramas in 1801, though for some time they also referred to them as "dramas," "pantomimes," or "pantomimes with dialogues." In other words, melodrama was just coming into its own as a genre during the late 1790s.[65]

Melodramas were self-consciously designed for a popular audience. Popular audiences had grown up on the monkey acts, circuses, mountebanks, bull fights, and pantomimes of the eighteenth-century boulevards, where theaters developed out of tightrope acts and puppet shows. In response to a critic of his style, Pixerécourt insisted: "I write for those who do not know how to read."[66] As a genre the melodrama emphasized the spectacular: a rapid succession of tragic events was leavened by various comic elements and an accompaniment of music and dance. The plot usually focused on persecuted innocence, but it was the setting and presentation that

---

65. For a discussion of early usages of the term, see Willie G. Hartog, *Guilbert de Pixerécourt: Sa Vie, son mélodrame, sa technique et son influence* (Paris, 1913), pp. 39–45.
66. Maurice Descotes, *Le Public de théâtre et son histoire* (Paris, 1964), p. 220.

really moved the audience, which soon learned that innocence always prevailed in the end.

Melodrama brought together many elements of eighteenth-century popular entertainment, but it only began to emerge as a distinctive form when the privileges of the royal theaters were abolished in January 1791.[67] The decree made it possible for anyone to open a theater and for any theater to produce any kind of entertainment it wanted. In the new atmosphere of effervescent experimentation, pantomimes developed into spectacular plays with spoken dialogue and music. Some critics have described the development of the melodrama as a convergence of a rising popular taste for depiction of sentiments rather than just spectacle, and a degeneration of the "bourgeois drama" and classical tragedy into a popular form that incorporated those spectacular elements previously limited to boulevard theater.[68]

As early as 1792 certain elements of melodrama were becoming apparent. Jean-Henri La Martelière adapted Schiller's play *The Robbers* under the title *Robert chef des brigands* (Robert, chief of the robbers) by simplifying the characters and substituting a happy ending for Schiller's tragic denouement. In the same year Joseph Loaisel de Tréogate presented his *Château du Diable* (Castle of the devil), which told the tale of a young girl who runs off to marry the man she loves in spite of the refusal of her guardian uncle. What distinguished the play was the author's use of horrible visions, slow and terrifying music, and lugubrious decors. The genre did not become more general until after 1795 because many playwrights were occupied during the years of the radical republic with the portrayal of revolutionary events: representations of the death of Marat and other political figures, political allegories such as Sylvain Maréchal's *The Last Judgment of Kings*, and the like. The popular theater still flourished during the years 1792–94, but it tended to present the same kinds of heroic pantomimes that had been popular before the Revolution.[69]

After 1795 the taste for thrilling action, terrifying music, and

---

67. On melodrama's origins in eighteenth-century popular entertainment, see E. C. Van Bellen, *Les Origines du mélodrame* (Utrecht, n.d.).

68. See, for example, Alexis Pitou, "Les Origines du mélodrame français à la fin du XVIIIe siècle," *Revue d'histoire littéraire de la France* 18 (1911): 256–96.

69. Ibid.

mysterious settings was combined with one of the major elements in the child novel, the scene of recognition. Pantomimes had always used recognition scenes of a sort, but they almost always revealed the truth of an identity in disguise. Now the hero him/herself was ignorant of his/her own identity or family lineage—precisely the defining characteristic of the child novel. Ducray-Duminil's story of Victor fitted this trope so well that no less than three adaptations of it appeared in 1798. Otherwise the depiction of the heroes of melodrama was rudimentary: the persecuted innocent, the traitor, the tyrant, and the liberator were all stock types taken from the pantomime tradition.[70]

Not surprisingly, many literary critics abhorred the very existence of the melodrama. Julien Geoffroy, a leading critic during the Napoleonic Empire, labeled melodramas "unformed productions of an unsettled imagination." Like the novel, he complained, the melodrama was based on escapism. In his view, melodramas were the product of political instability. They signaled a refusal of literary tradition, an attack on good taste, political anarchy, and lack of culture: "Everything is exaggeration and caricature; all the author knows of the world is novels and political clubs."[71]

Critics immediately noted the popular appeal of melodrama. The theater now drew in all manner of social types, from former lackeys to army suppliers, prostitutes, and apprentices. Everyone, including the respectable middle classes and newly rich, rushed to the popular theaters to see the latest successes. In 1796 a critic in the leading newspaper *La Décade philosophique* protested, "Our boxes and best seats are filled now with shopgirls, apprentice locksmiths, or market porters, who come to waste their time, and sometimes to show off their jewels." Others bemoaned the youth of the audience—"poor, ignorant, stupid, gross, and badly educated youth"—which seemed especially noteworthy for its "excess of frivolity, indolence, nullity." Early in the Napoleonic Empire, another critic linked the new audience to the politics of the Revolution: "The spirit, the tone, the operations of revolutionary anarchy have passed from the clubs to the theater. They listen, they judge, and they condemn with the

70. Ibid.
71. André Billaz, "Mélodrame et littérature: Le Cas de Pixerécourt," *Revue des sciences humaines* 41 (1976), pp. 239, 242.

same grossness, the same blindness, the same furor." From the very beginning of his rule in 1800, Napoleon acted to suppress any hint of disorder in the theater, and in 1807 he reduced the number of theaters in Paris from nineteen to eight, thus paralleling his control over the newspapers.[72] The melodrama nonetheless continued to play to large audiences.

The melodrama was a distinctively French creation. Although many English and German novels were adapted by French writers for the melodrama, the genre itself took shape first in France; it then spread quickly to neighboring countries. The first English play explicitly identified as a melodrama was Thomas Holcroft's *A Tale of Mystery,* performed at Covent Garden in 1802. It was based on Pixe-récourt's adaptation of Ducray-Duminil's *Coelina.*[73] Pixerécourt's *Coelina* (1800) played 378 times in Paris and 1089 times in the provinces, and it was translated into English, German, and Dutch.[74]

Since the melodrama was distinctively French in origin, and since it took shape in the late 1790s, it seems highly probable that it was tied in some way to the revolutionary experience itself. Many critics over the years have postulated a link to the Revolution, but they have tended to emphasize the need to relive strong emotions, to the exclusion of other considerations. In 1811 Geoffroy claimed that "the public needs strong emotions, violent shocks, no matter how and at what price." Critics in the late 1790s already associated "modern taste" with horror shows. In analyzing a recent production, one critic in 1798 explained: "None of the frightening scenes have been forgotten: the bloody wheel, the scene in the forest, the cellar of the abbey, the tombs."[75] Mercier complained that the vogue for specters, demons, and the apparatus of black magic, which he traced to the influence of the English gothic novel, was overshadowing the beauties of classic opera and theater. He tied the use of ghosts and specters to the most dramatic revolutionary events: "The people take pleasure in seeing the shadow of Robespierre in this phantasmagoria; it advances, a cry of horror is heard, all of a sudden his head is detached from his body, a terrible clap of thunder crushes

72. Descotes, *Le Public de théâtre,* pp. 215–17.
73. Joseph Donohue, *Theatre in the Age of Kean* (Totowa, N.J., 1975), p. 106.
74. Descotes, *Le Public de théâtre,* p. 223.
75. Ibid., p. 229.

the monster, and shouts of joy accompany the crashing fulmination."[76]

Dungeons, underground passages, conspiracies, intrigues, battles, double identities, robbery, and murder were all staples of the genre. Everything about the decor, the music, the characters, and the action was designed to create suspense. Yet everyone in the audience soon learned that good would triumph over evil in the end, and everyone could recognize from the beginning who were the good and who were the evil characters in the plot. As in the popular novel, the psychology of the characters had little place.

In his pathbreaking study *The Melodramatic Imagination,* Peter Brooks argues that melodrama was the principal mode for reinscribing morality in a postrevolutionary era. Like the oratory of the Revolution itself, the melodrama insistently reenacted the threat of evil and its inevitable defeat. According to Brooks, it was a response to a loss of a sense of the sacred, a loss which made tragedy as a genre impossible to sustain: "Melodrama starts from and expresses the anxiety brought by a frightening new world in which the traditional patterns of moral order no longer provide the necessary social glue." It resolves the anxiety by replaying again and again the triumph of virtue and by demonstrating "that the signs of ethical forces can be discovered and can be made legible." Melodrama is consequently always "radically democratic," even though it may be overtly either revolutionary or conservative, because it strives "to make its representations clear and legible to everyone."[77]

Brooks's analysis is appealing because it explains why the melodrama—and by implication, its related form, the popular child novel—could work to democratize cultural life, both in the audiences it solicited and in its modes of representation of action. His analysis also illuminates how the melodrama and the popular novel could originate in the late 1790s and yet continue to exercise their appeals well into the nineteenth century; the democratization of cultural life was able to continue under different political regimes.

This essentially positive view of melodrama has been challenged

---

76. Louis-Sébastien Mercier, *Le Nouveau Paris* (Paris, an VII [1799]), vol. 5, pp. 47–48.

77. Peter Brooks, *The Melodramatic Imagination: Balzac, Henry James, Melodrama, and the Mode of Excess* (New York, 1985; first published 1976), pp. 20, 15.

by Julia Przybos in her wide-ranging study, *L'Entreprise mélodramatique*. Although she, like Brooks, emphasizes the work that melodrama did in responding to the disaggregation of society during the French Revolution, she argues explicitly that the melodrama was "falsely democratic": "Our analysis throws into relief the conservative, if not reactionary, basis of melodramas, which exalted the happiness of a society founded on hierarchical order in the family, religion, and society and rejected in toto the ideals of the Revolution." She concludes in her final sentence, "The melodrama has perpetuated and will no doubt perpetuate forever the submission of the individual to the family, to the fatherland, to race, class, and humanity."[78]

Neither Brooks nor Przybos has devoted much attention to the formative period of melodrama, which is precisely the period that interests me here: 1795–1800. More study is needed before definitive conclusions about the early melodrama can be reached, yet at the very least it seems evident that the melodramas of the late 1790s, like the novels, were focused on the working through of particular family romances. Family identity is always in question in them, and the eventual triumph of good over evil depends upon the "child" (usually a young adult) being able to forge his or her own destiny.

Pixerécourt's own career is an illustration of the social and political and related artistic uncertainty of the late 1790s. After fighting in the counterrevolutionary armies of Condé, Pixerécourt returned to France to write plays. He seems to have tried just about everything, all of which failed until he "discovered" melodrama by adapting the novels of Ducray-Duminil. The opening of his adaptation of *Victor, ou l'Enfant de la forêt* makes the element of family romance absolutely crucial to the story. The first scene opens on Victor walking in the garden of a "gothic castle." His opening soliloquy explains his predicament:

> Yes, I must flee this place; honor requires it. This castle where I have been raised; this garden where I received a hundred times the innocent caresses of my Clémence, of Clémence who sees only a brother in me who is consumed by the most violent love for her. I will leave everything . . . yes, everything. But my protector! . . . This respectable and virtuous man who counts on me to soften the worries of his old age, will I really have the courage to abandon him?

78. Julia Przybos, *L'Entreprise mélodramatique* (Paris, 1987), pp. 72–73, 194.

All of the themes of the post-1795 family romance are present, but told from the point of view of the child of the family: the son abandoning his (adoptive) father; the potential for incest, which can only be removed by the revelation of Victor's true identity; the dependence on the goodwill of the daughter; and the difficulties for new men of making their way in the world. Can Victor—who describes himself as the "unfortunate child found in a forest . . . without parents, without friends, without support on this earth"—can he hope to become the son-in-law of one of the richest lords of Germany?[79]

The melodrama follows the novel in most respects except for certain significant elements of the ending. In the novel, both the baron of Fritzierne and Roger, Victor's real father, die before the end of the story. Roger dies defiant but also willing to admit that he has hidden his crimes "in the falsest and most dangerous systems" (presumably a reference to the radical revolution).[80] Victor is only saved from execution in his turn because of the intervention of Clémence, who pleads his case with the ruling duke. As in the many paintings of Oedipus of the late 1790s, a woman plays the key role in reconciling a son and his father, or a son and the law in this case. In the melodrama of Pixerécourt, in contrast, both the adoptive father and the real father are reunited with the son, underlining the theme of family reconciliation and circumventing the female role as well. Victor is saved from the battle between Roger's band and the emperor's troops when the baron cries out that Victor is his son. As Roger lies dying of his wounds, he asks to see Victor. He announces that the baron is the only one who deserves to be called Victor's father, and he asks Victor's pardon.

The theme of the band of robbers was a common one in melodrama. Schiller's *Robbers* had been adapted for the French stage in 1792, and both Ducray-Duminil and Pixerécourt had been influenced by the success of the play. Pixerécourt is known to have had a copy of the French translation of Schiller's play in his library.[81] A subtle transformation in the character of the chief robber had taken place since 1792, and this transformation signaled a change in atti-

79. René-Charles Guilbert-Pixerécourt, *Victor, ou l'Enfant de la forêt: Mélodrame en trois actes, en prose et à grand spectacle* (Paris, 1808; first presented 1798), pp. 3–4.

80. Ducray-Duminil, *Victor*, vol. 4, p. 262.

81. Van Bellen, *Les Origines du mélodrame*, p. 148.

tudes toward the Revolution itself. La Martelière had made Schiller's rebel against society into a kind of Robin Hood who was willing to lay down his arms and serve a reformed state. In other words, his Robert was a rebel turned patriot.

Five years later, Pixerécourt depicted his Roger as a failed revolutionary. Roger thought himself an avenger of humanity. "My love for humanity," he explained to Victor, had made him "defend the weak against the harassment of the insolent and oppressing rich." Victor rejects his father's rebellion as "a criminal ambition" because it does not follow the regular procedures of the law.[82] Victor, who is torn between his natural love for his rebellious father and his learned affection for his law-abiding protector, tries to win Roger over to a life within the law with the promise of loving grandchildren. His plea fails when the troops of the emperor arrive. Throughout Pixerécourt's version, then, family relations are at the center of the action. Castles, robbers, and fast action aside, the story is about refashioning family relations in a time of crisis. The family romance—Victor's feelings for both of his fathers and his desire to start his own family with Clémence—is the motor force of the plot.

The melodrama of the late 1790s is not only about reinscribing morality in the anxious postsacred (or postsacrificial) world—as in Brooks's argument—but also about the family as the frame for moral action. Melodramas such as *Victor* played on anxiety about lineage, father-son relationships, incest, and social mobility and then resolved it, again and again. Is this compulsion for repetition democratic or reactionary? Is this, as Przybos has it, an "apology for the patriarchal family and hierarchical society"?[83] I suppose the answer is yes and no. *Victor* taught a dual message: children had to be independent because fathers were sometimes in error, yet the melodrama also emphasized the need for respect for the law and love for the family. You can see at work what Freud called "the longing for the father" in Victor's love for his natural father, in his love for his adoptive one, and in his veneration of the law. Moreover, the melodrama, unlike the novel, emphasizes the redemptive quality of that love; the baron saves Victor from certain death by calling him son, and Victor tries to redeem his natural father with appeals to love of

82. Pixerécourt, *Victor*, p. 47.
83. Przybos, *L'Entreprise mélodramatique*, p. 173.

family. The family—however tortured and problematic—was the only haven in a dangerous and uncertain world. Significantly, however, mothers hardly ever figured in these stories; fathers were rediscovered and reconciled, but mothers remained absent, excluded from the story by some prior victimization.

The melodrama of the 1790s, like the popular novel, democratized the family romance by bringing fantasies of social ascension and familial replacement to a wider audience. The audience of shopgirls, matrons, apprentices, and gentlemen could all experience the shiver of anxiety that was produced by not knowing one's true identity—and the delightful release of knowing that anyone, even an infant abandoned in the forest, could become a useful citizen and happy husband or wife. Victor's reconciliation with the father did not come easily. Although the melodrama softened the edges of the popular novel and reduced its generic confusion into a much more homogenous presentation, it still incorporated the worries and anxieties of a revolutionary age. Any ritual resolution of a sacrificial crisis—to use René Girard's terms—must remind the participants of all the horror and terror they have just experienced.[84]

It may well be that the melodrama of the late 1790s was itself in the process of transformation, in a more conservative direction. A comparison between Pixerécourt's adaptation of *Coelina* with his earlier adaptation of *Victor* is significant. Again, uncertainties of lineage are at the heart of the story, and the emphasis is still on the independence of young people. In terms characteristic of eighteenth-century "good father" discourse, Monsieur Dufour insists that he will not force his ward Coelina to marry against her will (act 1, sc. 8), and Coelina plays a central role in unmasking Monsieur Truguelin. But Monsieur Dufour also turns into a despotic father when he discovers that Coelina is not his niece after all. Evil is much more clearly located than in *Victor*, where Roger was an ambivalent "traitor" figure. The stage directions in the play make the evil intentions of Truguelin obvious to everyone from the very first scenes, and the story is filled with obvious sentimentality.[85]

84. The Girardian framework is taken up at some length in Przybos, *L'Entreprise mélodramatique*, especially p. 52.
85. R. C. Guilbert de Pixerécourt, *Coelina ou l'Enfant du mystère*, ed. Norma Perry (Exeter, 1972). Perry's introduction gives a brief overview of Pixerécourt's life.

Something was happening to the melodrama around 1800. In the melodrama as it was reformulated in the Napoleonic period, domesticity, marriage, and reconciliations between fathers and their children dissolve the anxieties of making one's own way in the world. The stage directions themselves help eliminate the anxiety about identifying evil, excessive ambition, and criminal disguise. As part of this general stage-managing of anxiety, it may be that gender roles were also shifting. In the classic melodrama after 1800, the victim is almost always female; the traitor is male; and the source of knowledge is also male. Gender roles are clear-cut. In the popular novels of the 1790s, in contrast, young men are both the victims and the heroes. Their roles are very uncertain and success depends upon great personal initiative.

An enormous amount of cultural and ideological work had to be undertaken in the second half of the 1790s in order to assimilate and recast the revolutionary experience. I have only been able to scratch the surface of that cultural project, which included new directions in the sciences and social sciences, new forms of dress, and new kinds of youth culture.[86] In many areas—novels, paintings, engravings, festivals, melodramas, even legislation—we can see a move toward rehabilitation of the family as the model for a new kind of polity: one in which the terror of social disaggregation has been experienced and mastered and the individual is able to establish his or her own place in the world through a remodeled family affiliation.

Rehabilitation implied reconstruction and refashioning, not just a return to old values. Fathers were restored as rightful heads of the family, but only if they were willing to take on new roles as nurturers and guides rather than unfettered tyrants. Women were to confine themselves to motherhood, but motherhood was given greater value, and many questions remained about just what mothers should know. In the midst of this rearrangement of parental roles, children emerged as the iconic figures of the new society. The results were not necessarily liberating, as the tragic fate of the heroine of *Claire d'Albe* showed. Yet it is clear that things had changed, that enormous sources of anxiety had been uncovered, and that social reaggrega-

---

86. Some hint of this can be gleaned from Paolo Viola, *Il Trono vuoto* (Turin, 1989), especially chap. 6, "Antigiovanilismo, antifemminismo," pp. 76–88. See also the essays in Lévy, ed., *L'Enfant, la famille, et la Révolution française*.

tion could never be an easy or straightforward matter. The new forms of social organization did not simply incarnate the power of the father; they instituted a fragile, unstable, constantly shifting equilibrium between the individual and the family. There remained the vivid memory of that father's cut-off head.

Epilogue: Patriarchy in the
Past Tense?

As I was completing this book, I came upon a most unusual piece of information in the holiday gifts section of *The New Yorker* of 10 December 1990. Under the rubric "On and Off the Avenue" appeared a description of a mechanical toy dating from the French Revolution. The toy is shown on a videocassette titled *The Marvelous Toys of Dr. Athelstan Spilhaus*; it consists of two blacksmiths hammering at the severed head of an aristocrat while another figure tends the forge fire. The toy is dated 1791 and its motto reads: "Ici on reforge les têtes de familles [Here we reforge the heads of families]."[1]

The toy is a startling reminder of how revolutionary notions about politics and the family were intermixed and sometimes curiously and grimly sedimented out into artifacts that have been almost haphazardly preserved, like remnants of a lost civilization uncovered in an archaeological dig. My hope is that this book has provided a context in which to read the toy's motto. The most militant supporters of the Revolution imagined their enemies as more than individual aristocrats; they saw them also as heads of families and as heads of a national family whose character had to be irrevocably altered, pounded down and reinvented.

The facts and artifacts that I have discussed in these chapters have had their macabre side too; parricide, incest, and sodomy are hardly reassuring themes. It is a measure of the shattering impact of the French Revolution that it brought such matters into the open, not always to the level of self-conscious discussion, and rarely intentionally, but certainly to the point of suggestive appearances in a wide variety of forms. There is no evidence that parricide, incest, and sodomy were committed in greater numbers than before or even that they occupied the explicit attention of legislators, yet they came to the surface of cultural and political expression because the

---

1. *The New Yorker*, 10 December 1990, p. 144.

193

Revolution challenged every assumption about the basis of social order. Such themes, and the family romances that structured them, gave coherence to a multitude of experiences that ranged from the killing of the king to the staging of a melodrama.

Many writers have observed that the Revolution marked the destruction of traditional frames of authority. Monarchy, aristocracy, and religion all came under relentless attack. The revolutionaries pushed forward the desacralization of the world that had begun in the Renaissance; they dramatically enacted the annihilation of the signs and symbols that had given the Old Regime, and tradition itself, its meaning. For some, like Burke, this was the ruin and waste of all that was good, true, and beautiful in civilization. For others, like Marx, it was the still unfulfilled promise of a leap into the future of human beings' own self-fashioning.

I have taken no sustained stand here on the beauty or morality of this cultural and political program. My own sympathies are with those willing to leap, but I have been interested primarily in the anxieties attendant upon the revolutionary project and in the resources available for it. Such a fundamental questioning of the foundations of social and political order is bound to provoke great anxieties—anxieties expressed in the themes of parricide, incest, sodomy, the disorderly woman, and the orphan—and at the same time to release new, unsuspected energies. The anxieties and the energies went hand in hand.

Central to both the anxieties and the new energies were the often conflicting revolutionary notions of the individual personality. At one end of the spectrum of ideas and feelings about the individual was the Robespierrist insistence on consensus, the general will, and a communitarian form of universalism. According to this view, based on that of Rousseau, the virtuous individual would naturally feel kinship with all other French citizens, and if the new ceremonies and rituals of revolution could not evoke this feeling of community, it would have to be compelled. At the other end was Sade's particular vision of the egotistical, pleasure-seeking, self-regarding, Hobbesian man, whose autonomy was expressed by his—almost always *his*—ability to compel other, weaker beings to submit to his will. Rather than highlighting the inevitable tensions between the two opposing ends of the spectrum, or their inextricable interconnections, I have tried to draw attention to the range of options in between.[2]

The tensions between the two visions of the individual's relationship to society were important, and my previous work on the Revolution took them as a major theme.[3] Yet the experience of those who made the Revolution in its various phases was always much more contradictory, ambiguous, and ambivalent than such neat juxtapositions might imply. There was much talk of the freely contracting individual and many rituals to develop the new consensus, but officials and ordinary people alike still lived for the most part within the family, that is, somewhere in between the experience of the isolated, independent, atomistic individual and the exaltation of a revivified community. They might reject monarchy, aristocracy, deference, and even religion, but they still married and had children. In his letters to his brother, for example, Nicolas Ruault described all the major political events in Paris, yet the most affecting moment of his correspondence came when he told of the death of his only child, who was "all that we had that was most dear in the world." "What point is there in living now?" he exclaimed. As far as Ruault was concerned, he and his wife were both "widows" and life was henceforth only "a horrible nightmare."[4]

I do not mean to imply by this that politics did not matter in the face of ordinary life concerns. On the contrary, politics invaded every aspect of life, including the most intimate details of daily existence. Sade's writings were one fantastic example of this invasion; the desire of the women of the Société des Républicaines Révolutionnaires to give birth to little Marats was another; there were countless other, less controversial instances. How did people understand this remarkable expansion of politics? For the most part, they probably didn't. The experience was so new that it did not fit into the available categories of political explanation. For some, the available categories were the only categories imaginable. As Burke protested, "When antient opinions and rules of life are taken away,

2. On the tension between bourgeois individualism and universalism, see Patrice Higonnet, *Class, Ideology, and the Rights of Nobles during the French Revolution* (Oxford, 1981).

3. Lynn Hunt, *Politics, Culture, and Class in the French Revolution* (Berkeley, 1984).

4. Nicolas Ruault, *Gazette d'un parisien sous la Révolution: Lettres à son frère, 1783–1796*, texts assembled by Anne Vassal (Paris, 1976), p. 343.

the loss cannot possibly be estimated. From that moment we have no compass to govern us; nor can we know distinctly to what port we steer."[5] The revolutionaries may have felt uncertain about what they were doing, but contrary to Burke's prediction, they felt far from totally lost; they thought they had the surest possible compass in reason and the principles of the Enlightenment.

Reason, however, whether in the form of universal rights, imagined social contracts, or the general will, was a rather abstract standard of measurement. In the new state of affairs, everyone needed a touchstone for political thinking, a way of comparing options and thinking through alternatives. Only the educated classes were familiar with past writings about politics, and even they had not expected to find themselves in such a novel situation, a situation completely unpredicted by Voltaire, Montesquieu, or even Rousseau. It has been my contention throughout this book that the most obvious material at hand for thinking politically was the family, not the family as some kind of modal social experience, but the family as an imaginative construct of power relations.

The family romance was a kind of prepolitical category for organizing political experience. If kinship is the basis of most if not all organized social relations, then it is also an essential category for understanding political power. Traditionalists in European history had long pointed to the family as the first experience of power and consequently as a sure model of its working; just as the father was "naturally" the head of the family, so too the king was naturally the head of the body politic. I hope that it is clear by now that family romances, like kinship systems, could take many different forms and serve many different political ends. The family was indeed every individual's first experience of politics, but the family experience was not immutable, especially in revolutionary times. It was much more variable than Freud, for instance, maintained.

In these pages, I have traced the development of different family romances at the various defining moments of the Revolution, but I have almost always emphasized their unifying functions rather than their effects of difference or fragmentation. The good father, the aggressive band of brothers, the disorderly women, the rehabilitated

5. Edmund Burke, *Reflections on the Revolution in France* (New York, 1973), p. 91.

family, and the enterprising orphan did not follow upon each other in lockstep. The deputies voted to kill the king, for instance, but the image of the band of brothers did not push the figure of the good father completely aside. Competing and contradictory images of family figures, such as the threatening bad mother and the good republican mother, overlapped in time and none of them ever completely disappeared. A more exhaustive account would address not only these competitions but also the differences in family romances between social groups, between men and women, between people in different regions of the country, between competing political formations, and perhaps even between adults and children. These differences are no doubt important, but I have consciously limited myself to getting at the most persistent and powerful unifying features of the political imagination.

The revolutionary family romances were linked to the two most important categories of the revolutionary understanding of politics: the location of charisma and the sense of political time. I cannot hope to develop here the ways in which I align with and differentiate my analysis from Max Weber and Emile Durkheim, both of whom made charisma or the location of the sacred essential categories of political analysis: suffice it to say that I believe that any political system must be sacralized in some fashion, that this weight of sacredness or charisma must be located somewhere, and that differences in the location and operation of the sacred have great implications for the general operation of politics in any society. The French Revolution may have marked a gigantic leap forward in the longterm process of western desacralization by cutting politics off from its roots in religion and tradition and making it in theory subject to human will alone, but the revolutionaries at the same time sought their own sources of resacralization.

Under the Old Regime in France, the "mystic fiction" had it that the sacred was located quite precisely in the king's body, and as a consequence, the ceremonial and political life of the country revolved around that body.[6] The French Revolution attacked this notion and replaced it with another, in which charisma was dis-

6. For the mystic fiction of the king's two bodies, see Ernst H. Kantorowicz, *The King's Two Bodies: A Study in Mediaeval Political Theology* (Princeton, 1957).

placed and dispersed, to be located in language, symbols, and the new ceremonies of power, that is, in the collective representations of revolutionary fraternity.[7] In Freudian terms, no one individual was to be venerated above the rest after the murder of the father.

Along with this dispersion of charisma went a profound revolution in the notion of political time: the monarchy with its dependence on tradition and simple longevity was replaced by a republic that declared itself the inauguration of a new era. The revolutionary calendar announced the revolutionary desire to break with the past and install a new present. The names of its months were based on nature (*brumaire* to suggest the fog of autumn; *ventôse*, the winds of spring), its days on rational apportionment (*primidi* for the first day, *décadi* for the tenth), and its years (the year 1 began with the proclamation of the republic) on the gospel of revolution. Moreover, this present was meant to be enduring, or what I have called a mythic present.[8]

The revolutionary transformation of charisma and of time worked together to produce a revolution that was at once the most radical, the most violent, the most volatile in the short term and the most enduring in its longterm effects, of any revolution that the world had heretofore seen. The revolutionary sense of charisma and time were tied together and made possible by the new family romances of power and especially by the romance of fraternity in which the band of brothers replaced the father-king. The family romance of fraternity enabled the French to imagine a complete rupture with their past and to construct a different model of the location of the sacred. In the fraternal model, all the brothers shared in the father's charisma just as they all shared in the guilt of his sacrifice. They had killed him and metaphorically eaten his body together. The political clock started again on new terms when the brothers had done their deed.

The rupture in time and the dispersion of charisma so essential to the Revolution as a political and cultural process could not be imagined without some kind of image in which to express it. I do not mean to say that each individual had a clear or self-conscious image of him- or herself as part of the revolutionary fraternity in, for example, 1792 or 1793. Yet partial narratives and half-glimpsed im-

7. This is my argument in *Politics, Culture, and Class.*
8. Ibid., pp. 27–28.

ages did help organize political perceptions. The family romances were metaphors for political life, metaphors that were developed in response to changing events (and in response to longterm cultural trends), but also metaphors that drove the revolutionary process forward. The images of good fathers, of the killing of the king and the queen, of revolutionary child-martyrs, and of the denunciation of disorderly women—all these had a pervasive, if sometimes unconscious, effect. Each deputy had his own individual views of kings and fathers, for instance, and the variability in the general population must have been greater still. Yet, even if consensus was never enforced, reactions to the major events of the Revolution did crystallize around a few main story lines thanks to the dissemination of a few central family types.

The French could imagine themselves as the politically orphaned children—and there was always ambiguity about whether these children were brothers and sisters or just brothers—having to make their way in the new world of modern politics without any help from tradition or convention. This self-image, unfolding in festivals, rituals, and everyday political gestures, had dramatic consequences. It was easily associated with a belligerent sense of national autonomy and a feeling of being beleaguered from within and without. Because power could now be located anywhere, enemies could be found anywhere too. The sacralization of any document, such as a constitution, was made nearly impossible by the unwillingness to fix charisma in any particular location, where it might become the reserve of a privileged few.[9]

No brother, and no particular text, except perhaps the Declaration of the Rights of Man and Citizen, was to be venerated above the rest. There were no French founding fathers, and there was no official patrimony to be deposited in a document. The declaration could not function as a stabilizing text because it provided the principles for a continual revision of revolutionary constitutions. Its opening paragraph makes this clear:

> The representatives of the French people, constituted in a National Assembly, considering that ignorance, neglect or disdain for the

9. Some comparisons with the American situation are developed in Lynn Hunt, "Family Narrative and Political Discourse in Revolutionary France and America," in *Quaderno 2: The Language of Revolution*, ed. Loretta Valtz Mannucci (Milan, 1989), pp. 161–76.

rights of man are the only causes of public discontent and of the corruption of governments, have resolved to expose, in a solemn declaration, the natural, inalienable and sacred rights of man, so that this declaration, *constantly present* to all the members of the social body, will remind them without cease of their rights and their duties; so that the acts of legislative power and those of executive power *can be at every instant compared with the goal of all political institutions.* [My emphasis]

This is a vision of brotherhood in which charisma, like the declaration itself, is "constantly present to all the members of the social body."

The rhetoric of the American constitution, in contrast, assumes that the new social contract is being signed and hence in some sense fixed with the process of ratification:

> We the People of the United States, in Order to form a more perfect Union, . . . do ordain and establish this Constitution for the United States of America.

It is assumed here that the constitution will henceforth stand in for the social contract and be the repository of the national patrimony. Ratifying the constitution is signing the social contract. Charisma is thereby transferred from the American revolutionary sons of liberty to the founding fathers and to their documentary legacy. In France, no constitution could ever have this fixity, and such a transfer did not take place (at least not until Napoleon).

In the absence of a sacred text such as a constitution, it became enormously difficult to establish political parties that could compete over the text's meaning. In this sense, the French family romance of fraternity worked against the establishment of a liberal, representative government. On the other side of the coin, however, the same romance had farreaching effects on western political alternatives. The idea of a permanent revolution, a permanent suspension of patriarchal authority, a constant reopening of the terms of the social contract—these had their own enduring legacy in the modern world. In a sense, then, the family romance of fraternity gave patriarchy a past tense. It was a way of imagining the political world without fathers.

The revolutionary family romances also had profound implications for the view of women in the nineteenth century: the French ideology of domesticity can be traced in part to reactions against the revolutionary experiment under the Napoleonic and Restoration regimes, but it can also be traced to the positions developed by the revolutionary leadership itself. Because it was molded in the varying images of the family, the political imagination was inherently gendered, and its gendering had important, often unforeseen consequences for the construction of the social order. When revolutionaries proclaimed the sanctity of the universal rights of man, they raised inevitable questions about the identity of the brotherhood. Why were men of color excluded? Were women not citizens and "men" too in the generic sense? It turned out to be harder to resist the abolition of slavery and the admission of men of color into the fraternity than to resist the admission of women to the full rights of citizenship.

According to Carole Pateman, the subordination of women to men *as men,* to men as a fraternity, is a defining feature of modern civil society. She distinguishes between patriarchal right, that is, the right of a man (as husband) over a woman (his wife), and paternal right, that is, a man's power as a father. Contract theorists contested paternal right, not patriarchal right. Thus modern civil society, in her view, is most properly termed a fraternal patriarchy. Patriarchy, in the sense of the subordination of women, is not destroyed but only transformed into a new version in which men act politically as men.[10] Once the power of fathers as fathers is destroyed, the original political right of men over women is concealed by relegating it to the nonpolitical realm of the familial and the private. Patriarchy remains patriarchy by becoming private life. Patriarchy is not relegated to the past after all, but cunningly transformed into an up-to-date mechanism for the continued subjection of women.

Pateman's argument is part of a growing trend within feminism that attacks liberal political theory for its bias against women. "Universal" human rights turn out to be embodied rights, and they are embodied in (usually white) males. In Pateman's words, "The body of the 'individual' is very different from women's bodies. His body is tightly enclosed within boundaries, but women's bodies are permeable." Women's supposedly special relationship to nature through childbirth make them "incapable of entering the original contract

10. Carole Pateman, *The Sexual Contract* (Stanford, 1988).

and transforming themselves into the civil individuals who uphold its terms."[11] In a recent article on Olympe de Gouges, Joan Scott makes a similar point for the period of the French Revolution. She argues that feminism was "poised in critical opposition to liberal political theory," which set the terms of political discussion. Political meant rational, public, and universal, and women were defined as natural and hence outside of politics. Both Pateman and Scott conclude that the feminist project cannot be fulfilled within the terms of liberal political theory.[12]

For all its virtues in calling attention to the gaps and inconsistencies in liberal political theory, this line of criticism overlooks the serious historical difficulties encountered in the establishment of a "liberal" legal framework (i.e., one based on a notion of the freely contracting individual) and underestimates the shock that such a theory gave to the old order. Rather than cast the debate about liberal political theory in the binary mode of equality versus difference, I have tried to put it into the context of the family romance. The history of the family romance in French revolutionary politics shows that the individual was always imagined as embedded in family relationships and that these relationships were always potentially unstable. The liberal notion of the individual in the Revolution, for instance, depended upon a model of the family in which fathers granted autonomy to their children, daughters and sons had equal rights of inheritance, and wives as well as husbands could sue for divorce. The revolutionary legislation that established this model did not resolve all the issues, however. Some men and women immediately recognized that the status of women was paradoxical. Women had been incorporated into the new civil order, they were civil individuals under the law; but they had been excluded from certain political rights, with no evident explanation.

It is no accident that Olympe de Gouges published her *Declaration of the Rights of Woman and Citizen* in 1791, just when this new liberal, civil order was being legally established. The articulation of the new

11. Ibid., p. 96.
12. Pateman is more ambiguous on this point than Scott, who concludes "that the democratic promise of liberal (and socialist and republican) political theory is as yet unfulfilled, but also that it may be impossible of fulfilment in the terms in which it has so far been conceived." Joan Wallach Scott, "French Feminists and the Rights of 'Man': Olympe de Gouges's Declarations," *History Workshop Journal* 28 (1989): pp. 17–18.

principles enabled critics to ask new kinds of questions about the paradox of women's civil status. Likewise, it is no accident that there was a self-conscious feminist movement, however small, in France, and nowhere else, not even in America. Feminism, that is, a movement of sustained questioning about the status of women, was made possible by the conjunction in France of the legal establishment of a liberal notion of the individual, with a challenge to the basis of the family as well as the state. Liberal political theory was actualized in France in the midst of an extensive political and cultural crisis, and it continued to bear the marks of that uncertainty. The appearance of feminist writing was both brief and intense because it was associated with a crisis about familial authority. It would not have appeared without the crisis, but because it was born in this crisis it was also tainted by its association with an attack on the family.

Misogyny has been a nearly continuous feature of social life throughout western history, but it does have a history; that is, it has not remained the same over time. The exclusion of women was not theoretically necessary in liberal politics; because of its notions of the autonomous individual, liberal political theory actually made the exclusion of women much more problematic. It made the exclusion of women into an issue. The mobilization of medical opinion to support the view that women's nature was different and disabling was a critical element in the continued exclusion of women, but it was also a new element at the end of the eighteenth century.[13] Medical opinion was mobilized in this way, as I have tried to show, in order to answer the pressing questions raised about, and raised by, women's political participation. Domestic ideology only emerged in France because political and cultural leaders felt the need to justify in some systematic way the continuing exclusion of women from politics, even while they were admitted to many of the legal rights of civil society. Domestic ideology was the attempt to institute one kind of family romance.

As revolutionary leaders groped for models of the family that would keep women out of politics, they also tried to retain the main elements of the liberal notion of the individual and restrain the

---

13. For the role of eighteenth-century medical opinion on sex itself, see Thomas Laqueur, *Making Sex: Body and Gender from the Greeks to Freud* (Cambridge, Mass., 1990).

powers of fathers. This turned out to be quite difficult and certainly not logically consistent. Liberal political theory and the exclusion of women did not go so neatly together. By making this point, I do not mean to rehabilitate liberal political theory against the charge that it assumes that the individual in question is male and white. I do mean to argue, however, that the association of individualism with male (economically independent, white) persons was historically contingent and thus subject to immediate as well as longterm criticism and alteration. As Freud has shown us, male control of the world never went without saying after the father had been killed.

Index

Compositor:	Keystone Typesetting, Inc.
Text:	10/13 Baskerville
Display:	Baskerville
Printer:	Malloy Lithographing, Inc.
Binder:	John H. Dekker & Sons